G.I. JOE

BEST OF

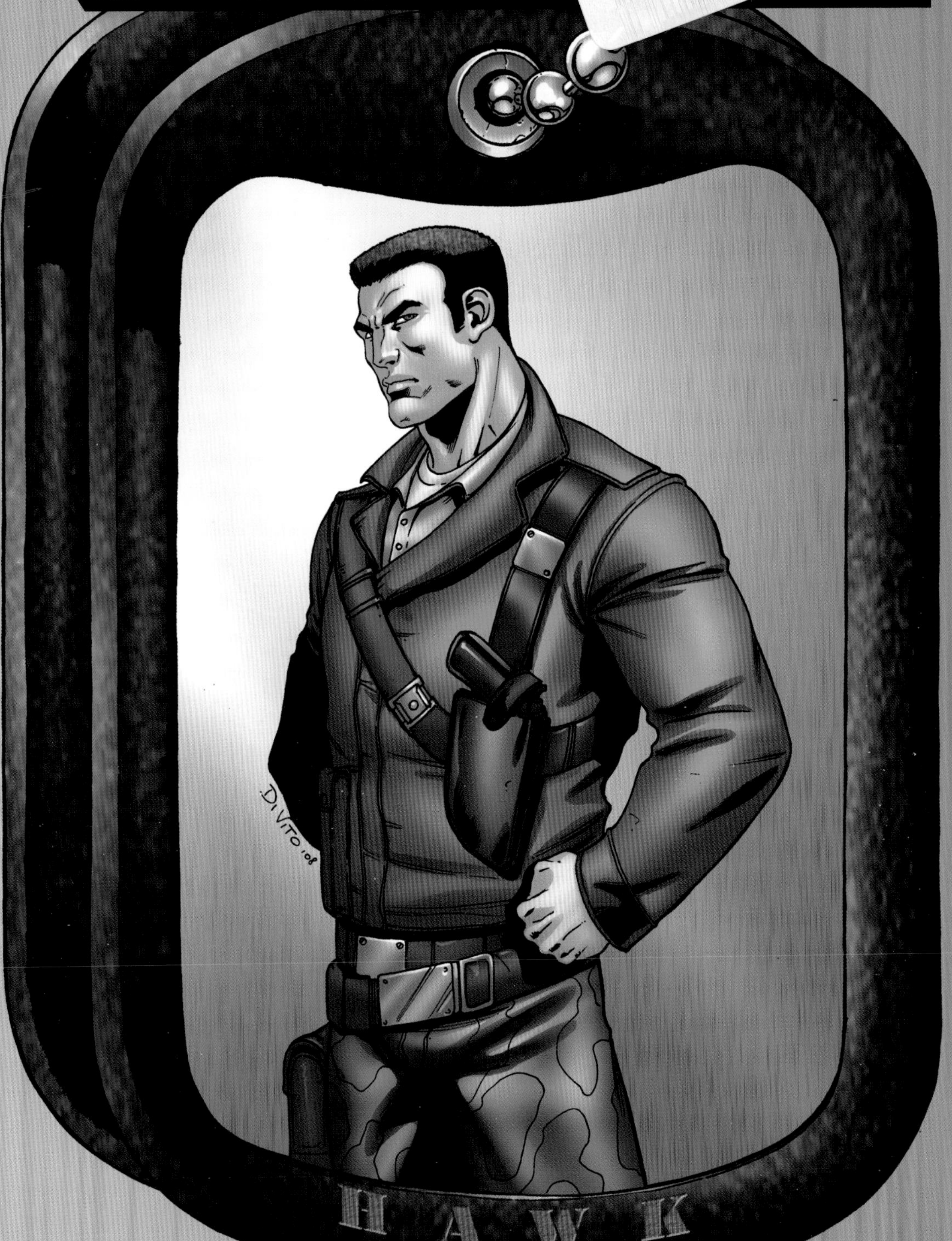
HAWK

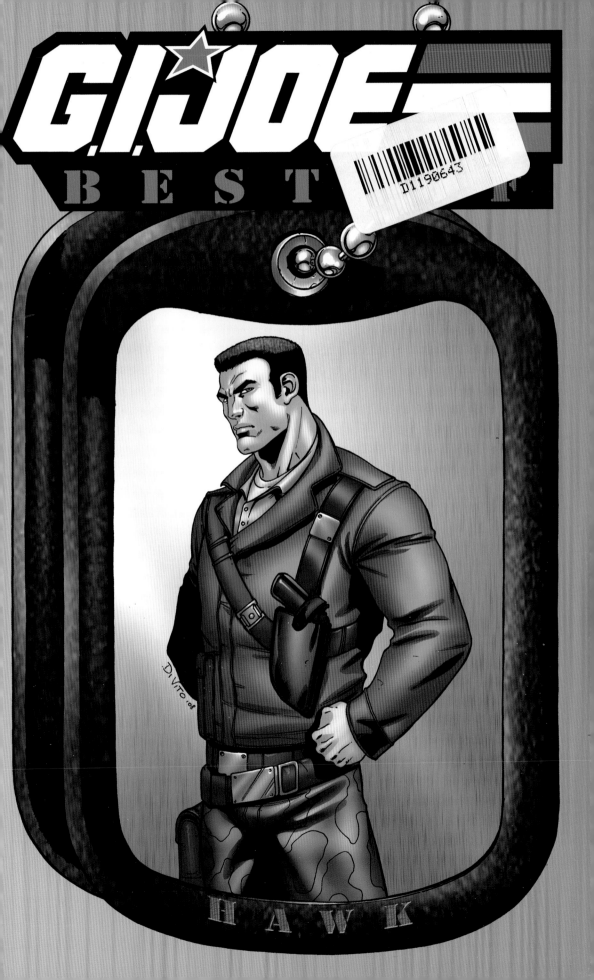

HAWK

All stories written by
Larry Hama

Collection Edits by **Justin Eisinger** & **Mariah Huehner**
Collection Design by **Chris Mowry**
Collection Production by **Amauri Osorio**

ISBN: 978-160010-427-5

12 11 10 09   1 2 3 4

www.idwpublishing.com

IDW Publishing
Operations:
Ted Adams, Chief Executive Officer
Greg Goldstein, Chief Operating Officer
Matthew Ruzicka, CPA, Chief Financial Officer
Alan Payne, VP of Sales
Lorelei Bunjes, Dir. of Digital Services
AnnaMaria White, Marketing & PR Manager
Marci Hubbard, Executive Assistant
Alonzo Simon, Shipping Manager

Editorial:
Chris Ryall, Publisher/Editor-in-Chief
Scott Dunbier, Editor, Special Projects
Andy Schmidt, Senior Editor
Justin Eisinger, Editor
Kris Oprisko, Editor/Foreign Lic.
Denton J. Tipton, Editor
Tom Waltz, Editor
Mariah Huehner, Associate Editor

Design:
Robbie Robbins, EVP/Sr. Graphic Artist
Ben Templesmith, Artist/Designer
Neil Uyetake, Art Director
Chris Mowry, Graphic Artist
Amauri Osorio, Graphic Artist
Gilberto Lozcano, Production Assistant

Special thanks to Hasbro's Aaron Archer, Michael Kelly,
Amie Lozanski, Ed Lane, Michael Provost, Michael Richie,
Sarah Baskin, Samantha Lomow, Joe Furfaro and
Michael Verrecchia for their invaluable assistance.

Additional thanks to Dan Buckley, David Bogart, and Jeff
Youngquist at Marvel Entertainment for their assistance in
acquiring the re-colored pages presented in this collection.

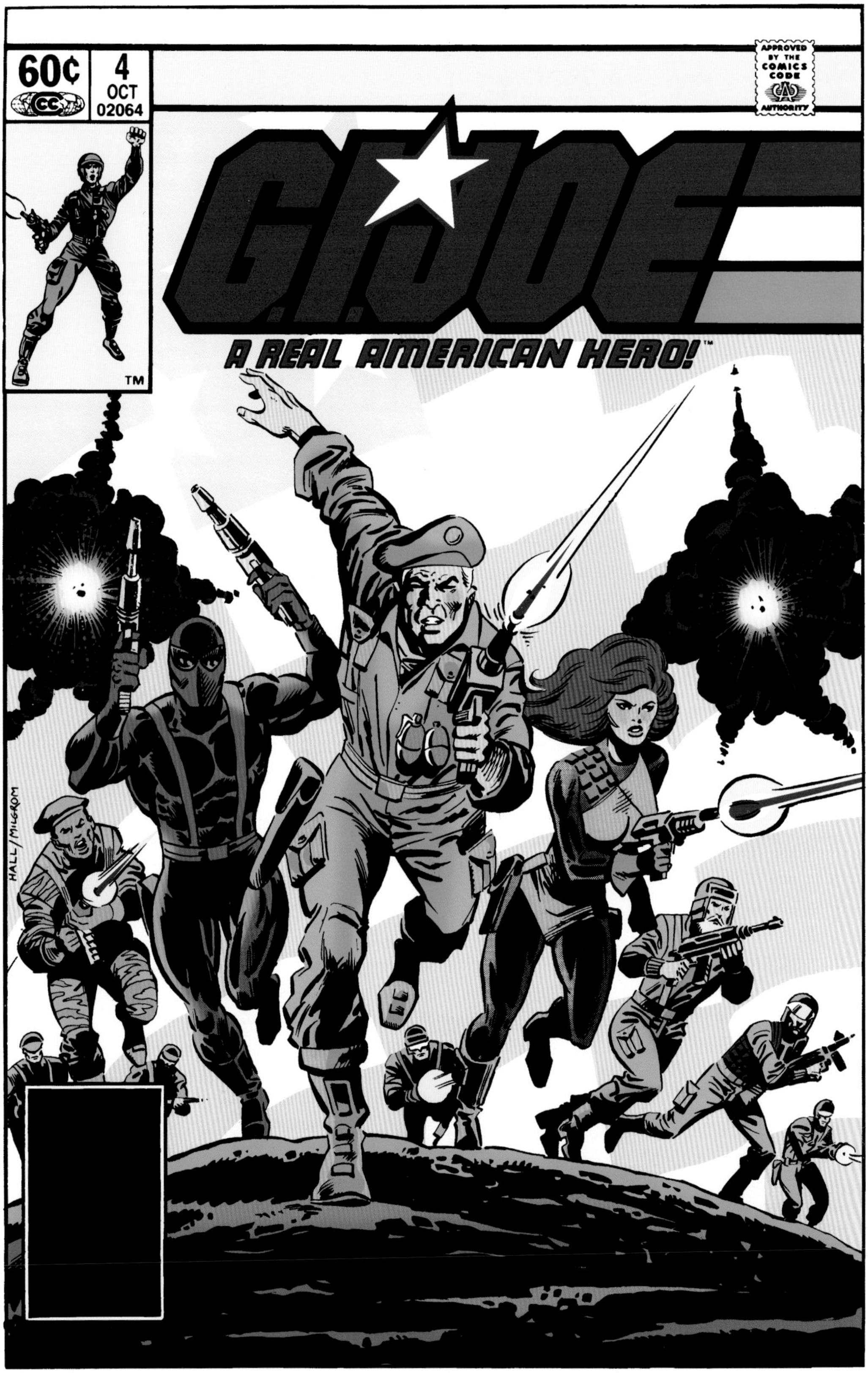

60¢
4
OCT
02064
APPROVED BY THE COMICS CODE AUTHORITY
G.I. JOE
A REAL AMERICAN HERO!™
TM
HALL/MILGROM

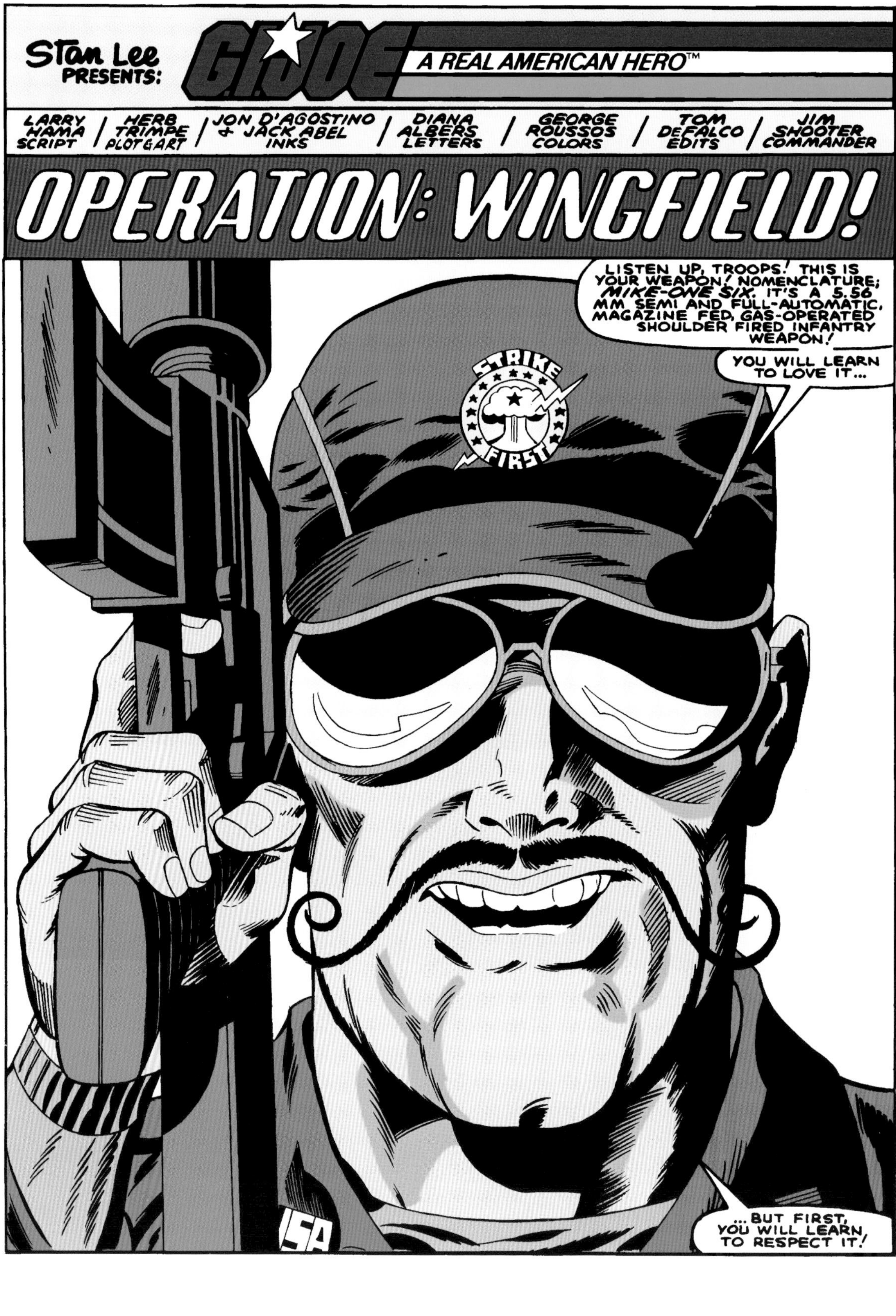
Stan Lee PRESENTS:
G.I. JOE
A REAL AMERICAN HERO™
LARRY HAMA SCRIPT / HERB TRIMPE PLOT & ART / JON D'AGOSTINO & JACK ABEL INKS / DIANA ALBERS LETTERS / GEORGE ROUSSOS COLORS / TOM DEFALCO EDITS / JIM SHOOTER COMMANDER
OPERATION: WINGFIELD!
LISTEN UP, TROOPS! THIS IS YOUR WEAPON! NOMENCLATURE; MIKE-ONE SIX. IT'S A 5.56 MM SEMI AND FULL-AUTOMATIC, MAGAZINE FED, GAS-OPERATED SHOULDER FIRED INFANTRY WEAPON!
YOU WILL LEARN TO LOVE IT...
STRIKE FIRST
...BUT FIRST, YOU WILL LEARN TO RESPECT IT!

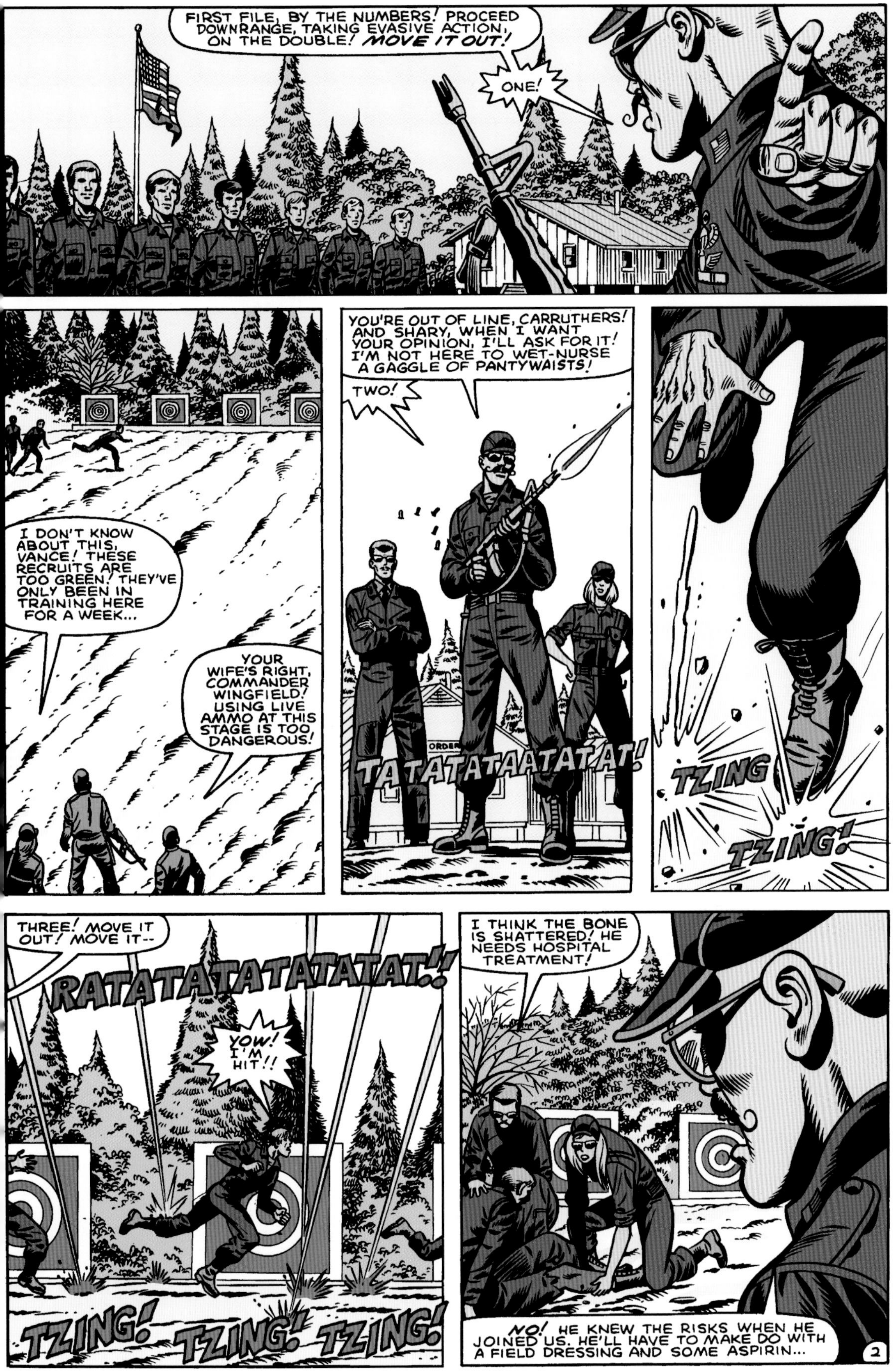
FIRST FILE, BY THE NUMBERS! PROCEED DOWNRANGE, TAKING EVASIVE ACTION, ON THE DOUBLE! MOVE IT OUT!
ONE!
I DON'T KNOW ABOUT THIS, VANCE! THESE RECRUITS ARE TOO GREEN! THEY'VE ONLY BEEN IN TRAINING HERE FOR A WEEK...
YOUR WIFE'S RIGHT, COMMANDER WINGFIELD! USING LIVE AMMO AT THIS STAGE IS TOO DANGEROUS!
YOU'RE OUT OF LINE, CARRUTHERS! AND SHARY, WHEN I WANT YOUR OPINION, I'LL ASK FOR IT! I'M NOT HERE TO WET-NURSE A GAGGLE OF PANTYWAISTS!
TWO!
TATATATAATATATAT!
TZING
TZING!
THREE! MOVE IT OUT! MOVE IT--
RATATATATATATATAT!!
YOW! I'M HIT!!
TZING! TZING! TZING!
I THINK THE BONE IS SHATTERED! HE NEEDS HOSPITAL TREATMENT!
NO! HE KNEW THE RISKS WHEN HE JOINED US. HE'LL HAVE TO MAKE DO WITH A FIELD DRESSING AND SOME ASPIRIN...
2

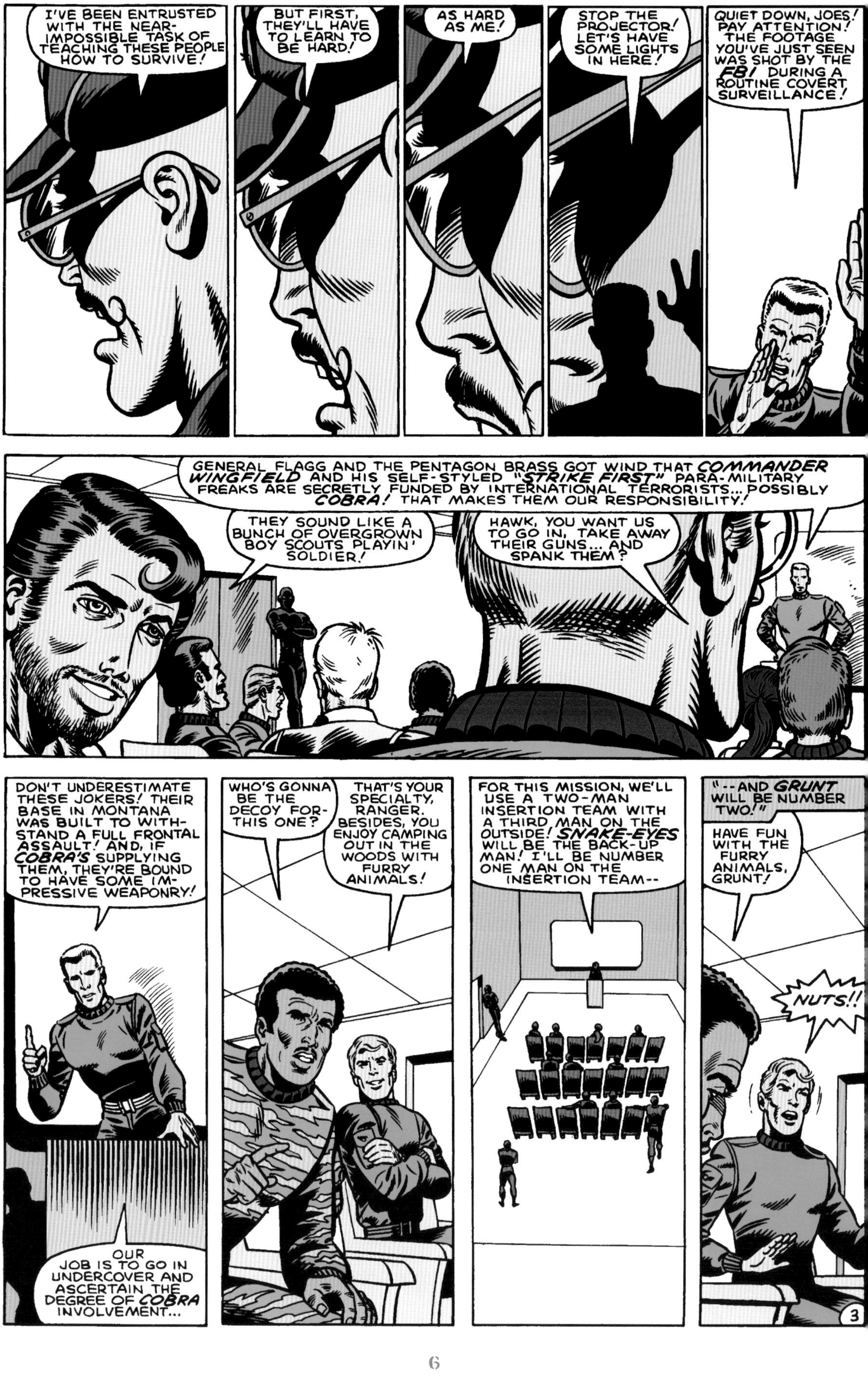
I'VE BEEN ENTRUSTED WITH THE NEAR-IMPOSSIBLE TASK OF TEACHING THESE PEOPLE HOW TO SURVIVE!
BUT FIRST, THEY'LL HAVE TO LEARN TO BE HARD!
AS HARD AS ME!
STOP THE PROJECTOR! LET'S HAVE SOME LIGHTS IN HERE!
QUIET DOWN, JOES! PAY ATTENTION! THE FOOTAGE YOU'VE JUST SEEN WAS SHOT BY THE FBI DURING A ROUTINE COVERT SURVEILLANCE!
GENERAL FLAGG AND THE PENTAGON BRASS GOT WIND THAT COMMANDER WINGFIELD AND HIS SELF-STYLED "STRIKE FIRST" PARA-MILITARY FREAKS ARE SECRETLY FUNDED BY INTERNATIONAL TERRORISTS... POSSIBLY COBRA! THAT MAKES THEM OUR RESPONSIBILITY!
THEY SOUND LIKE A BUNCH OF OVERGROWN BOY SCOUTS PLAYIN' SOLDIER!
HAWK, YOU WANT US TO GO IN, TAKE AWAY THEIR GUNS... AND SPANK THEM?
DON'T UNDERESTIMATE THESE JOKERS! THEIR BASE IN MONTANA WAS BUILT TO WITHSTAND A FULL FRONTAL ASSAULT! AND, IF COBRA'S SUPPLYING THEM, THEY'RE BOUND TO HAVE SOME IMPRESSIVE WEAPONRY!
OUR JOB IS TO GO IN UNDERCOVER AND ASCERTAIN THE DEGREE OF COBRA INVOLVEMENT...
WHO'S GONNA BE THE DECOY FOR THIS ONE?
THAT'S YOUR SPECIALTY, RANGER. BESIDES, YOU ENJOY CAMPING OUT IN THE WOODS WITH FURRY ANIMALS!
FOR THIS MISSION, WE'LL USE A TWO-MAN INSERTION TEAM WITH A THIRD MAN ON THE OUTSIDE! SNAKE-EYES WILL BE THE BACK-UP MAN! I'LL BE NUMBER ONE MAN ON THE INSERTION TEAM--
"--AND GRUNT WILL BE NUMBER TWO!"
HAVE FUN WITH THE FURRY ANIMALS, GRUNT!
NUTS!!
3

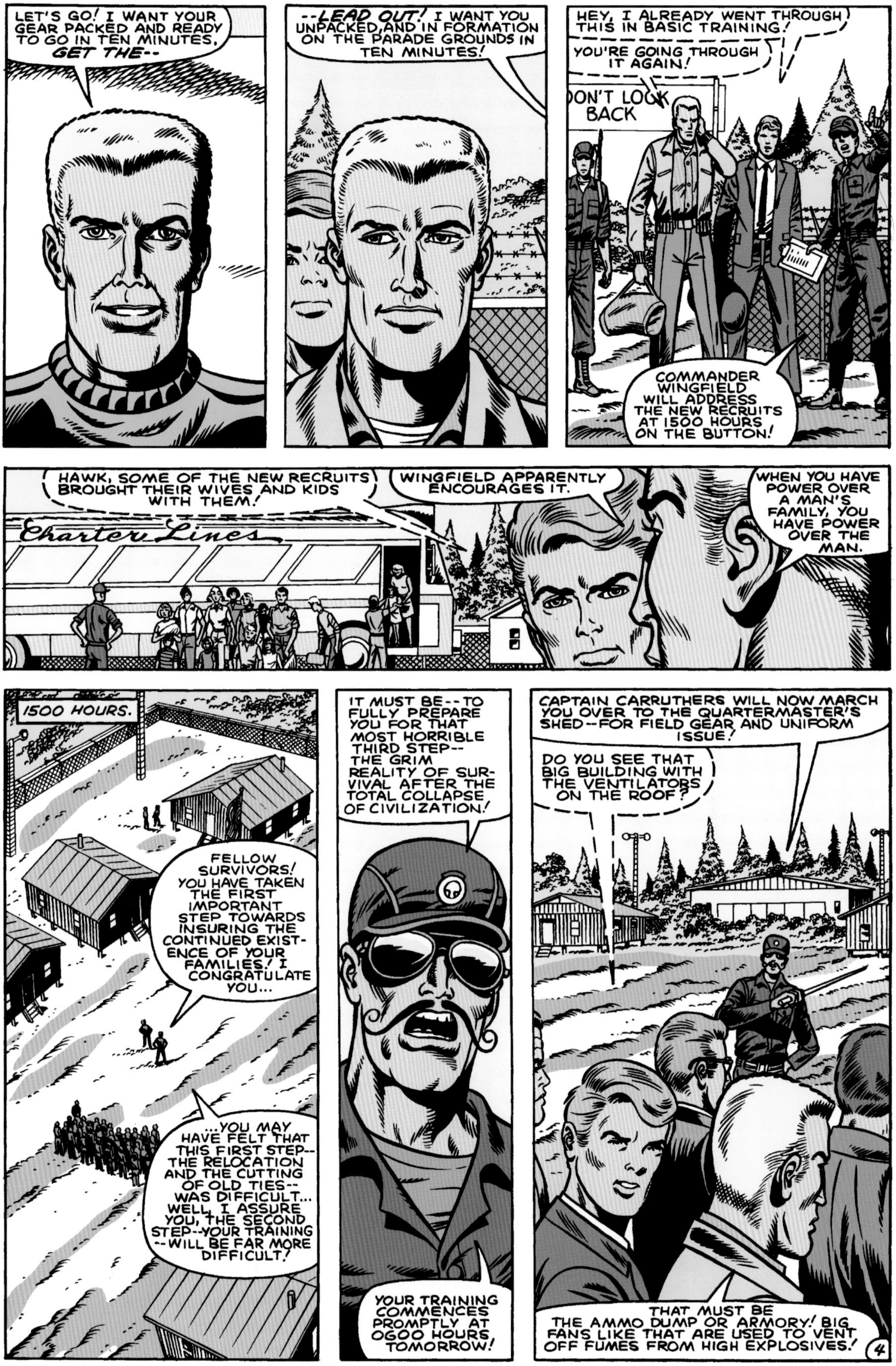
LET'S GO! I WANT YOUR GEAR PACKED AND READY TO GO IN TEN MINUTES. GET THE--
--LEAD OUT! I WANT YOU UNPACKED, AND IN FORMATION ON THE PARADE GROUNDS IN TEN MINUTES!
HEY, I ALREADY WENT THROUGH THIS IN BASIC TRAINING!
YOU'RE GOING THROUGH IT AGAIN!
DON'T LOOK BACK
COMMANDER WINGFIELD WILL ADDRESS THE NEW RECRUITS AT 1500 HOURS ON THE BUTTON!
HAWK, SOME OF THE NEW RECRUITS BROUGHT THEIR WIVES AND KIDS WITH THEM!
WINGFIELD APPARENTLY ENCOURAGES IT.
WHEN YOU HAVE POWER OVER A MAN'S FAMILY, YOU HAVE POWER OVER THE MAN.
Charter Lines
1500 HOURS.
FELLOW SURVIVORS! YOU HAVE TAKEN THE FIRST IMPORTANT STEP TOWARDS INSURING THE CONTINUED EXISTENCE OF YOUR FAMILIES! I CONGRATULATE YOU...
...YOU MAY HAVE FELT THAT THIS FIRST STEP--THE RELOCATION AND THE CUTTING OF OLD TIES--WAS DIFFICULT... WELL, I ASSURE YOU, THE SECOND STEP--YOUR TRAINING--WILL BE FAR MORE DIFFICULT!
IT MUST BE--TO FULLY PREPARE YOU FOR THAT MOST HORRIBLE THIRD STEP--THE GRIM REALITY OF SURVIVAL AFTER THE TOTAL COLLAPSE OF CIVILIZATION!
YOUR TRAINING COMMENCES PROMPTLY AT 0600 HOURS TOMORROW!
CAPTAIN CARRUTHERS WILL NOW MARCH YOU OVER TO THE QUARTERMASTER'S SHED--FOR FIELD GEAR AND UNIFORM ISSUE!
DO YOU SEE THAT BIG BUILDING WITH THE VENTILATORS ON THE ROOF?
THAT MUST BE THE AMMO DUMP OR ARMORY! BIG FANS LIKE THAT ARE USED TO VENT OFF FUMES FROM HIGH EXPLOSIVES!
4

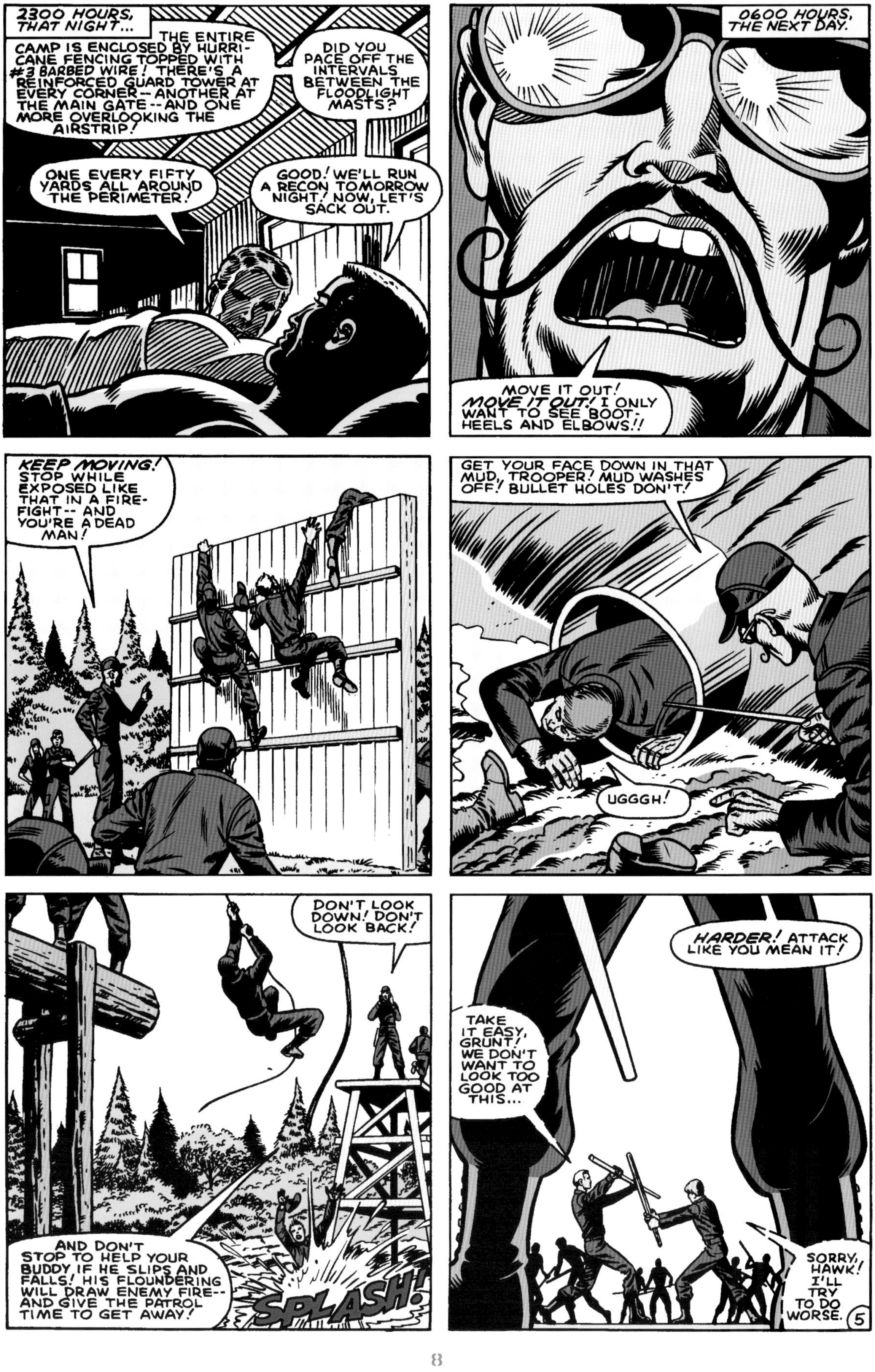
2300 HOURS, THAT NIGHT...
THE ENTIRE CAMP IS ENCLOSED BY HURRICANE FENCING TOPPED WITH #3 BARBED WIRE! THERE'S A REINFORCED GUARD TOWER AT EVERY CORNER -- ANOTHER AT THE MAIN GATE -- AND ONE MORE OVERLOOKING THE AIRSTRIP!
DID YOU PACE OFF THE INTERVALS BETWEEN THE FLOODLIGHT MASTS?
ONE EVERY FIFTY YARDS ALL AROUND THE PERIMETER!
GOOD! WE'LL RUN A RECON TOMORROW NIGHT! NOW, LET'S SACK OUT.
0600 HOURS, THE NEXT DAY.
MOVE IT OUT! MOVE IT OUT! I ONLY WANT TO SEE BOOT-HEELS AND ELBOWS!!
KEEP MOVING! STOP WHILE EXPOSED LIKE THAT IN A FIRE-FIGHT -- AND YOU'RE A DEAD MAN!
GET YOUR FACE DOWN IN THAT MUD, TROOPER! MUD WASHES OFF! BULLET HOLES DON'T!
UGGGH!
DON'T LOOK DOWN! DON'T LOOK BACK!
AND DON'T STOP TO HELP YOUR BUDDY IF HE SLIPS AND FALLS! HIS FLOUNDERING WILL DRAW ENEMY FIRE -- AND GIVE THE PATROL TIME TO GET AWAY!
SPLASH!
HARDER! ATTACK LIKE YOU MEAN IT!
TAKE IT EASY, GRUNT! WE DON'T WANT TO LOOK TOO GOOD AT THIS...
SORRY, HAWK! I'LL TRY TO DO WORSE.
5

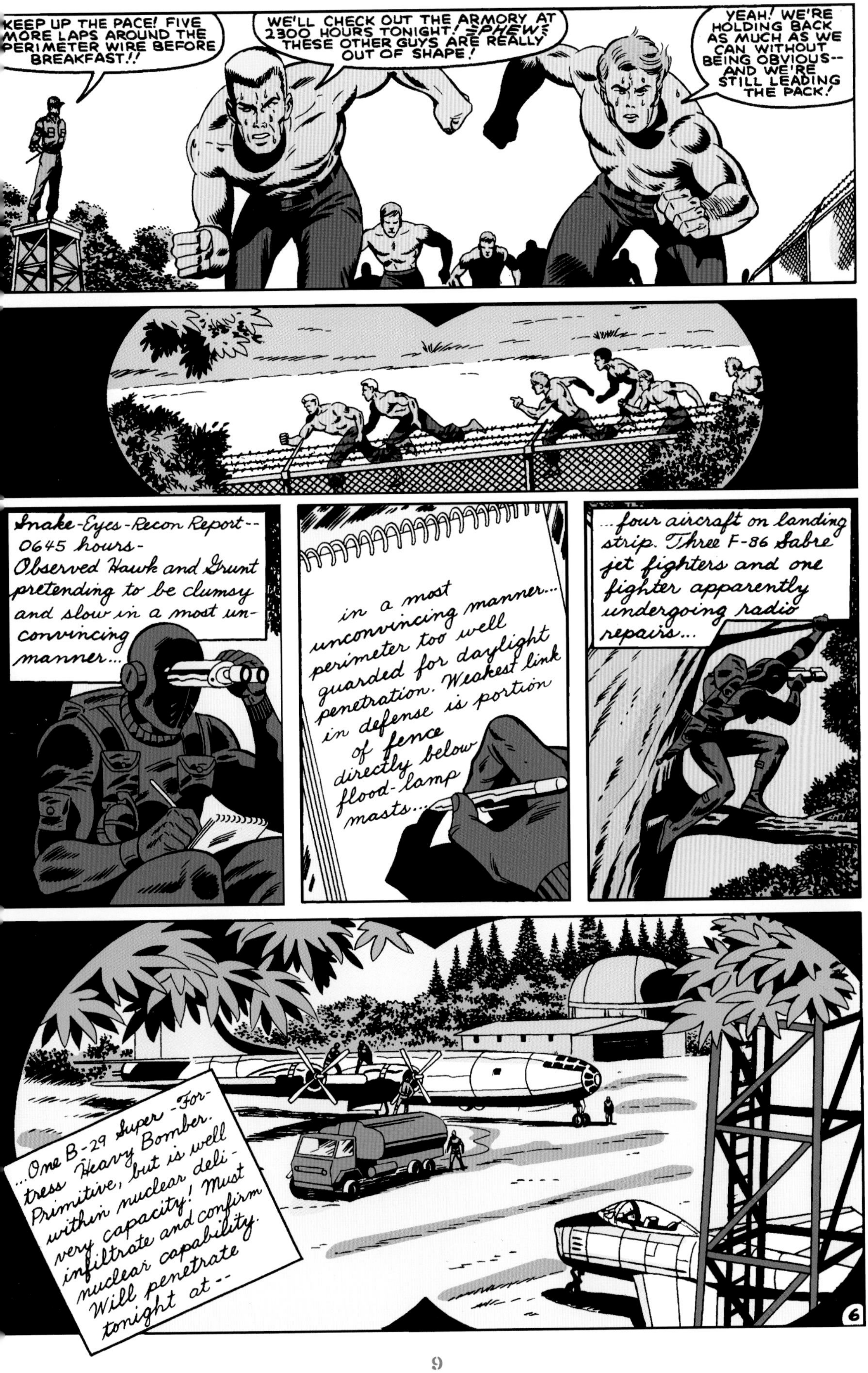
KEEP UP THE PACE! FIVE MORE LAPS AROUND THE PERIMETER WIRE BEFORE BREAKFAST!!
WE'LL CHECK OUT THE ARMORY AT 2300 HOURS TONIGHT! PHEW! THESE OTHER GUYS ARE REALLY OUT OF SHAPE!
YEAH! WE'RE HOLDING BACK AS MUCH AS WE CAN WITHOUT BEING OBVIOUS-- AND WE'RE STILL LEADING THE PACK!
Snake-Eyes-Recon Report-- 0645 hours- Observed Hawk and Grunt pretending to be clumsy and slow in a most un-convincing manner...
in a most unconvincing manner... perimeter too well guarded for daylight penetration. Weakest link in defense is portion of fence directly below flood-lamp masts...
...four aircraft on landing strip. Three F-86 Sabre jet fighters and one fighter apparently undergoing radio repairs...
...One B-29 Super-Fortress Heavy Bomber. Primitive, but is well within nuclear deli-very capacity! Must infiltrate and confirm nuclear capability. Will penetrate tonight at--
6

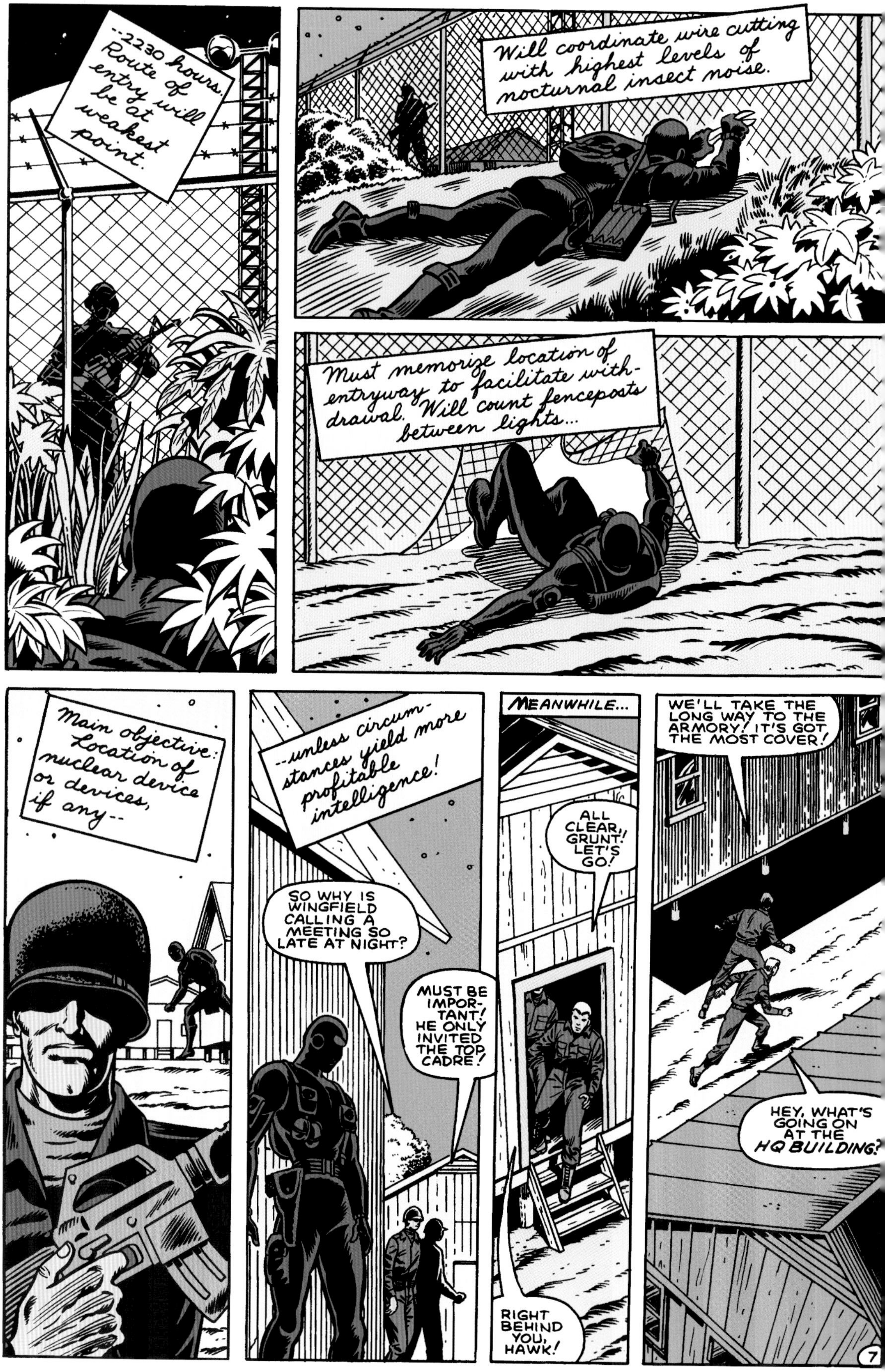
--2230 hours. Route of entry will be at weakest point.
Will coordinate wire cutting with highest levels of nocturnal insect noise.
Must memorize location of entryway to facilitate withdrawal. Will count fenceposts between lights...
Main objective: Location of nuclear device or devices, if any--
--unless circumstances yield more profitable intelligence!
SO WHY IS WINGFIELD CALLING A MEETING SO LATE AT NIGHT?
MUST BE IMPORTANT! HE ONLY INVITED THE TOP CADRE!
MEANWHILE...
ALL CLEAR, GRUNT! LET'S GO!
RIGHT BEHIND YOU, HAWK!
WE'LL TAKE THE LONG WAY TO THE ARMORY! IT'S GOT THE MOST COVER!
HEY, WHAT'S GOING ON AT THE HQ BUILDING?
7

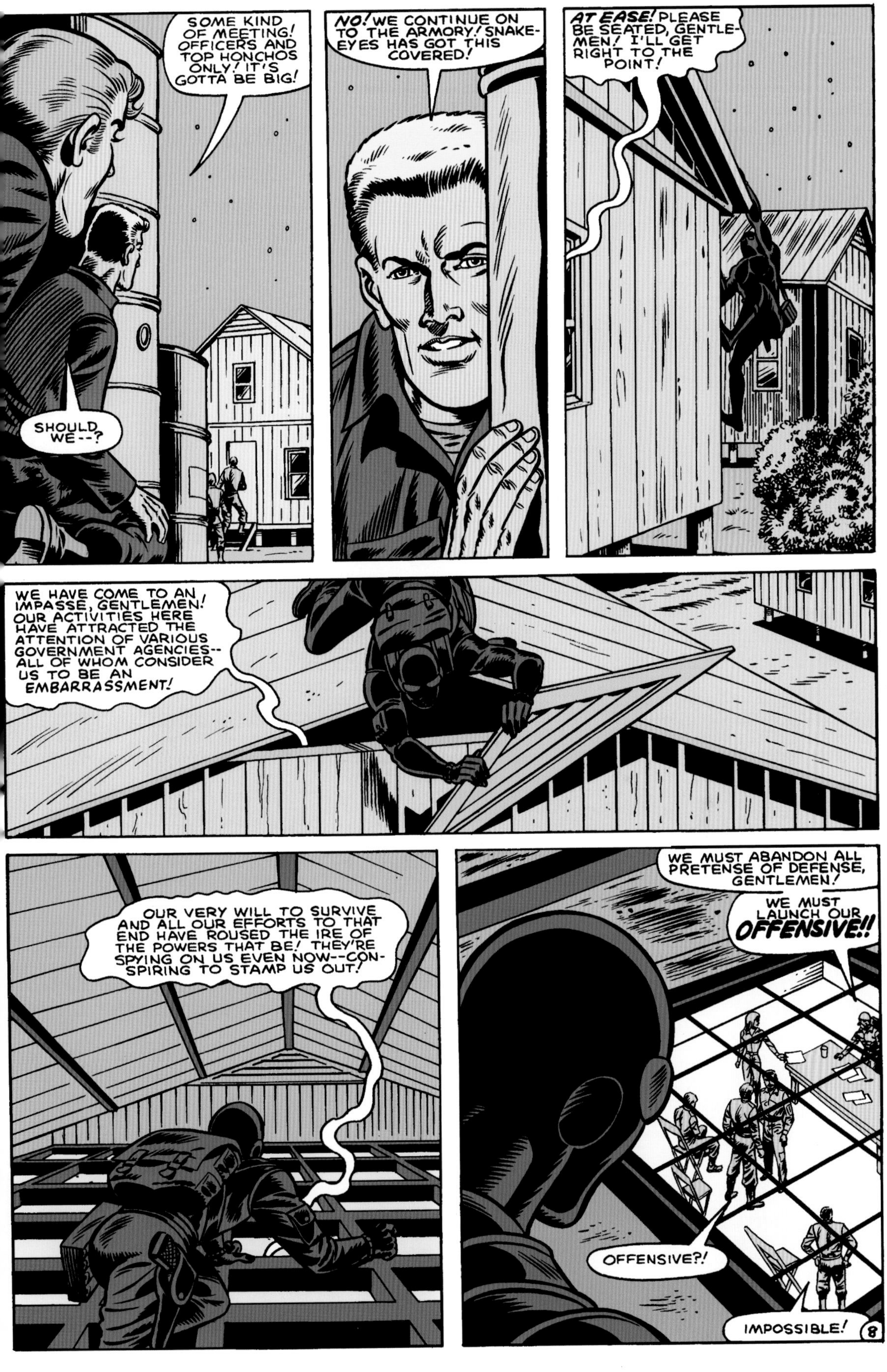
SOME KIND OF MEETING! OFFICERS AND TOP HONCHOS ONLY! IT'S GOTTA BE BIG!
SHOULD WE--?
NO! WE CONTINUE ON TO THE ARMORY! SNAKE-EYES HAS GOT THIS COVERED!
AT EASE! PLEASE BE SEATED, GENTLE-MEN! I'LL GET RIGHT TO THE POINT!
WE HAVE COME TO AN IMPASSE, GENTLEMEN! OUR ACTIVITIES HERE HAVE ATTRACTED THE ATTENTION OF VARIOUS GOVERNMENT AGENCIES-- ALL OF WHOM CONSIDER US TO BE AN EMBARRASSMENT!
OUR VERY WILL TO SURVIVE AND ALL OUR EFFORTS TO THAT END HAVE ROUSED THE IRE OF THE POWERS THAT BE! THEY'RE SPYING ON US EVEN NOW--CON-SPIRING TO STAMP US OUT!
WE MUST ABANDON ALL PRETENSE OF DEFENSE, GENTLEMEN!
WE MUST LAUNCH OUR OFFENSIVE!!
OFFENSIVE?!
IMPOSSIBLE!
8

NOT IMPOSSIBLE, GENTLEMEN! THE TECHNICIANS FROM *COBRA* WHO INSTALLED THE SILENT ALARM SYSTEM THAT GUARDS OUR ARMORY--

--HAVE ALSO PROVIDED US WITH TWO NUCLEAR WARHEADS!

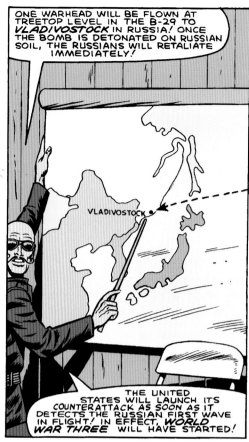

ONE WARHEAD WILL BE FLOWN AT TREETOP LEVEL IN THE B-29 TO *VLADIVOSTOCK* IN RUSSIA! ONCE THE BOMB IS DETONATED ON RUSSIAN SOIL, THE RUSSIANS WILL RETALIATE IMMEDIATELY!

VLADIVOSTOCK

THE UNITED STATES WILL LAUNCH ITS COUNTERATTACK AS SOON AS IT DETECTS THE RUSSIAN FIRST WAVE IN FLIGHT! IN EFFECT, *WORLD WAR THREE* WILL HAVE STARTED!

AFTER THE SWINE HAVE WIPED EACH OTHER OUT, *WE* SHALL EMERGE FROM OUR WELL-STOCKED FORTIFIED SHELTERS BENEATH THIS COMPOUND --TO REBUILD A NEW WORLD IN OUR IMAGE!

THE SECOND WARHEAD IS BURIED UNDER OUR CAMP--IN A LOCATION KNOWN ONLY TO CARRUTHERS, MY WIFE AND ME! I CAN ARM AND SET THE DETONATOR TIMER BY REMOTE CONTROL!

ONCE SET, ONLY I CAN DISARM IT!

IF OUR BOMBING ATTEMPT ON VLADIVO-STOCK FAILS--WE ARE UTTERLY DOOMED! BOTH GOVERNMENTS WILL TRACK US TO THE ENDS OF THE EARTH...

HOWEVER, IF WE DETONATE THE BOMB HERE IN MONTANA, THE UNITED STATES WILL HAVE TO ASSUME THAT THE RUSSIANS HAVE OPTED FOR A RETALIATORY STRIKE...

AND, ALTHOUGH WE WILL PERISH IN THE FIRST BLAST, THE SCUM THAT PERSECUTE US SHALL JOIN US IN THE BLASTS THAT FOLLOW!

9

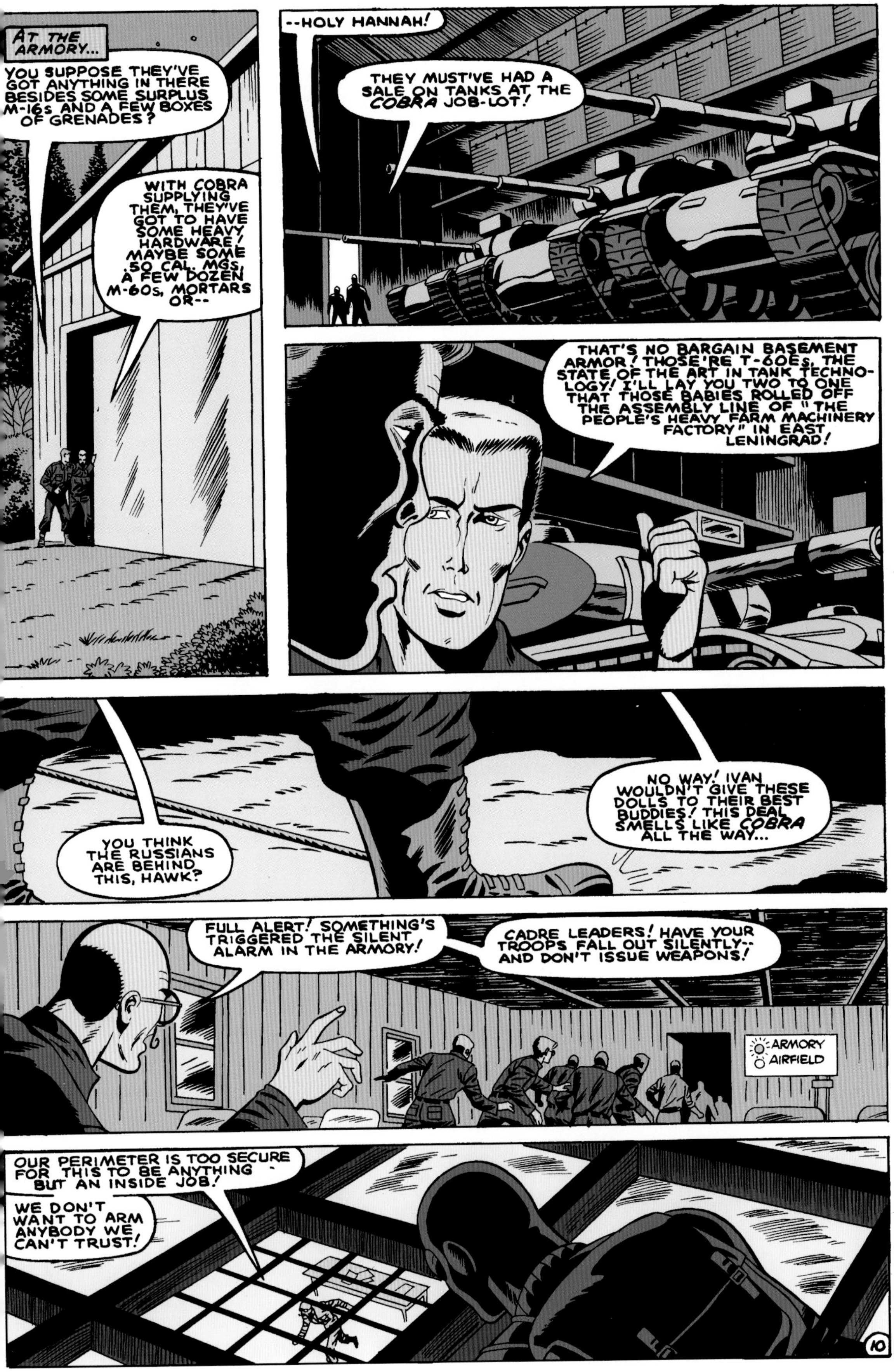
AT THE ARMORY...
YOU SUPPOSE THEY'VE GOT ANYTHING IN THERE BESIDES SOME SURPLUS M-16s AND A FEW BOXES OF GRENADES?
WITH COBRA SUPPLYING THEM, THEY'VE GOT TO HAVE SOME HEAVY HARDWARE! MAYBE SOME .50 CAL. MGs, A FEW DOZEN M-60s, MORTARS OR--
--HOLY HANNAH!
THEY MUST'VE HAD A SALE ON TANKS AT THE COBRA JOB-LOT!
THAT'S NO BARGAIN BASEMENT ARMOR! THOSE'RE T-60Es, THE STATE OF THE ART IN TANK TECHNOLOGY! I'LL LAY YOU TWO TO ONE THAT THOSE BABIES ROLLED OFF THE ASSEMBLY LINE OF "THE PEOPLE'S HEAVY FARM MACHINERY FACTORY" IN EAST LENINGRAD!
YOU THINK THE RUSSIANS ARE BEHIND THIS, HAWK?
NO WAY! IVAN WOULDN'T GIVE THESE DOLLS TO THEIR BEST BUDDIES! THIS DEAL SMELLS LIKE COBRA ALL THE WAY...
FULL ALERT! SOMETHING'S TRIGGERED THE SILENT ALARM IN THE ARMORY!
CADRE LEADERS! HAVE YOUR TROOPS FALL OUT SILENTLY-- AND DON'T ISSUE WEAPONS!
ARMORY
AIRFIELD
OUR PERIMETER IS TOO SECURE FOR THIS TO BE ANYTHING BUT AN INSIDE JOB!
WE DON'T WANT TO ARM ANYBODY WE CAN'T TRUST!
10

SURROUND THE ARMORY! SECURE ALL EXITS AND WINDOWS!

FIRST PLATOON, IN THROUGH THE FRONT DOOR!

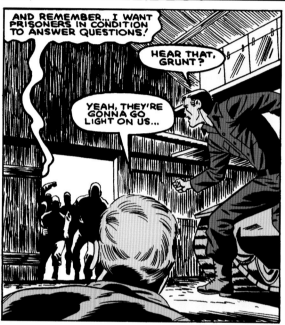

AND REMEMBER... I WANT PRISONERS IN CONDITION TO ANSWER QUESTIONS!

HEAR THAT, GRUNT?

YEAH, THEY'RE GONNA GO LIGHT ON US...

THINK MAYBE WE OUGHTA PULL OUR PUNCHES, TOO?

NAAAH!

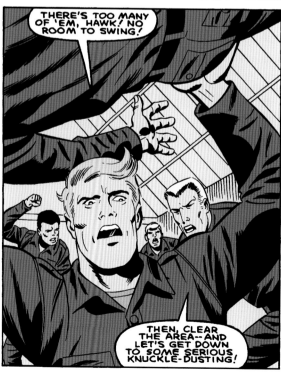

THERE'S TOO MANY OF 'EM, HAWK! NO ROOM TO SWING!

THEN, CLEAR THE AREA-- AND LET'S GET DOWN TO SOME SERIOUS KNUCKLE-DUSTING!

YOU GOT IT, HAWK!

SLAMM!!

11

TEN MINUTES LATER...

COMMANDER WINGFIELD! THE INTRUDERS PUT A DOZEN OF OUR MEN OUT OF COMMISSION, BUT WE HAVE FINALLY SUBDUED THEM!

DO YOU WANT TO INTERROGATE THEM NOW?

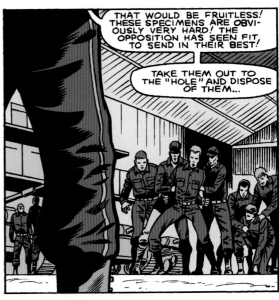

THAT WOULD BE FRUITLESS! THESE SPECIMENS ARE OBVIOUSLY VERY HARD! THE OPPOSITION HAS SEEN FIT, TO SEND IN THEIR BEST!

TAKE THEM OUT TO THE "HOLE" AND DISPOSE OF THEM...

THIS DRASTICALLY ALTERS THE SITUATION! I'M FORCED TO MOVE UP OUR SCHEDULE CONSIDERABLY!

SHARY, ACTUATE "PLAN ALPHA"... CARRUTHERS, "SUIT UP" AND REPORT TO THE AIRFIELD...

AT THE COMMUNICATIONS SHED...

≥URK!≤

DIT-DIT-DOT-DIT

12

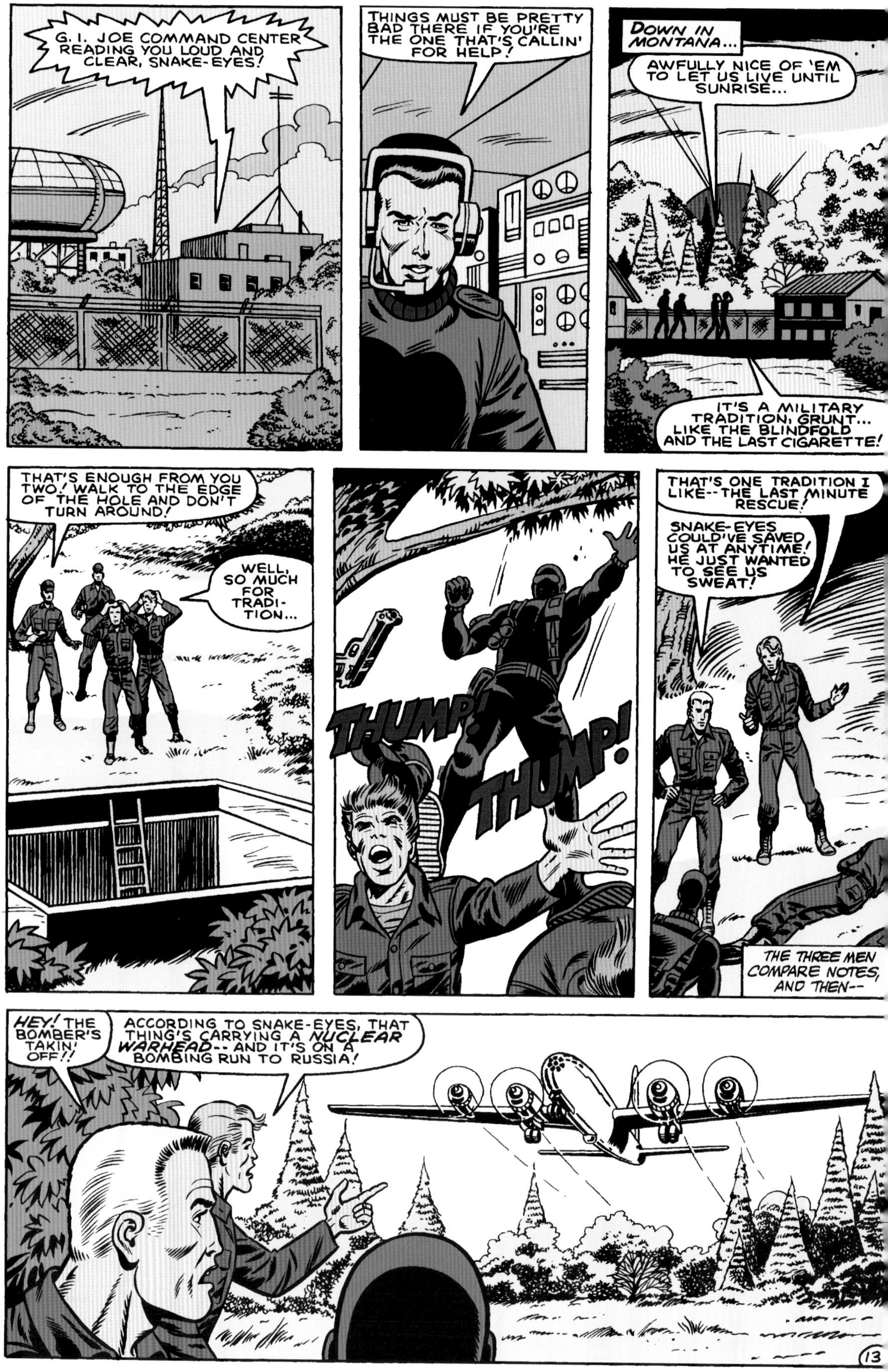

G. I. JOE COMMAND CENTER READING YOU LOUD AND CLEAR, SNAKE-EYES!
THINGS MUST BE PRETTY BAD THERE IF YOU'RE THE ONE THAT'S CALLIN' FOR HELP!
DOWN IN MONTANA...
AWFULLY NICE OF 'EM TO LET US LIVE UNTIL SUNRISE...
IT'S A MILITARY TRADITION, GRUNT... LIKE THE BLINDFOLD AND THE LAST CIGARETTE!
THAT'S ENOUGH FROM YOU TWO! WALK TO THE EDGE OF THE HOLE AND DON'T TURN AROUND!
WELL, SO MUCH FOR TRADI-TION...
THUMP!
THUMP!
THAT'S ONE TRADITION I LIKE--THE LAST MINUTE RESCUE!
SNAKE-EYES COULD'VE SAVED US AT ANYTIME! HE JUST WANTED TO SEE US SWEAT!
THE THREE MEN COMPARE NOTES, AND THEN--
HEY! THE BOMBER'S TAKIN' OFF!!
ACCORDING TO SNAKE-EYES, THAT THING'S CARRYING A NUCLEAR WARHEAD-- AND IT'S ON A BOMBING RUN TO RUSSIA!
13

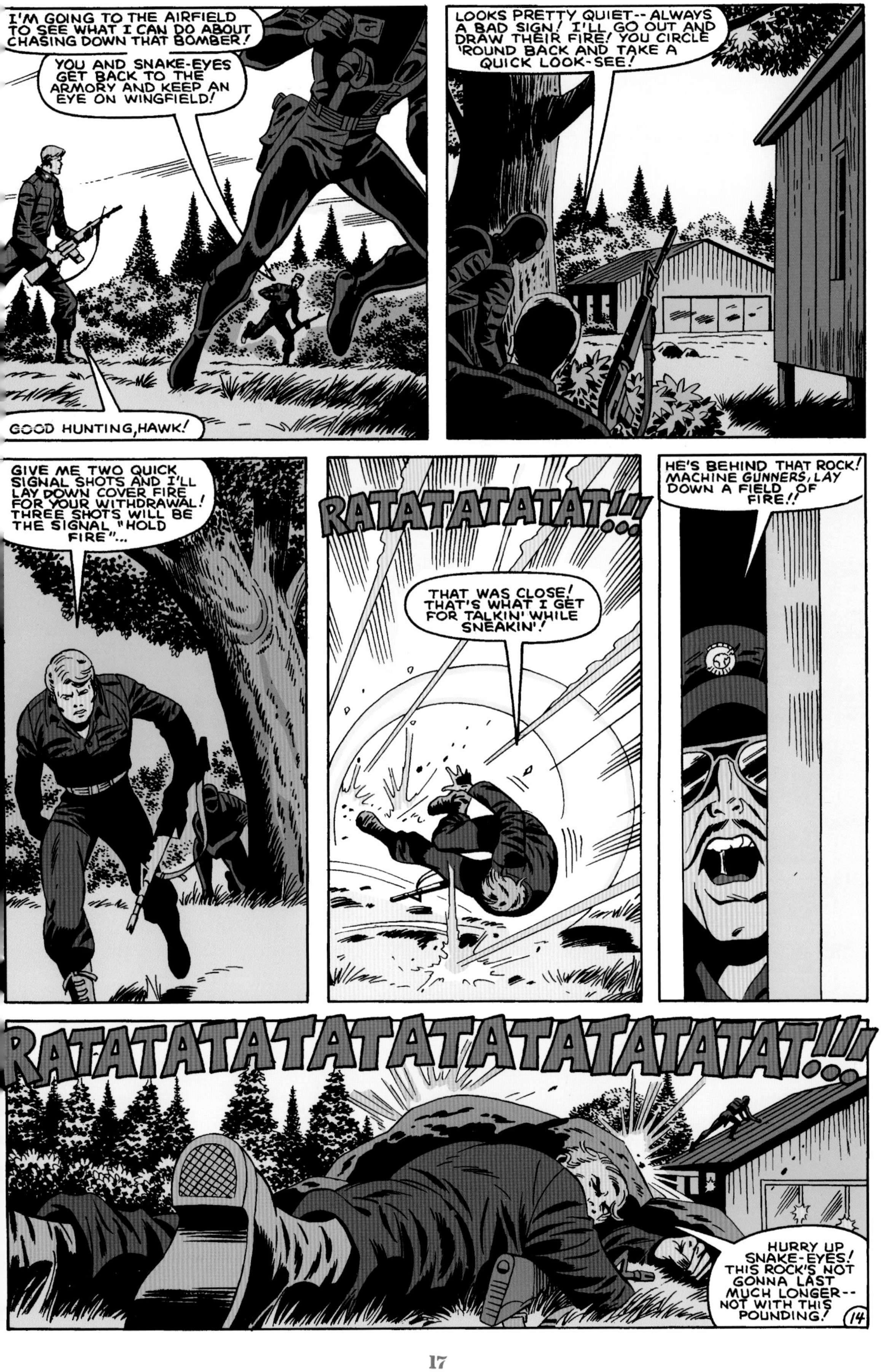
I'M GOING TO THE AIRFIELD TO SEE WHAT I CAN DO ABOUT CHASING DOWN THAT BOMBER!
YOU AND SNAKE-EYES GET BACK TO THE ARMORY AND KEEP AN EYE ON WINGFIELD!
GOOD HUNTING, HAWK!
LOOKS PRETTY QUIET-- ALWAYS A BAD SIGN! I'LL GO OUT AND DRAW THEIR FIRE! YOU CIRCLE 'ROUND BACK AND TAKE A QUICK LOOK-SEE!
GIVE ME TWO QUICK SIGNAL SHOTS AND I'LL LAY DOWN COVER FIRE FOR YOUR WITHDRAWAL! THREE SHOTS WILL BE THE SIGNAL "HOLD FIRE"...
RATATATATATAT!!...
THAT WAS CLOSE! THAT'S WHAT I GET FOR TALKIN' WHILE SNEAKIN'!
HE'S BEHIND THAT ROCK! MACHINE GUNNERS, LAY DOWN A FIELD OF FIRE!!
RATATATATATATATATATATATAT!!...
HURRY UP SNAKE-EYES! THIS ROCK'S NOT GONNA LAST MUCH LONGER-- NOT WITH THIS POUNDING!
14

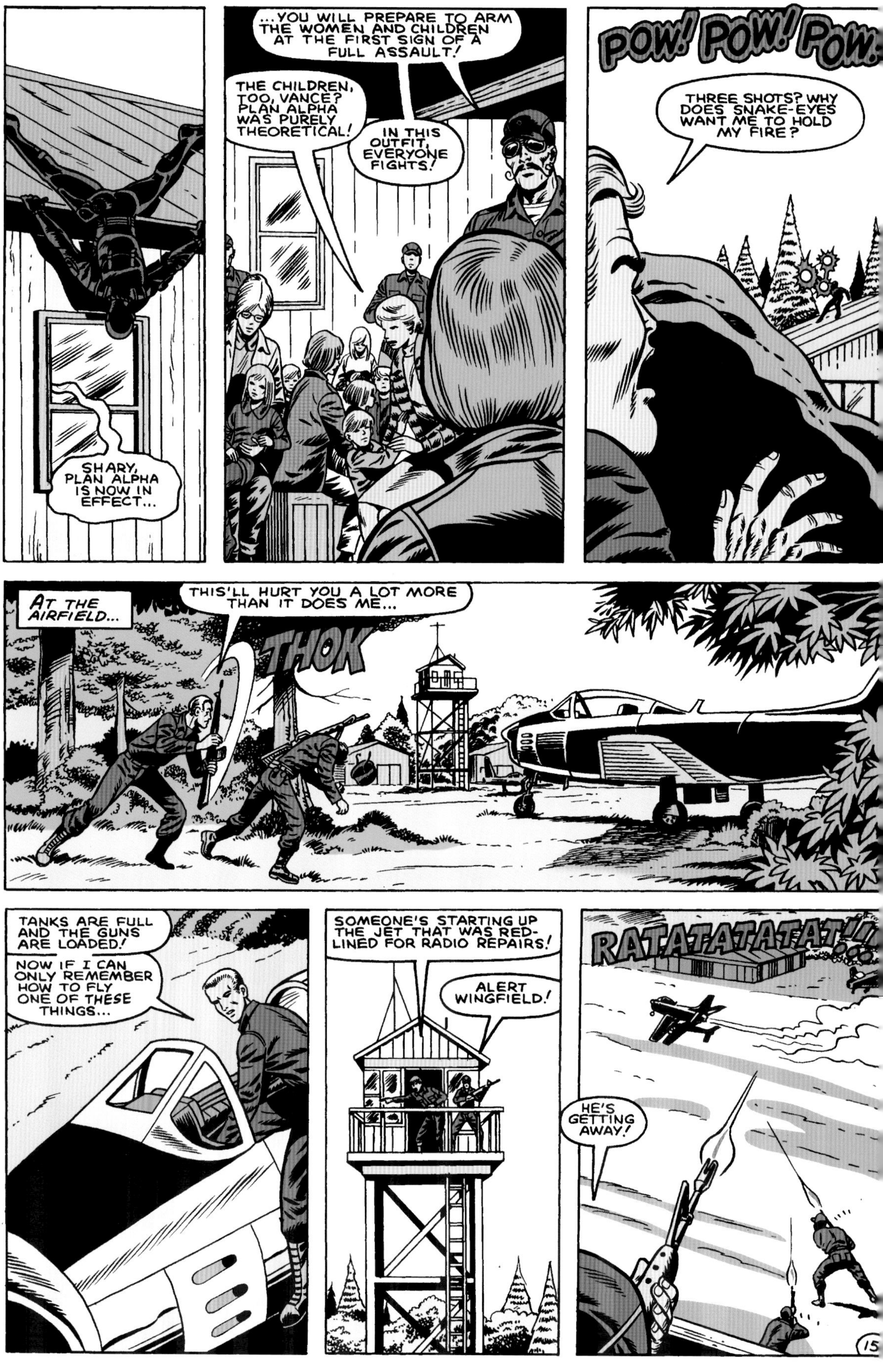
SHARY, PLAN ALPHA IS NOW IN EFFECT...
...YOU WILL PREPARE TO ARM THE WOMEN AND CHILDREN AT THE FIRST SIGN OF A FULL ASSAULT!
THE CHILDREN, TOO, VANCE? PLAN ALPHA WAS PURELY THEORETICAL!
IN THIS OUTFIT, EVERYONE FIGHTS!
POW! POW! POW!
THREE SHOTS? WHY DOES SNAKE-EYES WANT ME TO HOLD MY FIRE?
AT THE AIRFIELD...
THIS'LL HURT YOU A LOT MORE THAN IT DOES ME...
THOK
TANKS ARE FULL AND THE GUNS ARE LOADED!
NOW IF I CAN ONLY REMEMBER HOW TO FLY ONE OF THESE THINGS...
SOMEONE'S STARTING UP THE JET THAT WAS RED-LINED FOR RADIO REPAIRS!
ALERT WINGFIELD!
RATATATATAT!!
HE'S GETTING AWAY!
15

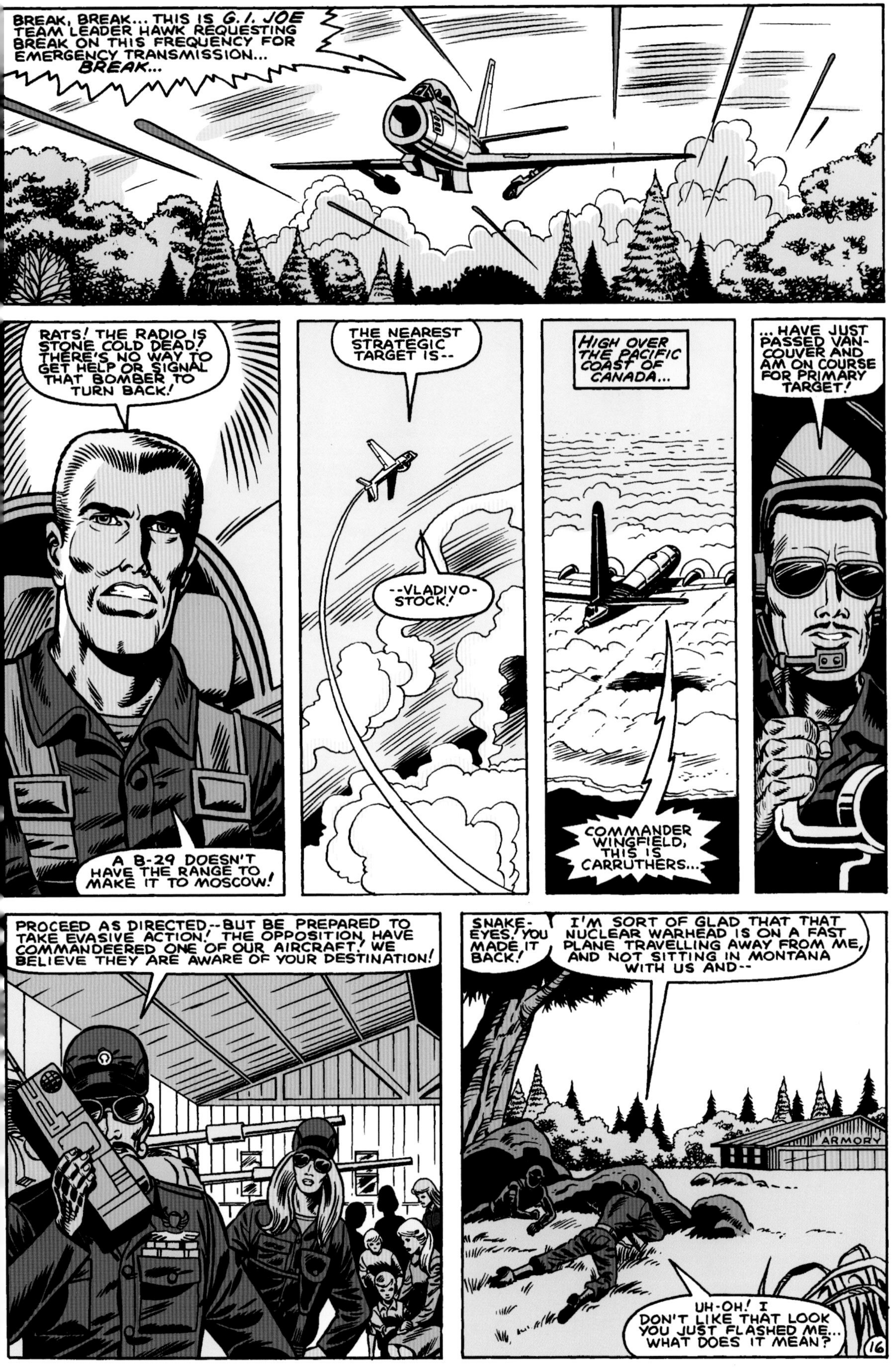
BREAK, BREAK... THIS IS G. I. JOE TEAM LEADER HAWK REQUESTING BREAK ON THIS FREQUENCY FOR EMERGENCY TRANSMISSION... BREAK...
RATS! THE RADIO IS STONE COLD DEAD! THERE'S NO WAY TO GET HELP OR SIGNAL THAT BOMBER TO TURN BACK!
A B-29 DOESN'T HAVE THE RANGE TO MAKE IT TO MOSCOW!
THE NEAREST STRATEGIC TARGET IS--
--VLADIVO-STOCK!
HIGH OVER THE PACIFIC COAST OF CANADA...
COMMANDER WINGFIELD, THIS IS CARRUTHERS...
...HAVE JUST PASSED VAN-COUVER AND AM ON COURSE FOR PRIMARY TARGET!
PROCEED AS DIRECTED--BUT BE PREPARED TO TAKE EVASIVE ACTION! THE OPPOSITION HAVE COMMANDEERED ONE OF OUR AIRCRAFT! WE BELIEVE THEY ARE AWARE OF YOUR DESTINATION!
SNAKE-EYES! YOU MADE IT BACK!
I'M SORT OF GLAD THAT THAT NUCLEAR WARHEAD IS ON A FAST PLANE TRAVELLING AWAY FROM ME, AND NOT SITTING IN MONTANA WITH US AND--
ARMORY
UH-OH! I DON'T LIKE THAT LOOK YOU JUST FLASHED ME... WHAT DOES IT MEAN?
16

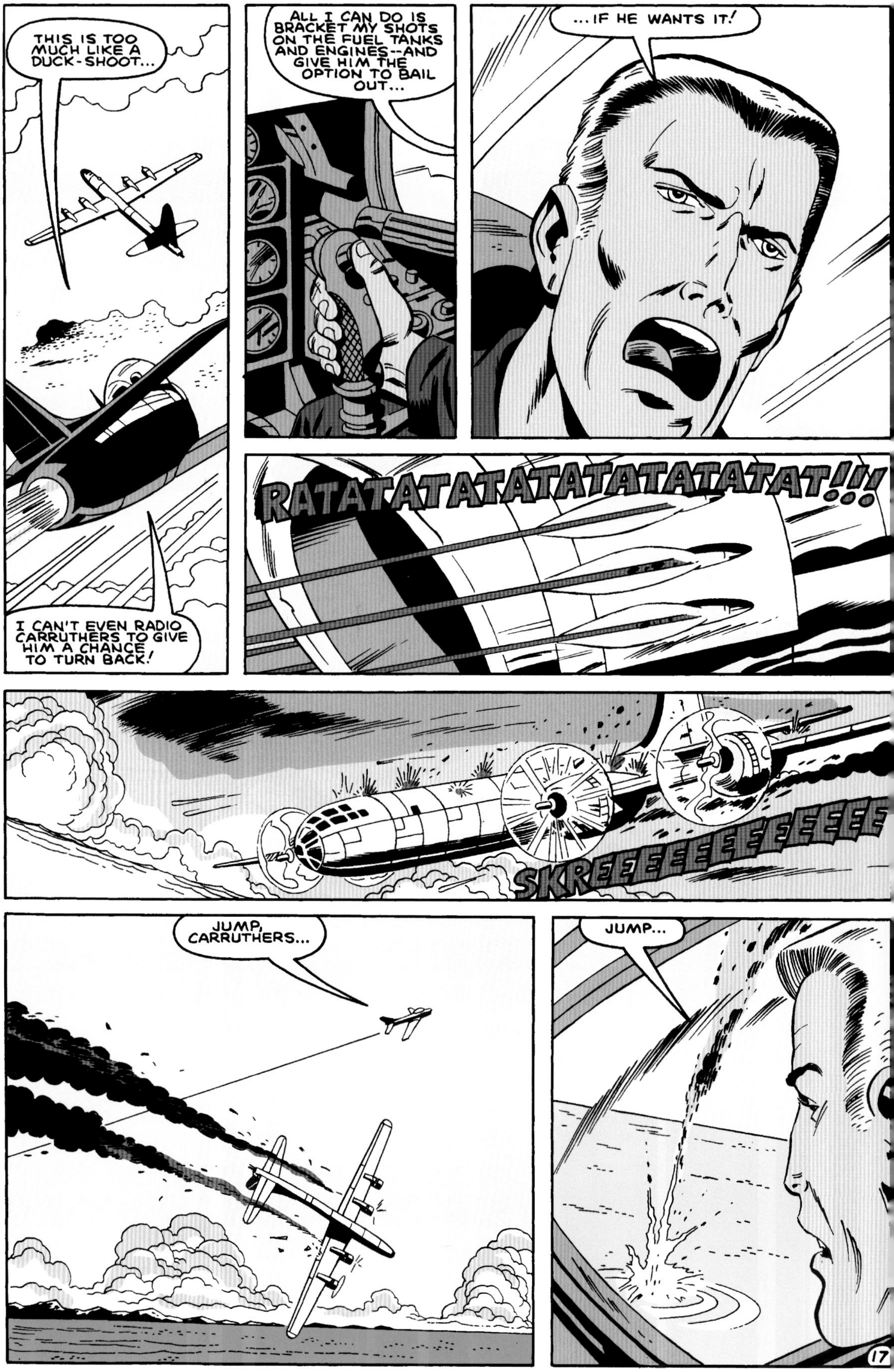
THIS IS TOO MUCH LIKE A DUCK-SHOOT...
I CAN'T EVEN RADIO CARRUTHERS TO GIVE HIM A CHANCE TO TURN BACK!
ALL I CAN DO IS BRACKET MY SHOTS ON THE FUEL TANKS AND ENGINES--AND GIVE HIM THE OPTION TO BAIL OUT...
...IF HE WANTS IT!
RATATATATATATATATATATAT!!!
SKREEEEEEEEEEEEEEE
JUMP, CARRUTHERS...
JUMP...
17

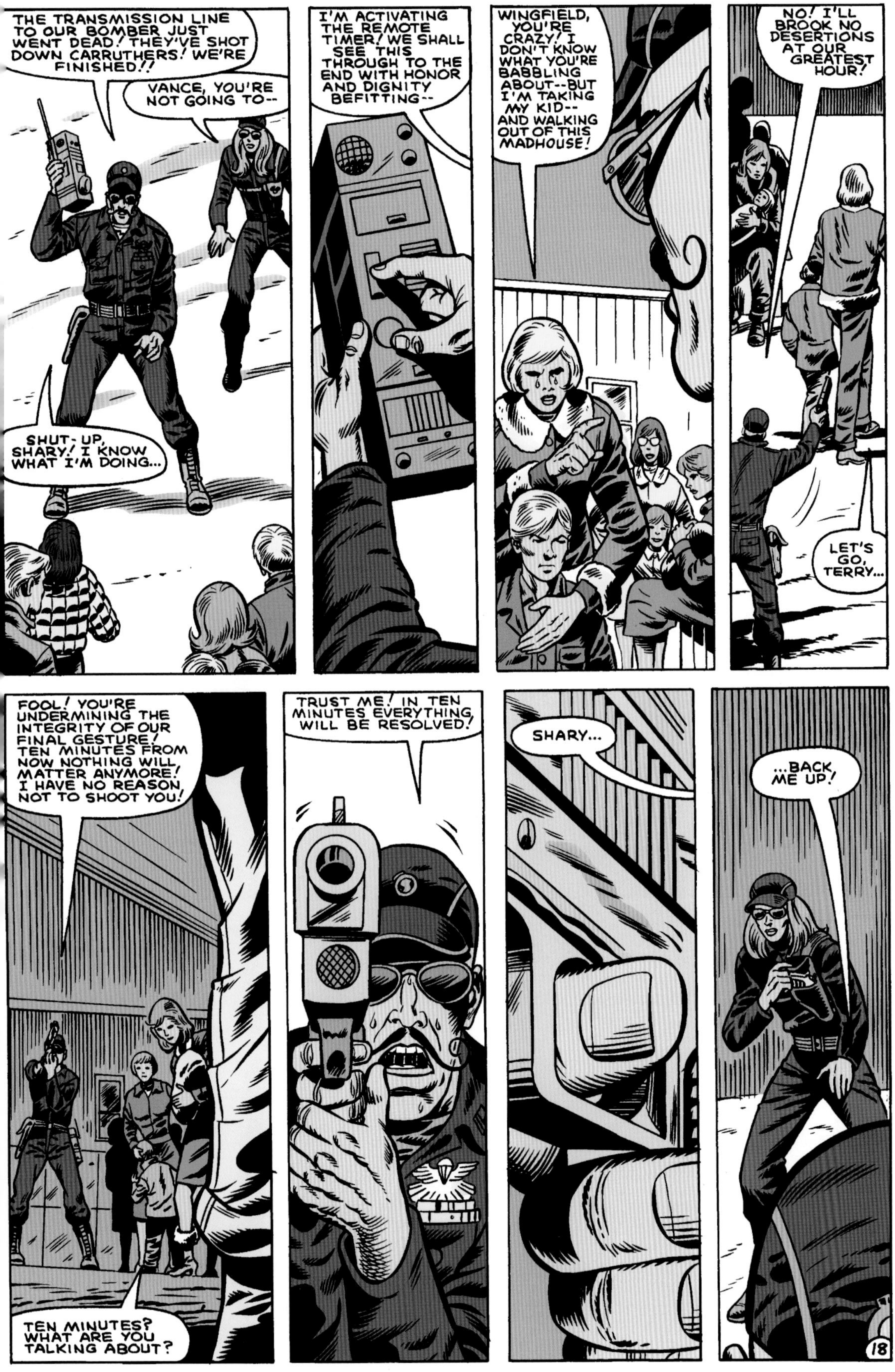
THE TRANSMISSION LINE TO OUR BOMBER JUST WENT DEAD! THEY'VE SHOT DOWN CARRUTHERS! WE'RE FINISHED!!
VANCE, YOU'RE NOT GOING TO--
SHUT-UP, SHARY! I KNOW WHAT I'M DOING...
I'M ACTIVATING THE REMOTE TIMER! WE SHALL SEE THIS THROUGH TO THE END WITH HONOR AND DIGNITY BEFITTING--
WINGFIELD, YOU'RE CRAZY! I DON'T KNOW WHAT YOU'RE BABBLING ABOUT--BUT I'M TAKING MY KID--AND WALKING OUT OF THIS MADHOUSE!
NO! I'LL BROOK NO DESERTIONS AT OUR GREATEST HOUR!
LET'S GO, TERRY...
FOOL! YOU'RE UNDERMINING THE INTEGRITY OF OUR FINAL GESTURE! TEN MINUTES FROM NOW NOTHING WILL MATTER ANYMORE! I HAVE NO REASON NOT TO SHOOT YOU!
TEN MINUTES? WHAT ARE YOU TALKING ABOUT?
TRUST ME! IN TEN MINUTES EVERYTHING WILL BE RESOLVED!
SHARY...
...BACK ME UP!
18

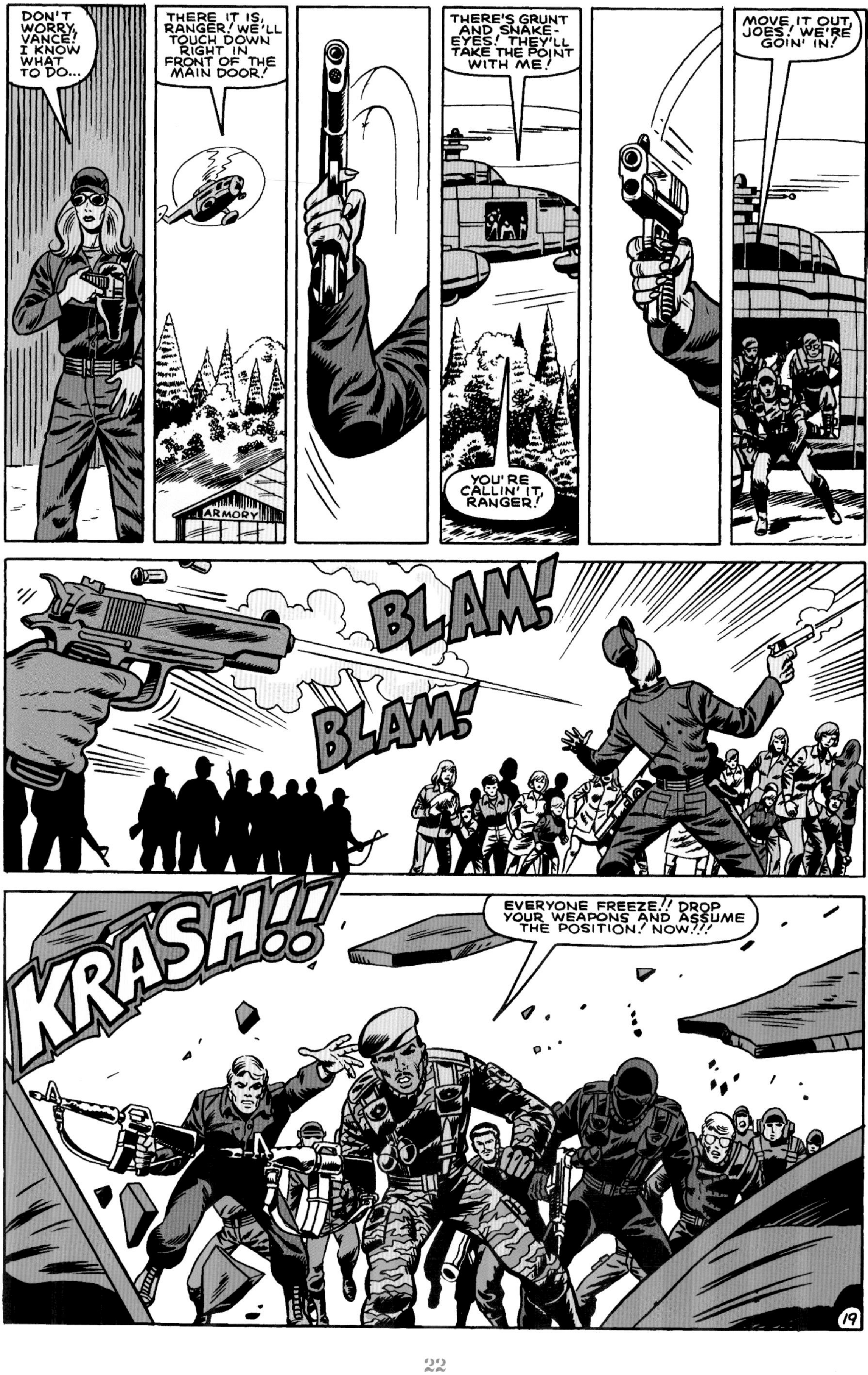
DON'T WORRY, VANCE! I KNOW WHAT TO DO...
THERE IT IS, RANGER! WE'LL TOUCH DOWN RIGHT IN FRONT OF THE MAIN DOOR!
ARMORY
THERE'S GRUNT AND SNAKE-EYES! THEY'LL TAKE THE POINT WITH ME!
YOU'RE CALLIN' IT, RANGER!
MOVE IT OUT, JOES! WE'RE GOIN' IN!
BLAM!
BLAM!
KRASH!!
EVERYONE FREEZE!! DROP YOUR WEAPONS AND ASSUME THE POSITION! NOW!!!
19

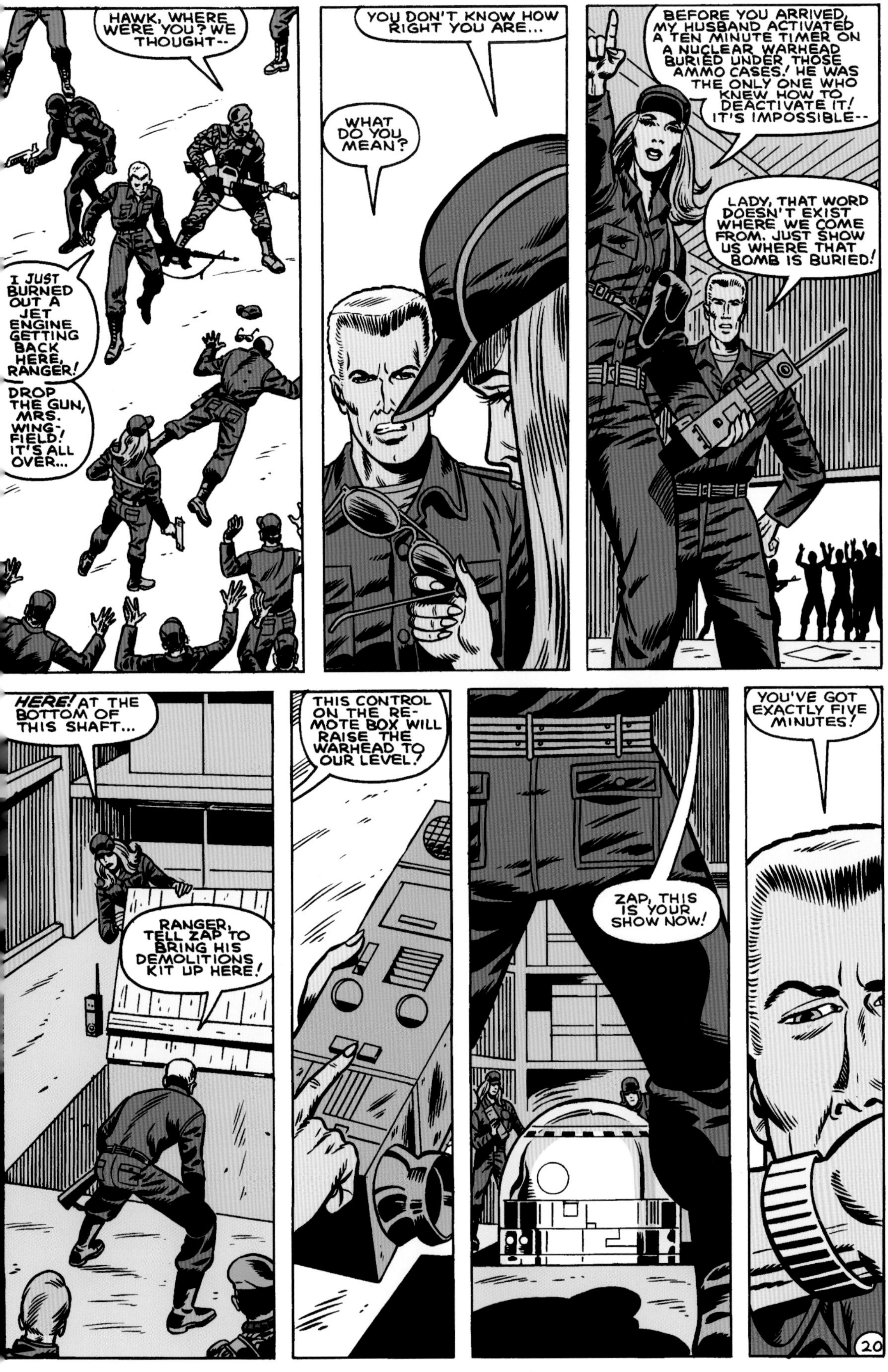
HAWK, WHERE WERE YOU? WE THOUGHT--
I JUST BURNED OUT A JET ENGINE GETTING BACK HERE, RANGER!
DROP THE GUN, MRS. WING-FIELD! IT'S ALL OVER...
YOU DON'T KNOW HOW RIGHT YOU ARE...
WHAT DO YOU MEAN?
BEFORE YOU ARRIVED, MY HUSBAND ACTIVATED A TEN MINUTE TIMER ON A NUCLEAR WARHEAD BURIED UNDER THOSE AMMO CASES! HE WAS THE ONLY ONE WHO KNEW HOW TO DEACTIVATE IT! IT'S IMPOSSIBLE--
LADY, THAT WORD DOESN'T EXIST WHERE WE COME FROM. JUST SHOW US WHERE THAT BOMB IS BURIED!
HERE! AT THE BOTTOM OF THIS SHAFT...
RANGER, TELL ZAP TO BRING HIS DEMOLITIONS KIT UP HERE!
THIS CONTROL ON THE RE-MOTE BOX WILL RAISE THE WARHEAD TO OUR LEVEL!
ZAP, THIS IS YOUR SHOW NOW!
YOU'VE GOT EXACTLY FIVE MINUTES!
20

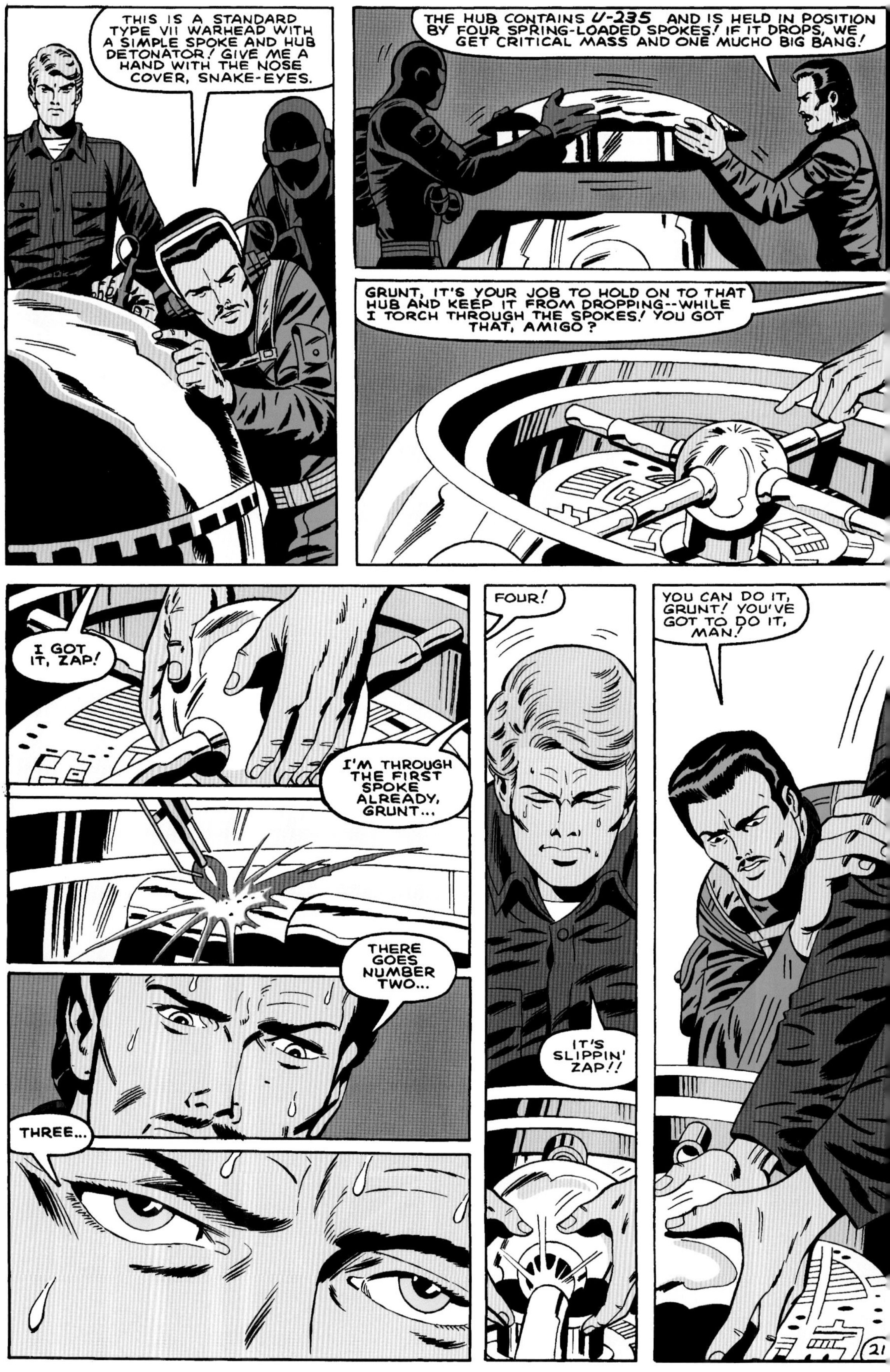
THIS IS A STANDARD TYPE VII WARHEAD WITH A SIMPLE SPOKE AND HUB DETONATOR! GIVE ME A HAND WITH THE NOSE COVER, SNAKE-EYES.
THE HUB CONTAINS U-235 AND IS HELD IN POSITION BY FOUR SPRING-LOADED SPOKES! IF IT DROPS, WE GET CRITICAL MASS AND ONE MUCHO BIG BANG!
GRUNT, IT'S YOUR JOB TO HOLD ON TO THAT HUB AND KEEP IT FROM DROPPING--WHILE I TORCH THROUGH THE SPOKES! YOU GOT THAT, AMIGO?
I GOT IT, ZAP!
I'M THROUGH THE FIRST SPOKE ALREADY, GRUNT...
THERE GOES NUMBER TWO...
THREE...
FOUR!
IT'S SLIPPIN' ZAP!!
YOU CAN DO IT, GRUNT! YOU'VE GOT TO DO IT, MAN!
21

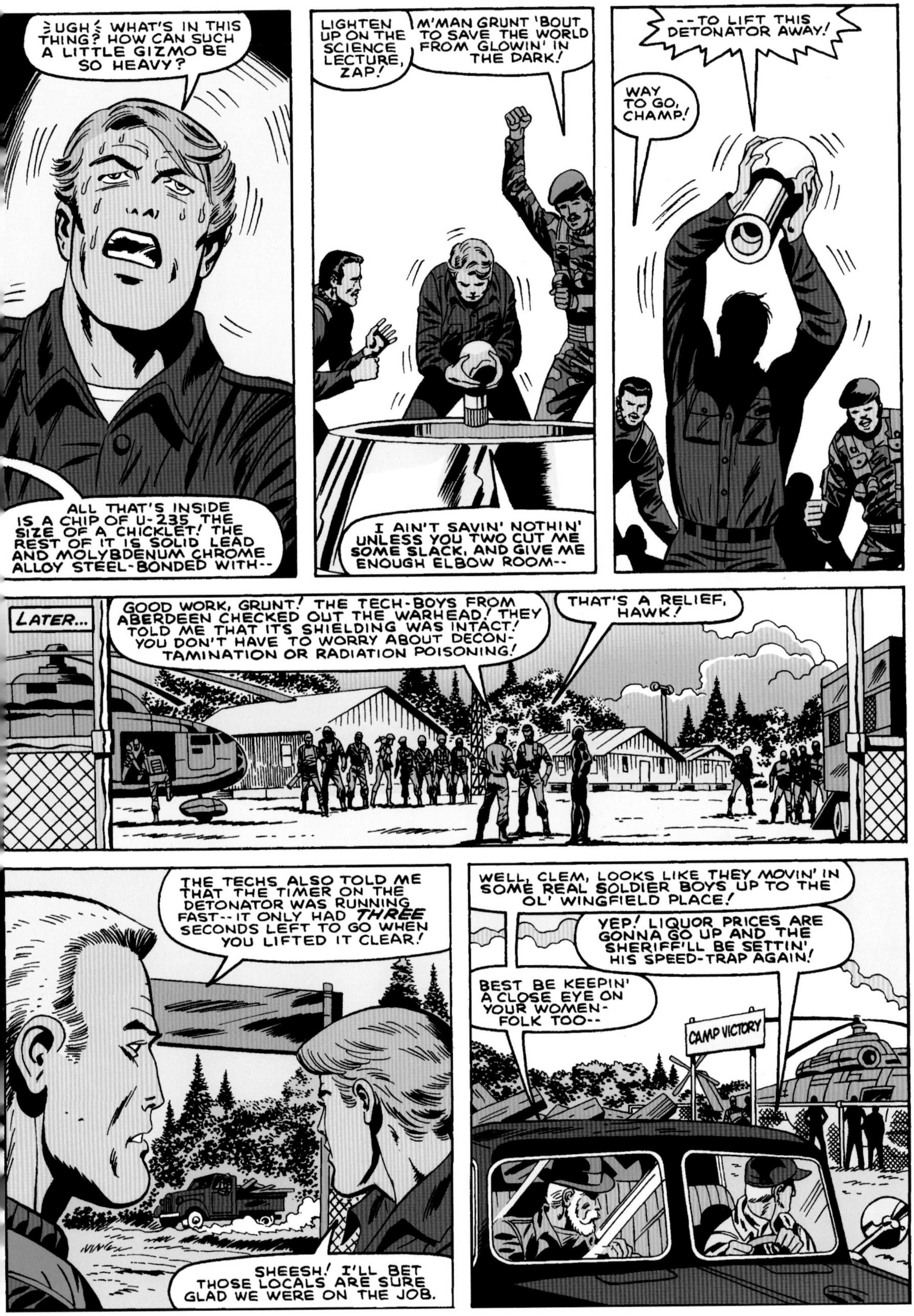
UGH! WHAT'S IN THIS THING? HOW CAN SUCH A LITTLE GIZMO BE SO HEAVY?
ALL THAT'S INSIDE IS A CHIP OF U-235 THE SIZE OF A CHICKLET! THE REST OF IT IS SOLID LEAD AND MOLYBDENUM CHROME ALLOY STEEL-BONDED WITH--
LIGHTEN UP ON THE SCIENCE LECTURE, ZAP!
M'MAN GRUNT 'BOUT TO SAVE THE WORLD FROM GLOWIN' IN THE DARK!
I AIN'T SAVIN' NOTHIN' UNLESS YOU TWO CUT ME SOME SLACK, AND GIVE ME ENOUGH ELBOW ROOM--
--TO LIFT THIS DETONATOR AWAY!
WAY TO GO, CHAMP!
LATER...
GOOD WORK, GRUNT! THE TECH-BOYS FROM ABERDEEN CHECKED OUT THE WARHEAD! THEY TOLD ME THAT ITS SHIELDING WAS INTACT! YOU DON'T HAVE TO WORRY ABOUT DECON-TAMINATION OR RADIATION POISONING!
THAT'S A RELIEF, HAWK!
THE TECHS ALSO TOLD ME THAT THE TIMER ON THE DETONATOR WAS RUNNING FAST--IT ONLY HAD THREE SECONDS LEFT TO GO WHEN YOU LIFTED IT CLEAR!
SHEESH! I'LL BET THOSE LOCALS ARE SURE GLAD WE WERE ON THE JOB.
WELL, CLEM, LOOKS LIKE THEY MOVIN' IN SOME REAL SOLDIER BOYS UP TO THE OL' WINGFIELD PLACE!
YEP! LIQUOR PRICES ARE GONNA GO UP AND THE SHERIFF'LL BE SETTIN' HIS SPEED-TRAP AGAIN!
BEST BE KEEPIN' A CLOSE EYE ON YOUR WOMEN-FOLK TOO--
CAMP VICTORY

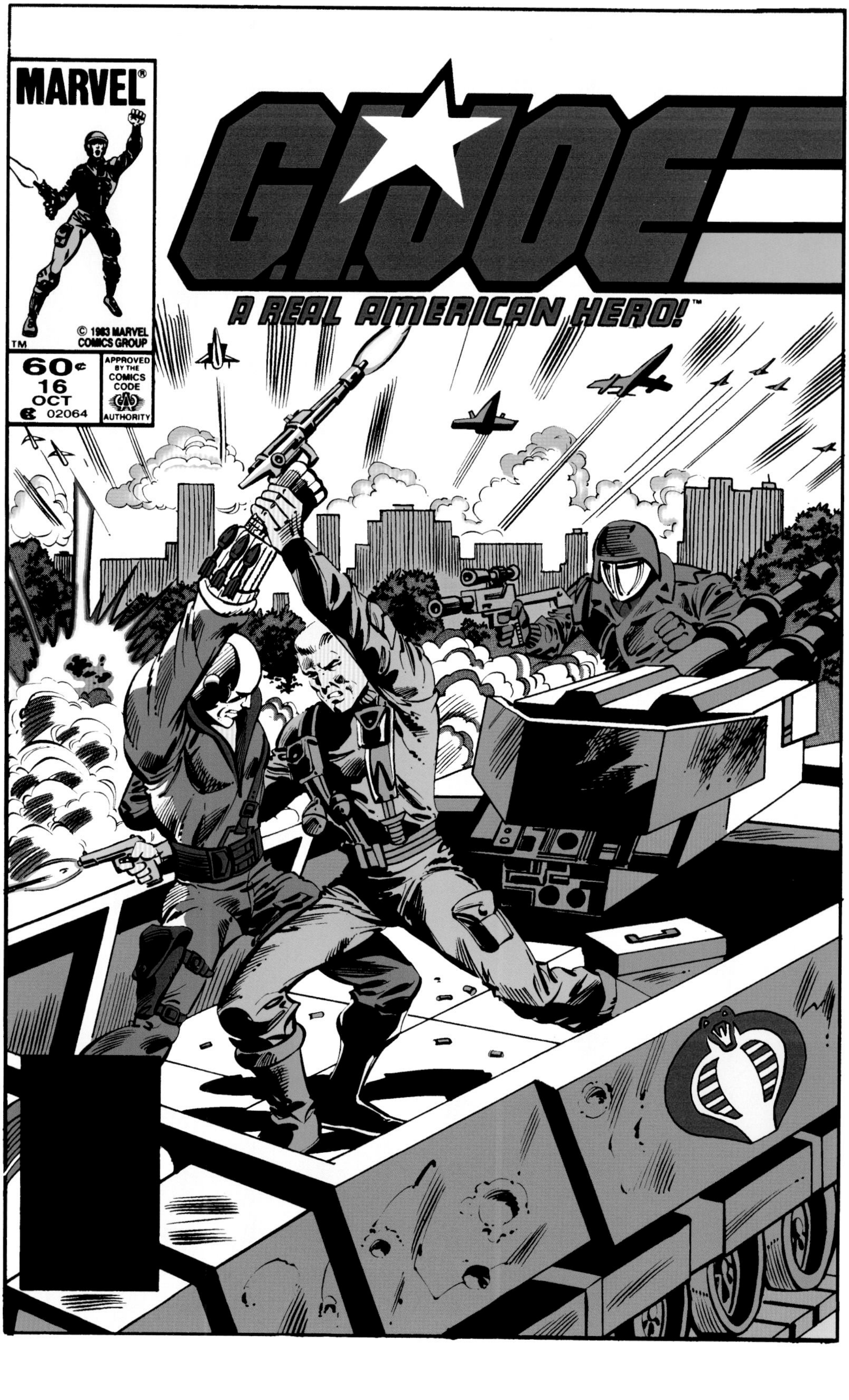
MARVEL
G.I. JOE
A REAL AMERICAN HERO!
© 1983 MARVEL COMICS GROUP
60¢
16
OCT
02064
APPROVED BY THE COMICS CODE AUTHORITY

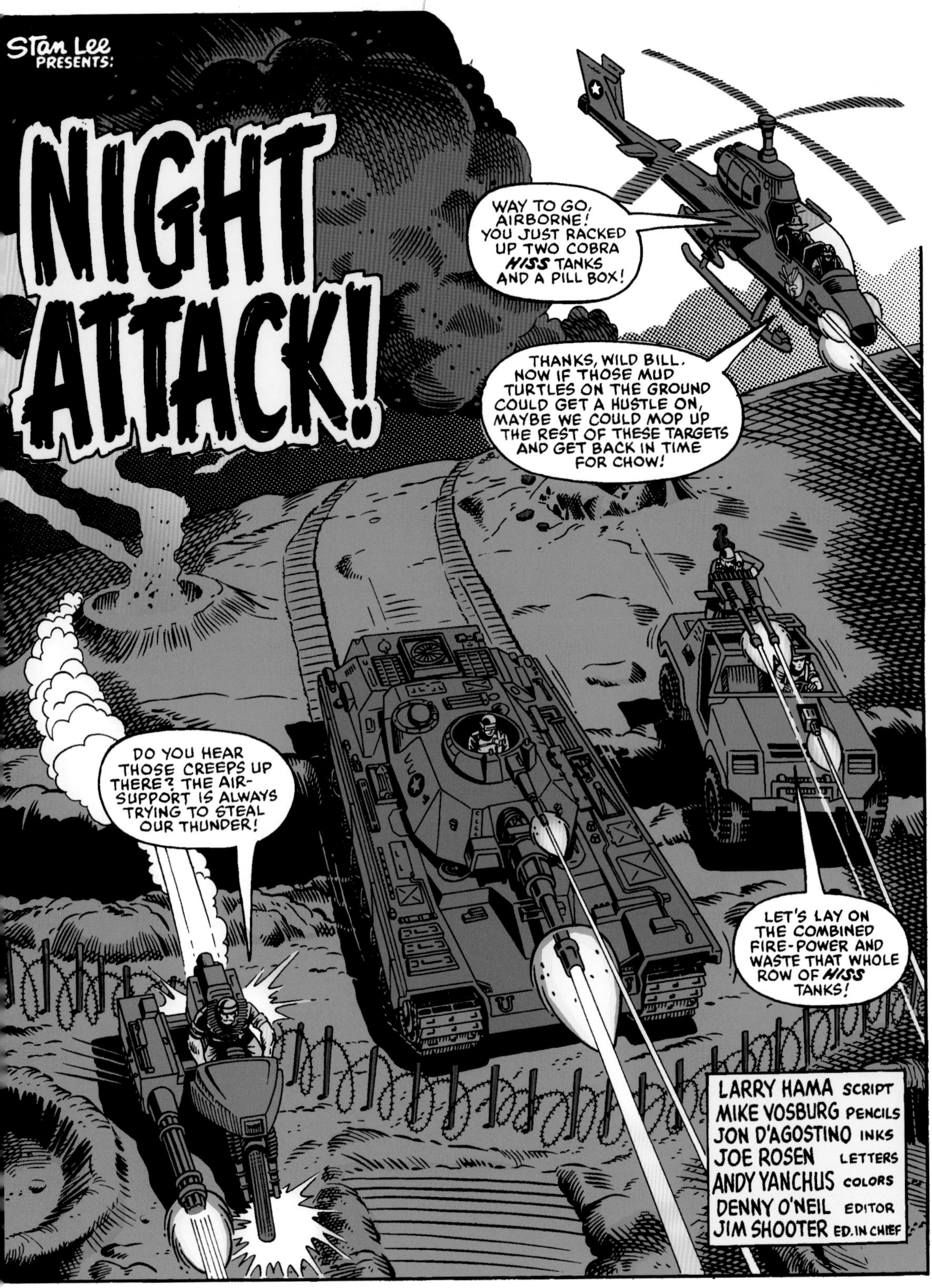
Stan Lee PRESENTS:
NIGHT ATTACK!
WAY TO GO, AIRBORNE! YOU JUST RACKED UP TWO COBRA HISS TANKS AND A PILL BOX!
THANKS, WILD BILL. NOW IF THOSE MUD TURTLES ON THE GROUND COULD GET A HUSTLE ON, MAYBE WE COULD MOP UP THE REST OF THESE TARGETS AND GET BACK IN TIME FOR CHOW!
DO YOU HEAR THOSE CREEPS UP THERE? THE AIR-SUPPORT IS ALWAYS TRYING TO STEAL OUR THUNDER!
LET'S LAY ON THE COMBINED FIRE-POWER AND WASTE THAT WHOLE ROW OF HISS TANKS!
LARRY HAMA SCRIPT
MIKE VOSBURG PENCILS
JON D'AGOSTINO INKS
JOE ROSEN LETTERS
ANDY YANCHUS COLORS
DENNY O'NEIL EDITOR
JIM SHOOTER ED. IN CHIEF

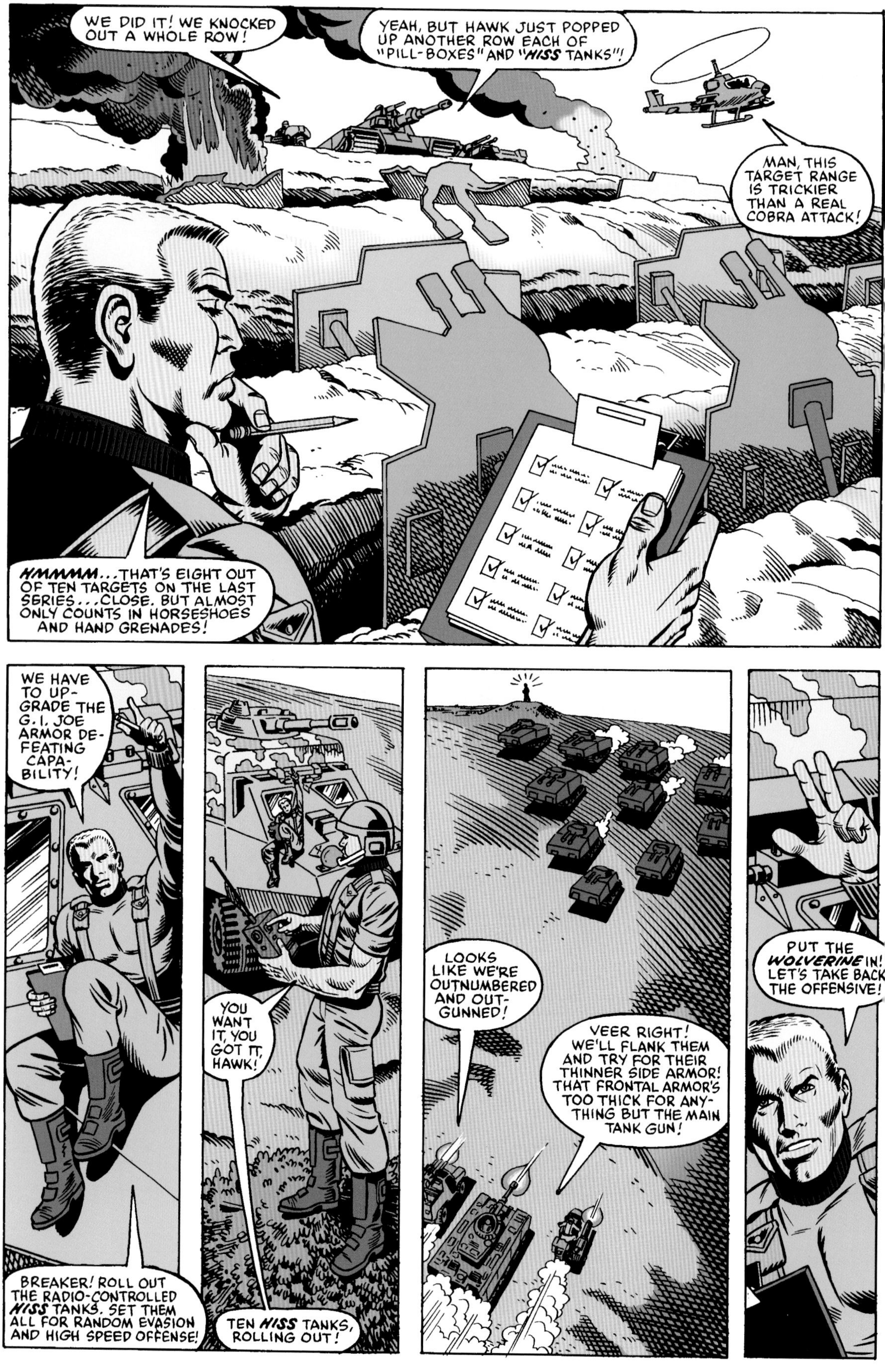
WE DID IT! WE KNOCKED OUT A WHOLE ROW!
YEAH, BUT HAWK JUST POPPED UP ANOTHER ROW EACH OF "PILL-BOXES" AND "HISS TANKS"!
MAN, THIS TARGET RANGE IS TRICKIER THAN A REAL COBRA ATTACK!
HMMMM... THAT'S EIGHT OUT OF TEN TARGETS ON THE LAST SERIES... CLOSE. BUT ALMOST ONLY COUNTS IN HORSESHOES AND HAND GRENADES!
WE HAVE TO UP-GRADE THE G.I. JOE ARMOR DE-FEATING CAPA-BILITY!
BREAKER! ROLL OUT THE RADIO-CONTROLLED HISS TANKS. SET THEM ALL FOR RANDOM EVASION AND HIGH SPEED OFFENSE!
YOU WANT IT, YOU GOT IT, HAWK!
TEN HISS TANKS, ROLLING OUT!
LOOKS LIKE WE'RE OUTNUMBERED AND OUT-GUNNED!
VEER RIGHT! WE'LL FLANK THEM AND TRY FOR THEIR THINNER SIDE ARMOR! THAT FRONTAL ARMOR'S TOO THICK FOR ANY-THING BUT THE MAIN TANK GUN!
PUT THE WOLVERINE IN! LET'S TAKE BACK THE OFFENSIVE!

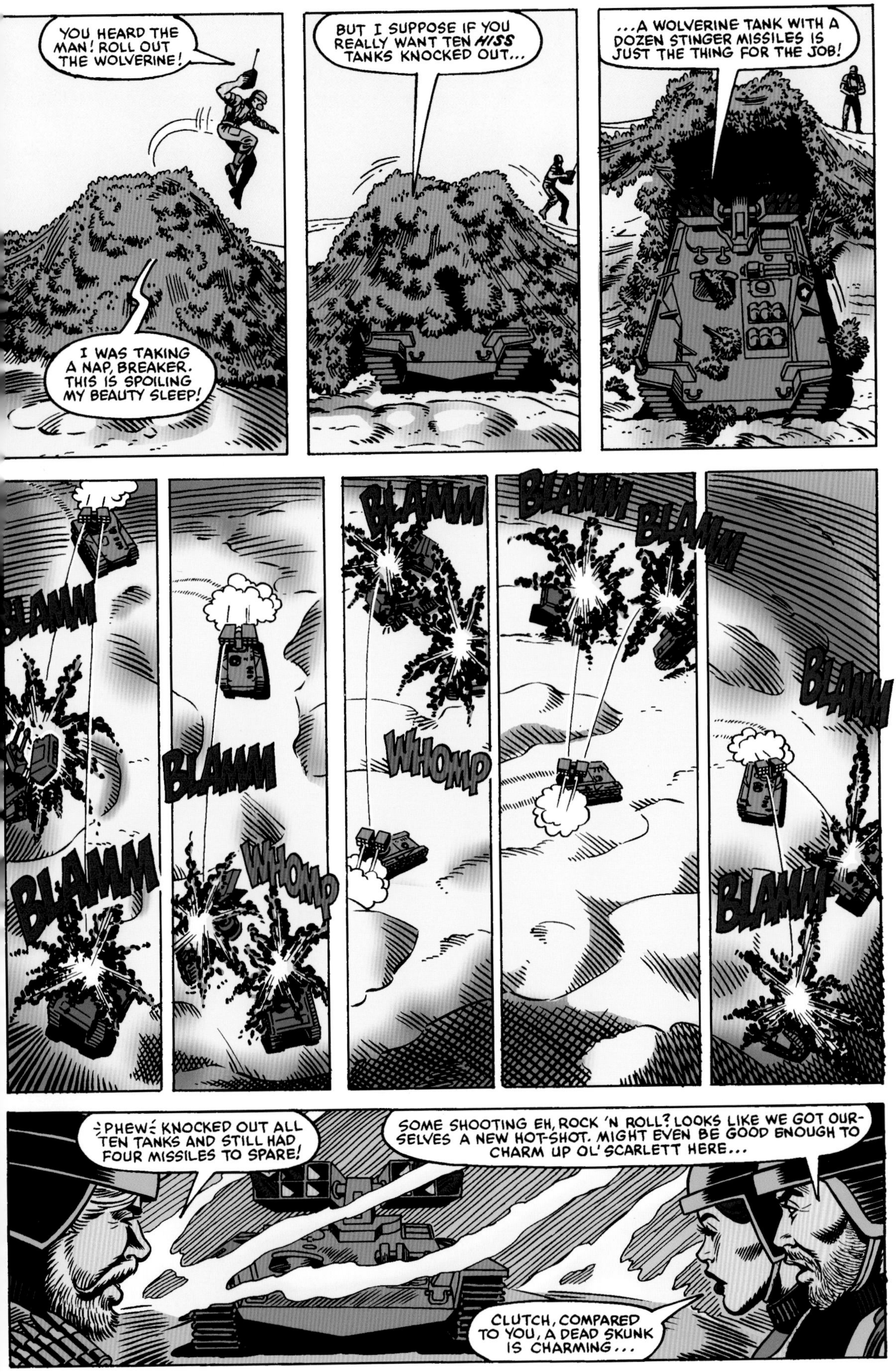
YOU HEARD THE MAN! ROLL OUT THE WOLVERINE!
I WAS TAKING A NAP, BREAKER. THIS IS SPOILING MY BEAUTY SLEEP!
BUT I SUPPOSE IF YOU REALLY WANT TEN HISS TANKS KNOCKED OUT...
...A WOLVERINE TANK WITH A DOZEN STINGER MISSILES IS JUST THE THING FOR THE JOB!
BLAMM
BLAMM
BLAMM
WHOMP
BLAMM
WHOMP
BLAMM
BLAMM
BLAMM
BLAMM
-PHEW- KNOCKED OUT ALL TEN TANKS AND STILL HAD FOUR MISSILES TO SPARE!
SOME SHOOTING EH, ROCK 'N ROLL? LOOKS LIKE WE GOT OURSELVES A NEW HOT-SHOT. MIGHT EVEN BE GOOD ENOUGH TO CHARM UP OL' SCARLETT HERE...
CLUTCH, COMPARED TO YOU, A DEAD SKUNK IS CHARMING...

WELL, I SHOULD CERTAINLY HOPE I'M MORE CHARMING THAN A DEAD SKUNK!

COVER GIRL, MEET ROCK 'N ROLL, SCARLETT AND CLUTCH.

THAT WAS *YOU*, TOOK OUT TEN TANKS? SOME PIECE O' WORK! GLAD TO HAVE YOU ON THE TEAM--

KEEPING YOUR COOL TO FIRE AT TARGETS THAT DON'T SHOOT BACK ON A PRACTICE RANGE IS ONE THING. A FIRE-FIGHT TENDS TO PUT FIRE IN YOUR BELLY, MOLASSES ON YOUR REFLEXES AND A DEAD LETTER STAMP ON YOUR JUDGMENT...

...LET'S RESERVE *OUR* JUDGMENT 'TIL WE SEE HOW SHE HOLDS UP IN A *REAL* BATTLE.

BETTER THAN YOUR FACE HAS, DEARIE...

WOOF! CHALK UP ONE FOR COVER GIRL!

I JUST REALIZED SOMETHING! YOU ONLY FIRED EIGHT MISSILES, BUT TEN TANKS WERE--

--SHE DIDN'T NEUTRALIZE ALL TEN TANKS. *I* DISPOSED OF THE FOURTH AND SIXTH TANKS...

...I JUST WAITED UNTIL THE FUR WAS FLYING, SNUCK UP BEHIND THEM SUCKERS AND SLAPPED ON A COUPLE O' MAGNETIC SHAPED CHARGES!

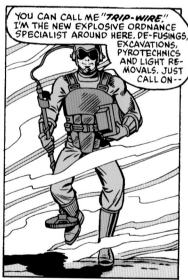

YOU CAN CALL ME *"TRIP-WIRE."* I'M THE NEW EXPLOSIVE ORDNANCE SPECIALIST AROUND HERE. DE-FUSINGS, EXCAVATIONS, PYROTECHNICS AND LIGHT RE-MOVALS. JUST CALL ON--

OOF!

WHAT IS THIS? A CARRYING CASE FOR OVERSIZED HOCKEY PUCKS?

THEY'S *MINES*...

I KNOW THEY'RE YOURS...

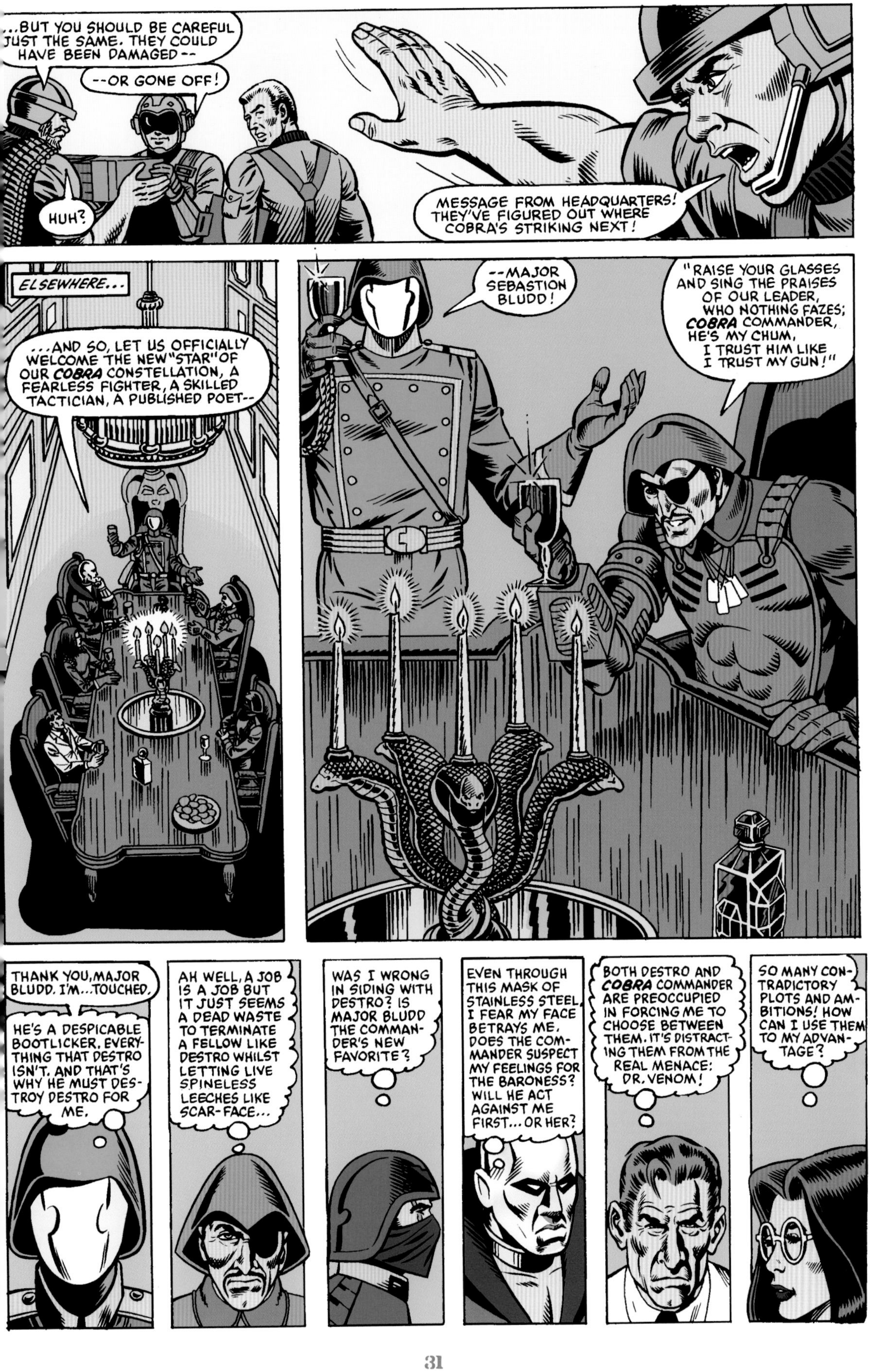
...BUT YOU SHOULD BE CAREFUL JUST THE SAME. THEY COULD HAVE BEEN DAMAGED--
--OR GONE OFF!
HUH?
MESSAGE FROM HEADQUARTERS! THEY'VE FIGURED OUT WHERE COBRA'S STRIKING NEXT!
ELSEWHERE...
...AND SO, LET US OFFICIALLY WELCOME THE NEW "STAR" OF OUR COBRA CONSTELLATION, A FEARLESS FIGHTER, A SKILLED TACTICIAN, A PUBLISHED POET--
--MAJOR SEBASTION BLUDD!
"RAISE YOUR GLASSES AND SING THE PRAISES OF OUR LEADER, WHO NOTHING FAZES; COBRA COMMANDER, HE'S MY CHUM, I TRUST HIM LIKE I TRUST MY GUN!"
THANK YOU, MAJOR BLUDD. I'M... TOUCHED.
HE'S A DESPICABLE BOOTLICKER, EVERYTHING THAT DESTRO ISN'T. AND THAT'S WHY HE MUST DESTROY DESTRO FOR ME.
AH WELL, A JOB IS A JOB BUT IT JUST SEEMS A DEAD WASTE TO TERMINATE A FELLOW LIKE DESTRO WHILST LETTING LIVE SPINELESS LEECHES LIKE SCAR-FACE...
WAS I WRONG IN SIDING WITH DESTRO? IS MAJOR BLUDD THE COMMANDER'S NEW FAVORITE?
EVEN THROUGH THIS MASK OF STAINLESS STEEL, I FEAR MY FACE BETRAYS ME. DOES THE COMMANDER SUSPECT MY FEELINGS FOR THE BARONESS? WILL HE ACT AGAINST ME FIRST... OR HER?
BOTH DESTRO AND COBRA COMMANDER ARE PREOCCUPIED IN FORCING ME TO CHOOSE BETWEEN THEM. IT'S DISTRACTING THEM FROM THE REAL MENACE: DR. VENOM!
SO MANY CONTRADICTORY PLOTS AND AMBITIONS! HOW CAN I USE THEM TO MY ADVANTAGE?

COBRA COMRADES! I PROPOSE A TOAST! TO VICTORY THROUGH... UNITY!

IN G.I. JOE HEADQUARTERS...

GENERAL FLAGG, OUR BOYS HAVE IDENTIFIED THE INK WE FOUND IN THE COBRA LAB IN VERMONT.* IT'S THE SAME INK USED TO PRINT UNITED STATES CURRENCY! ALSO PRESENT AT THE SITE WERE APPARATUSES COMMONLY USED IN THE HANDLING OF BIOLOGICAL TOXINS!

THERE IS EVERY REASON TO BELIEVE THAT COBRA INTENDS TO POISON AMERICAN MONEY AT THE SOURCE--THE BUREAU OF PRINTING AND ENGRAVING!

*SEE G.I. JOE #14! --DENNY.

ASSIGN ME ENOUGH TROOPS TO THROW A CORDON AROUND THE TREASURY BUILDINGS AND I CAN SCOOP UP COBRAS AS THEY--

THAT'S A NEGATIVE, HAWK. COBRA HAS THREATENED TO BLOW UP THE THE CAPITOL BUILDING. ALL AVAILABLE TROOPS ARE EARMARKED FOR DEFENSIVE DUTIES. NO EXCEPTIONS.

THE GOVERNMENT IS KEEPING THIS WHOLE THING UNDER WRAPS TO AVOID A PUBLIC PANIC BUT THEY ARE NOT ABOUT TO BE TAKING ANY CHANCES. BESIDES, THE TREASURY THREAT MAY BE THE DIVERSION AND THE REAL TARGET MAY JUST BE THE CAPITOL AFTER ALL!

YOU REALLY CAN'T BLAME THE BRASS FOR TRYING TO COVER THEIR OWN TAILS IN THIS MESS. AND HAWK, IF I WERE YOU, I'D COVER MYSELF AS WELL...

I WILL, GENERAL FLAGG...

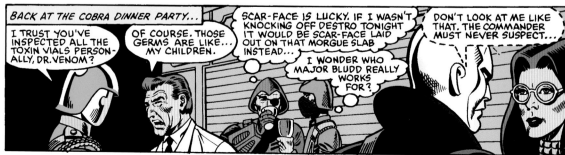

BACK AT THE COBRA DINNER PARTY...

I TRUST YOU'VE INSPECTED ALL THE TOXIN VIALS PERSONALLY, DR. VENOM?

OF COURSE. THOSE GERMS ARE LIKE... MY CHILDREN.

SCAR-FACE IS LUCKY. IF I WASN'T KNOCKING OFF DESTRO TONIGHT IT WOULD BE SCAR-FACE LAID OUT ON THAT MORGUE SLAB INSTEAD...

I WONDER WHO MAJOR BLUDD REALLY WORKS FOR?

DON'T LOOK AT ME LIKE THAT. THE COMMANDER MUST NEVER SUSPECT...

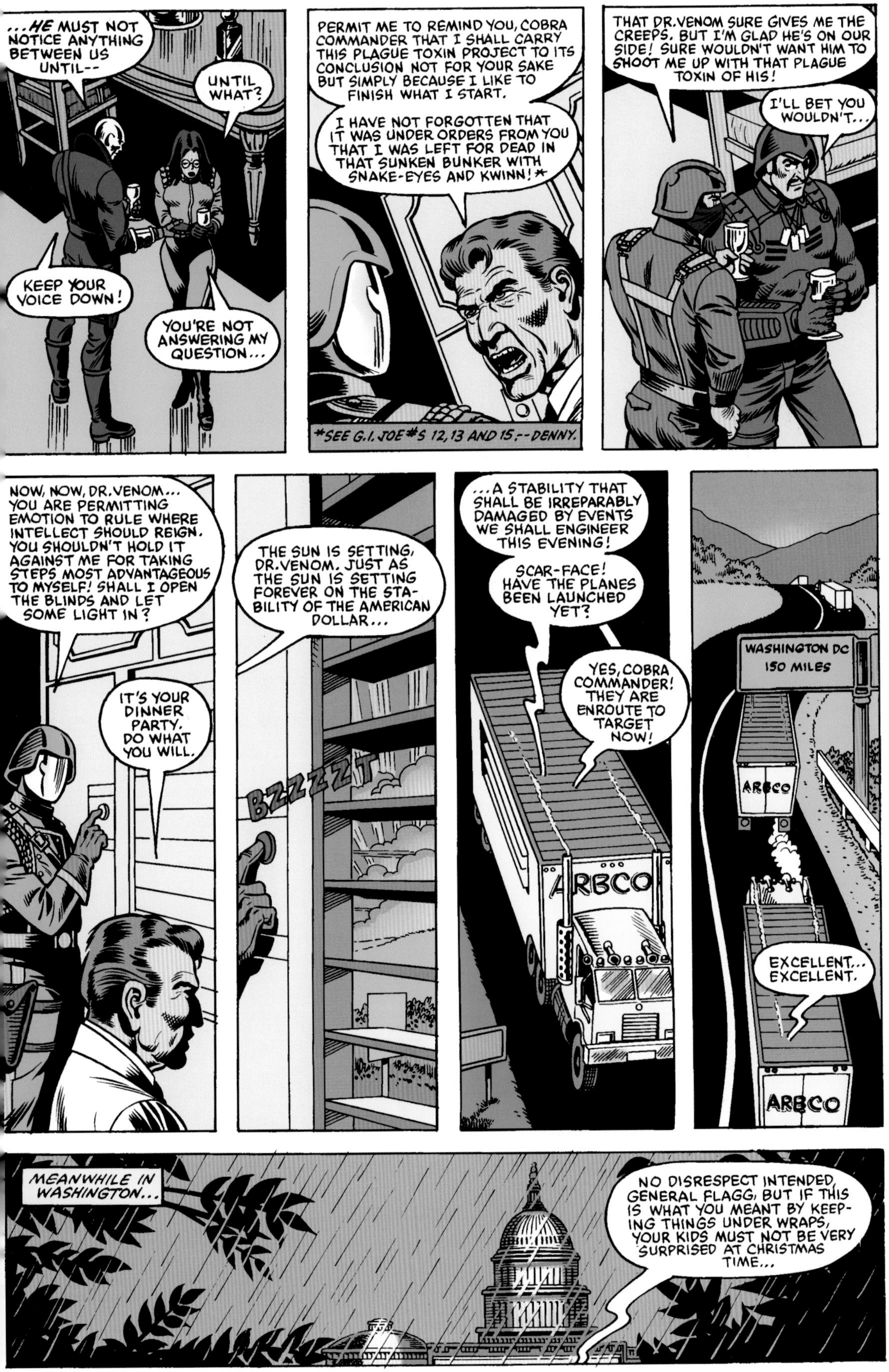
...HE MUST NOT NOTICE ANYTHING BETWEEN US UNTIL--
UNTIL WHAT?
KEEP YOUR VOICE DOWN!
YOU'RE NOT ANSWERING MY QUESTION...
PERMIT ME TO REMIND YOU, COBRA COMMANDER THAT I SHALL CARRY THIS PLAGUE TOXIN PROJECT TO ITS CONCLUSION NOT FOR YOUR SAKE BUT SIMPLY BECAUSE I LIKE TO FINISH WHAT I START.
I HAVE NOT FORGOTTEN THAT IT WAS UNDER ORDERS FROM YOU THAT I WAS LEFT FOR DEAD IN THAT SUNKEN BUNKER WITH SNAKE-EYES AND KWINN!*
*SEE G.I. JOE#S 12, 13 AND 15.--DENNY.
THAT DR. VENOM SURE GIVES ME THE CREEPS. BUT I'M GLAD HE'S ON OUR SIDE! SURE WOULDN'T WANT HIM TO SHOOT ME UP WITH THAT PLAGUE TOXIN OF HIS!
I'LL BET YOU WOULDN'T...
NOW, NOW, DR. VENOM... YOU ARE PERMITTING EMOTION TO RULE WHERE INTELLECT SHOULD REIGN. YOU SHOULDN'T HOLD IT AGAINST ME FOR TAKING STEPS MOST ADVANTAGEOUS TO MYSELF! SHALL I OPEN THE BLINDS AND LET SOME LIGHT IN?
IT'S YOUR DINNER PARTY. DO WHAT YOU WILL.
THE SUN IS SETTING, DR. VENOM. JUST AS THE SUN IS SETTING FOREVER ON THE STABILITY OF THE AMERICAN DOLLAR...
BZZZZT
...A STABILITY THAT SHALL BE IRREPARABLY DAMAGED BY EVENTS WE SHALL ENGINEER THIS EVENING!
SCAR-FACE! HAVE THE PLANES BEEN LAUNCHED YET?
YES, COBRA COMMANDER! THEY ARE ENROUTE TO TARGET NOW!
ARBCO
WASHINGTON DC 150 MILES
ARBCO
EXCELLENT... EXCELLENT.
ARBCO
MEANWHILE IN WASHINGTON...
NO DISRESPECT INTENDED, GENERAL FLAGG, BUT IF THIS IS WHAT YOU MEANT BY KEEPING THINGS UNDER WRAPS, YOUR KIDS MUST NOT BE VERY SURPRISED AT CHRISTMAS TIME...

...YOU'VE GOT THE ENTIRE VIRGINIA NATIONAL GUARD OUT HERE IN FULL BATTLE KIT! I SEE AIRBORNE RANGERS FROM FORT BRAGG, ARMOR FROM KNOX, INTELLIGENCE HONCHOS FROM HOLABIRD AND A 76 PIECE BAND FROM FORT DIX!

IF YOU WERE TO LOAN ME A SMALL BATTALION NOBODY WOULD EVEN MISS THEM! WE COULD SET UP A PERIMETER AROUND THE TREASURY BUILDING AND TAKE A LOT OF HEAT OFF MY JOES!

NO, HAWK. THE DEFENSE OF THE CAPITOL IS TOP PRIORITY.

SIR, WON'T YOU RECONSIDER? IF COBRA DOES HIT THE TREASURY BUILDING, THE JOE TEAM IS IN THERE WITH NO SUPPORT--

THE JOES ARE SUPPOSED TO BE CAPABLE OF OPERATING FOR PROTRACTED PERIODS WITH NO SUPPORT AT ALL--

TAKE COVER! COBRA AIRCRAFT COMING IN LOW AND FAST!!

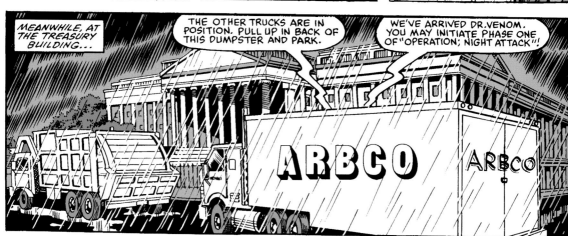

MEANWHILE, AT THE TREASURY BUILDING...

THE OTHER TRUCKS ARE IN POSITION. PULL UP IN BACK OF THIS DUMPSTER AND PARK.

WE'VE ARRIVED DR. VENOM. YOU MAY INITIATE PHASE ONE OF "OPERATION; NIGHT ATTACK"!

ARBCO

ARBCO

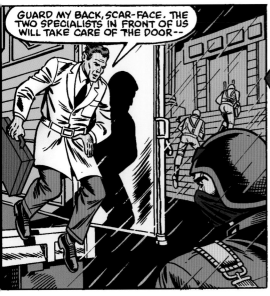

GUARD MY BACK, SCAR-FACE. THE TWO SPECIALISTS IN FRONT OF US WILL TAKE CARE OF THE DOOR--

BLAMM!

KA-POW!

BRAAAPP!

--AND ANY GUARDS THAT ARE FOOLISH ENOUGH TO BOTHER US!

SCAR-FACE. SEND THOSE TWO LOUTS ON TO THE PRESSES AND HAVE THEM PRY LOOSE THE PLATES FOR TWENTY DOLLAR BILLS. THE PLATE THEFT WILL BE OUR COVER TO DIVERT SUSPICION FROM THE INK...

YOU HEARD THE DOC! GET THOSE PLATES!

YES, SIR!

WITH MY NEW TIME-DELAY TOXIN, THE EVIL EFFECTS WON'T BE NOTICEABLE FOR WEEKS. THEN, EVERYBODY WHO HAS HANDLED THE CONTAMINATED MONEY WILL START DROPPING LIKE FLIES! WE COULD KILL MILLIONS!

AT THE CAPITOL...

SOME DIVERSION, HUH? LOOK AT THIS! THEY'RE DROPPING HALF A REGIMENT ON US!

THIS IS UNBELIEVABLE, SIR...EVEN COBRA WOULDN'T--

WOULDN'T? THEY'RE DARN-WELL DOING IT, AREN'T THEY?

PATCH ME THROUGH TO CENTRAL COMM-LINK! I WANT ALL AVAILABLE UNITS ON IMMEDIATE ALERT AND STANDING BY TO MOVE INTO THE CAPITOL AREA!

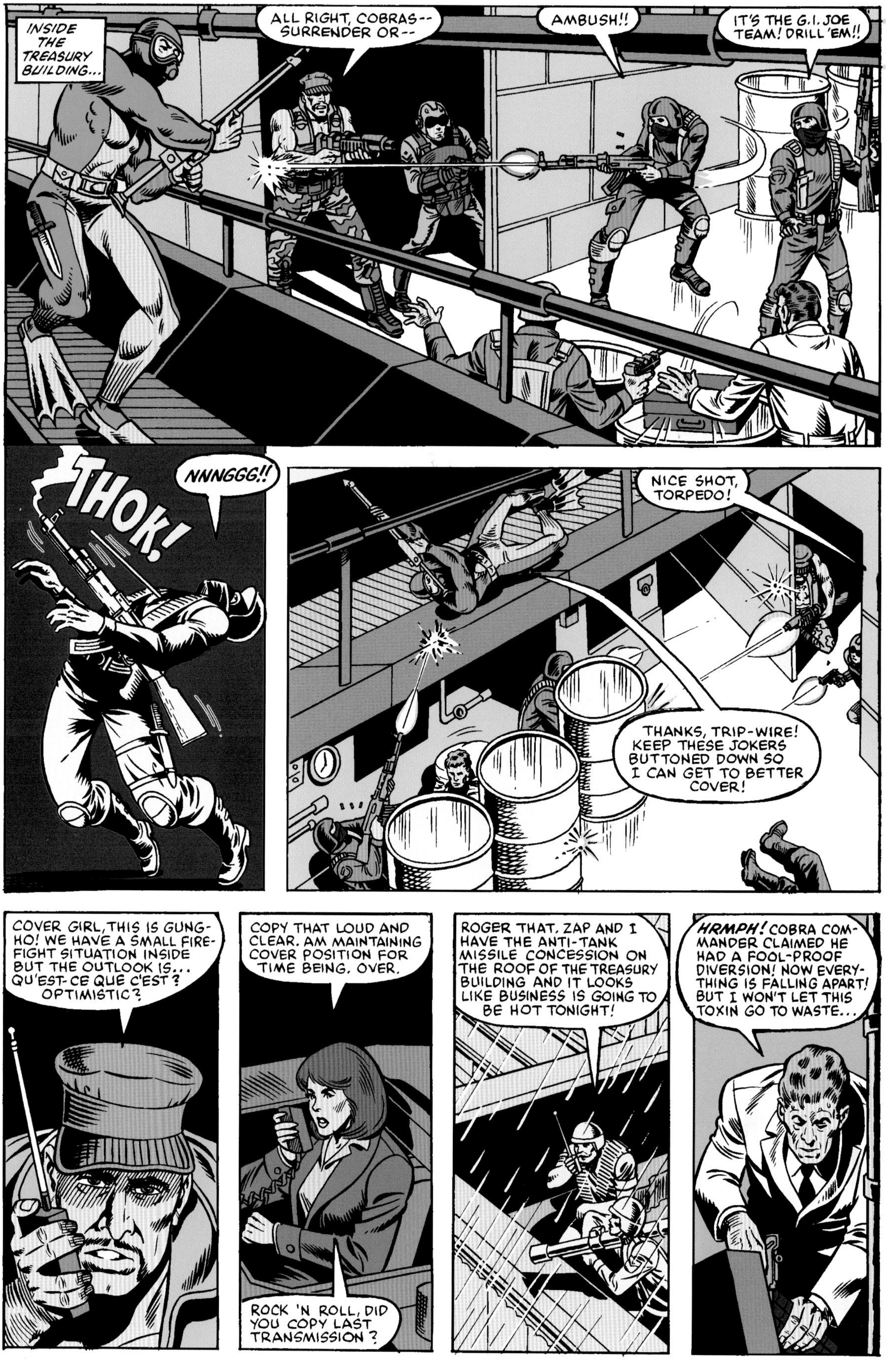

INSIDE THE TREASURY BUILDING...
ALL RIGHT, COBRAS-- SURRENDER OR--
AMBUSH!!
IT'S THE G.I. JOE TEAM! DRILL 'EM!!
THOK!
NNNGGG!!
NICE SHOT, TORPEDO!
THANKS, TRIP-WIRE! KEEP THESE JOKERS BUTTONED DOWN SO I CAN GET TO BETTER COVER!
COVER GIRL, THIS IS GUNG-HO! WE HAVE A SMALL FIRE-FIGHT SITUATION INSIDE BUT THE OUTLOOK IS... QU'EST-CE QUE C'EST? OPTIMISTIC?
COPY THAT LOUD AND CLEAR. AM MAINTAINING COVER POSITION FOR TIME BEING. OVER.
ROCK 'N ROLL, DID YOU COPY LAST TRANSMISSION?
ROGER THAT. ZAP AND I HAVE THE ANTI-TANK MISSILE CONCESSION ON THE ROOF OF THE TREASURY BUILDING AND IT LOOKS LIKE BUSINESS IS GOING TO BE HOT TONIGHT!
HRMPH! COBRA COMMANDER CLAIMED HE HAD A FOOL-PROOF DIVERSION! NOW EVERYTHING IS FALLING APART! BUT I WON'T LET THIS TOXIN GO TO WASTE...

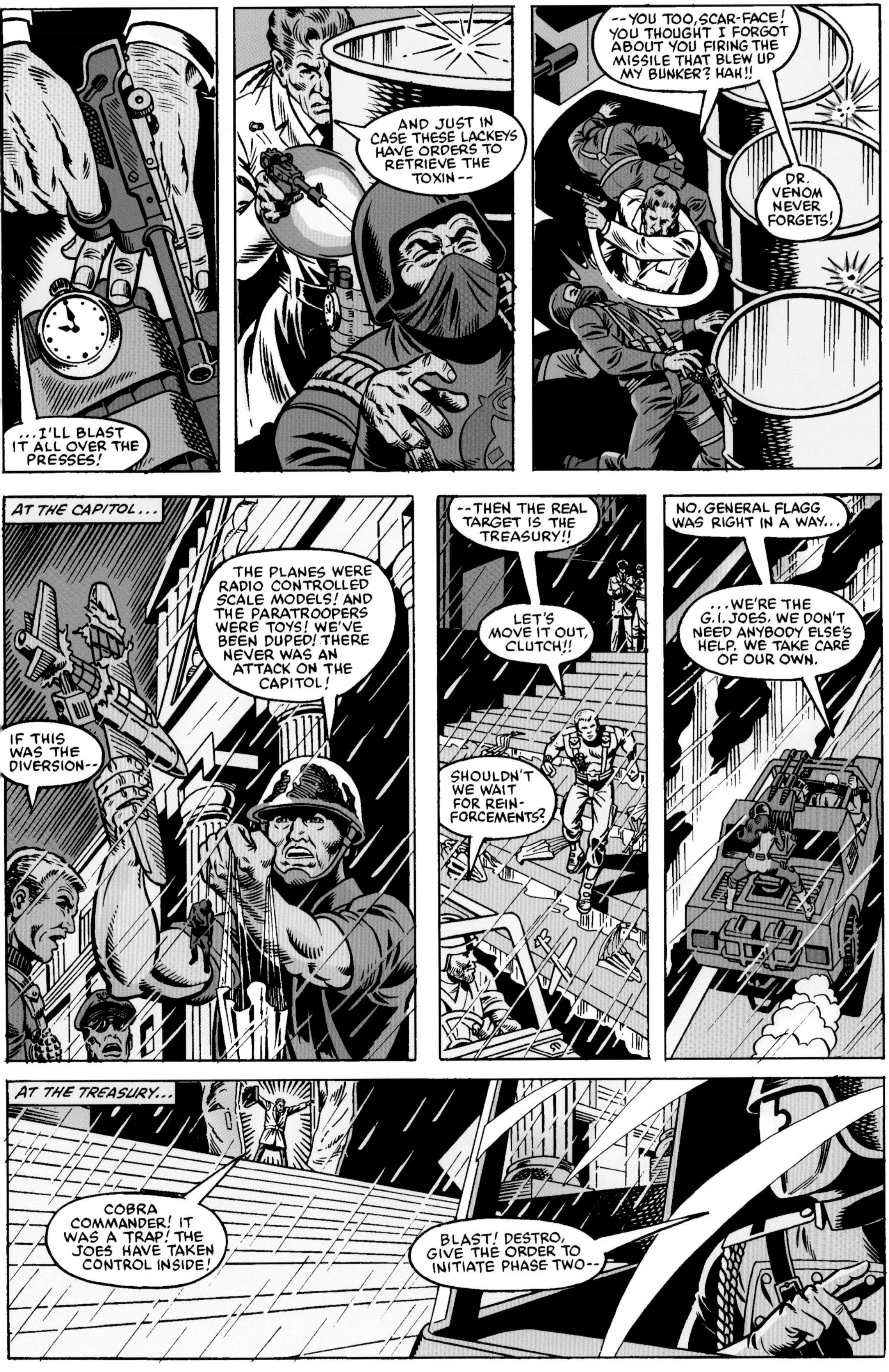
...I'LL BLAST IT ALL OVER THE PRESSES!
AND JUST IN CASE THESE LACKEYS HAVE ORDERS TO RETRIEVE THE TOXIN--
--YOU TOO, SCAR-FACE! YOU THOUGHT I FORGOT ABOUT YOU FIRING THE MISSILE THAT BLEW UP MY BUNKER? HAH!!
DR. VENOM NEVER FORGETS!
AT THE CAPITOL...
THE PLANES WERE RADIO CONTROLLED SCALE MODELS! AND THE PARATROOPERS WERE TOYS! WE'VE BEEN DUPED! THERE NEVER WAS AN ATTACK ON THE CAPITOL!
IF THIS WAS THE DIVERSION--
--THEN THE REAL TARGET IS THE TREASURY!!
LET'S MOVE IT OUT, CLUTCH!!
SHOULDN'T WE WAIT FOR REIN-FORCEMENTS?
NO. GENERAL FLAGG WAS RIGHT IN A WAY...
...WE'RE THE G.I. JOES. WE DON'T NEED ANYBODY ELSE'S HELP. WE TAKE CARE OF OUR OWN.
AT THE TREASURY...
COBRA COMMANDER! IT WAS A TRAP! THE JOES HAVE TAKEN CONTROL INSIDE!
BLAST! DESTRO, GIVE THE ORDER TO INITIATE PHASE TWO--

LOOKS LIKE IT'S ABOUT TIME TO SEE WHAT AN ANTI-TANK MISSILE CAN DO TO AN EIGHTEEN-WHEELER!

FOOOSH!

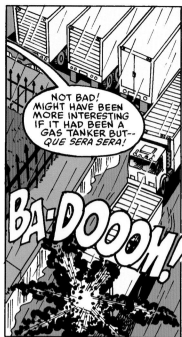

NOT BAD! MIGHT HAVE BEEN MORE INTERESTING IF IT HAD BEEN A GAS TANKER BUT-- *QUE SERA SERA!*

BA-DOOOH!

THEY WERE LUCKY! THEY ALMOST GOT US ALL! BUT THE COMMAND TRUCK IS--

FORGET IT! DESTRO, RIDES WITH ME...

BLUDD RIDES WITH THE BARONESS--

--IT'S TIME TO UNLEASH THE *HISS* TANKS!!

AR

INSIDE THE TREASURY BUILDING...

VERY QUIET OUT THERE. EITHER EVERYONE IS OUT FOR THE COUNT OR THEY'VE TAKEN THEIR BALL AND GONE HOME...

JUST THE SAME, DON'T BUNCH UP AND WATCH YOUR BACKS...

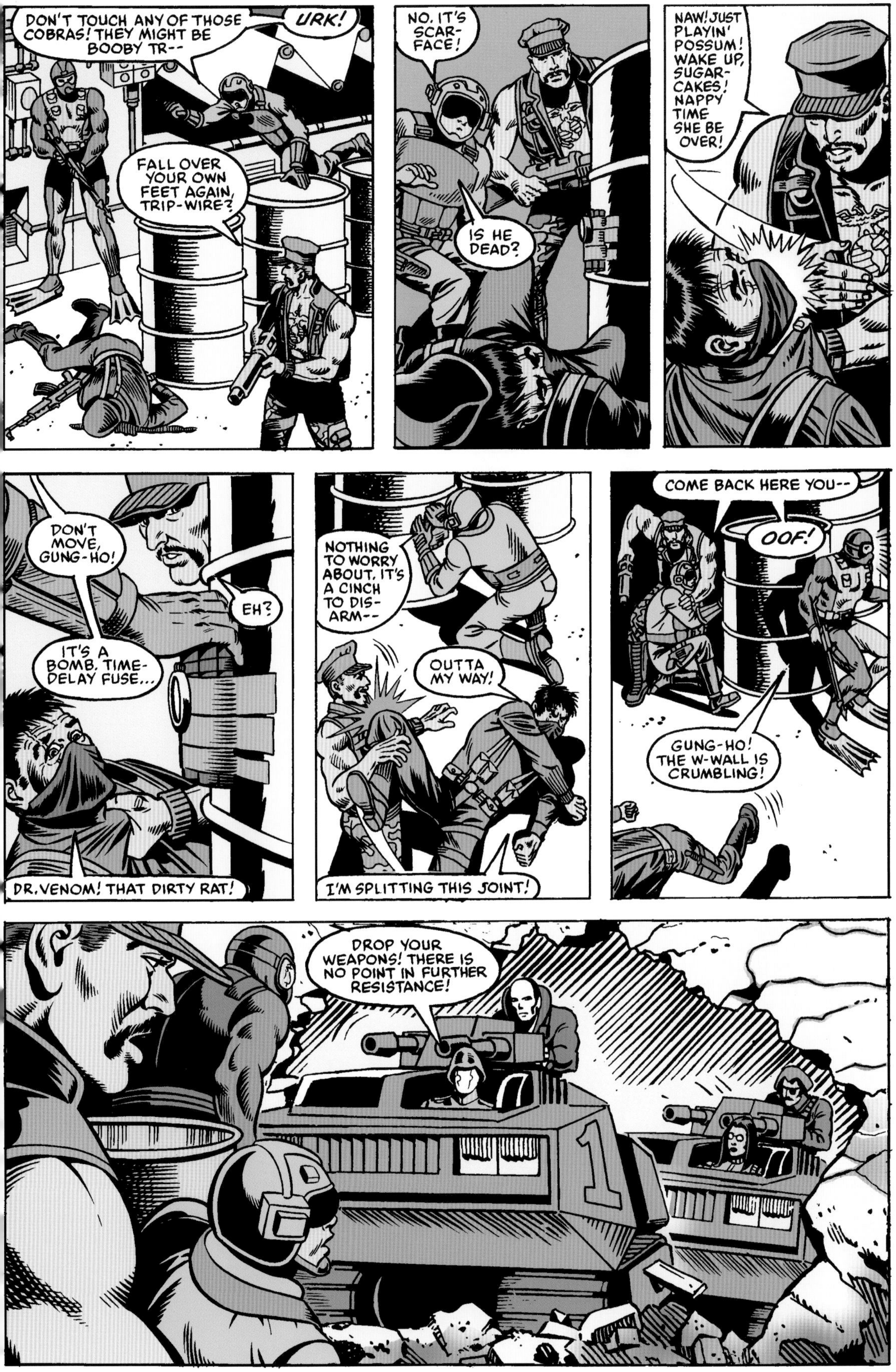
DON'T TOUCH ANY OF THOSE COBRAS! THEY MIGHT BE BOOBY TR--
URK!
FALL OVER YOUR OWN FEET AGAIN, TRIP-WIRE?
NO. IT'S SCAR-FACE!
IS HE DEAD?
NAW! JUST PLAYIN' POSSUM! WAKE UP, SUGAR-CAKES! NAPPY TIME SHE BE OVER!
DON'T MOVE, GUNG-HO!
EH?
IT'S A BOMB, TIME-DELAY FUSE...
DR. VENOM! THAT DIRTY RAT!
NOTHING TO WORRY ABOUT. IT'S A CINCH TO DIS-ARM--
OUTTA MY WAY!
I'M SPLITTING THIS JOINT!
COME BACK HERE YOU--
OOF!
GUNG-HO! THE W-WALL IS CRUMBLING!
DROP YOUR WEAPONS! THERE IS NO POINT IN FURTHER RESISTANCE!
1

IT'S DESTRO, AND COBRA COMMANDER HIMSELF IN THE DRIVER'S SEAT.

AND I'LL BET THAT'S THE BARONESS DRIVING THE SECOND TANK. BUT WHO'S MANNING THE TURRET?

MAJOR BLUDD...

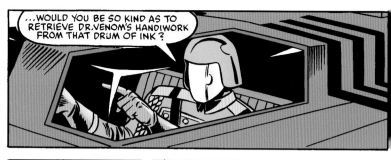

...WOULD YOU BE SO KIND AS TO RETRIEVE DR. VENOM'S HANDIWORK FROM THAT DRUM OF INK?

MY PLEASURE, COBRA COMMANDER.

NICE OF THESE CHAPS TO DISARM IT FOR US...

WHY ARE WE TAKING IT BACK? I THOUGHT--

THIS OPERATION IS BLOWN. IF THE TOXIN IS ANALYZED BY THE JOES, IT WILL BE USELESS TO US... FOR FUTURE OPERATIONS.

THESE THREE JOES ARE A CONSTANT THREAT AND DANGER TO US. I ADVISE TERMINATION WITH EXTREME PREJUDICE...

TERMINATION WITH EXTREME PREJUDICE? WHAT'S THAT MEAN?

IT MEANS, "A BULLET DON'T CARE WHAT COLOR YOU ARE."

NO, DESTRO. WE MAY NEED THEM AS HOSTAGES. THE EVENING IS NOT OVER YET...

BZZT POP COVER GIRL, THIS IS ZAP. I HAVE VISUAL CONTACT WITH OUR THREE LOST LAMBS. THEY ARE LEAVING BUILDING TO YOUR RIGHT...

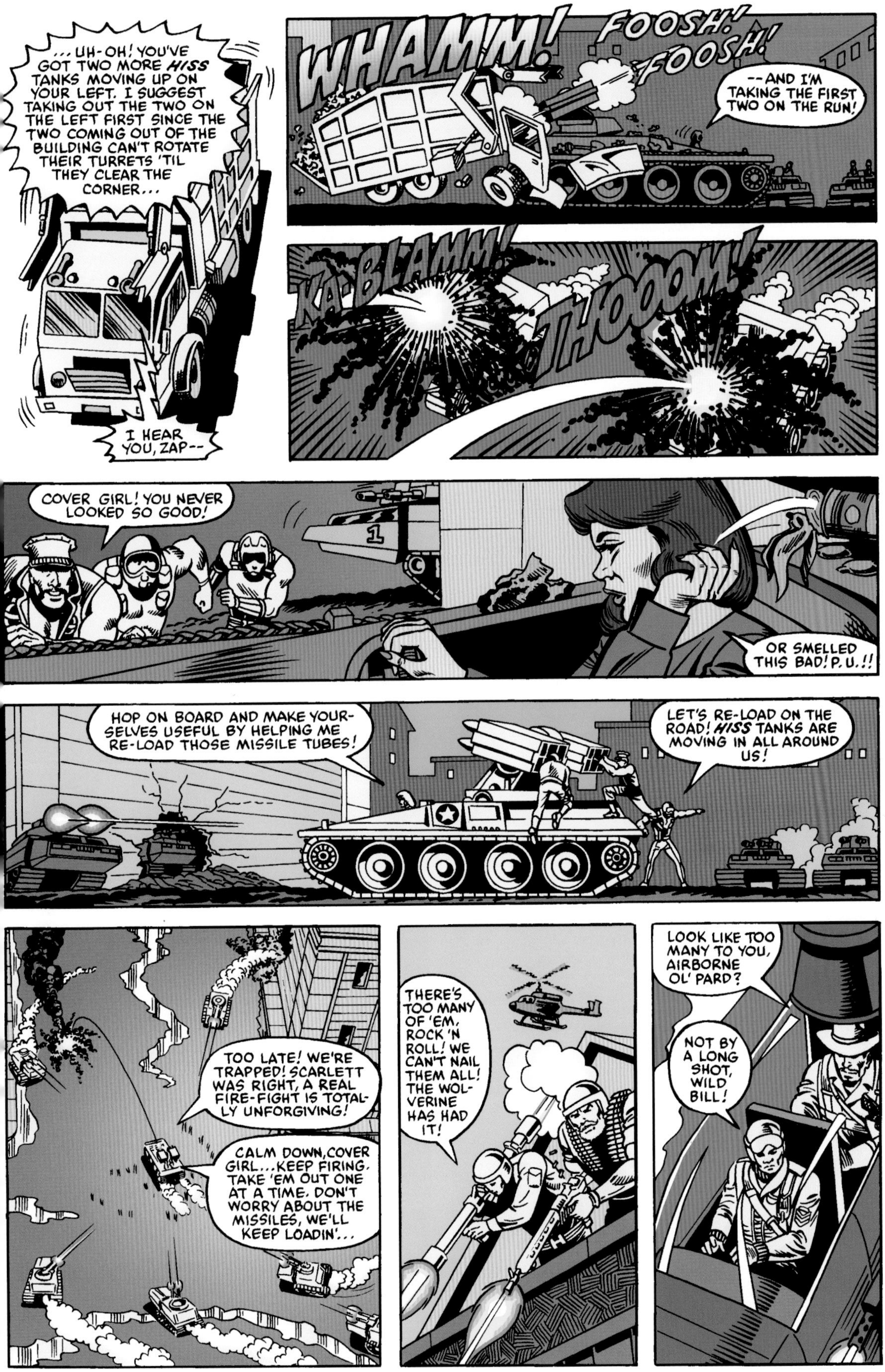
...UH-OH! YOU'VE GOT TWO MORE HISS TANKS MOVING UP ON YOUR LEFT. I SUGGEST TAKING OUT THE TWO ON THE LEFT FIRST SINCE THE TWO COMING OUT OF THE BUILDING CAN'T ROTATE THEIR TURRETS 'TIL THEY CLEAR THE CORNER...
I HEAR YOU, ZAP--
WHAMM!
FOOSH! FOOSH!
--AND I'M TAKING THE FIRST TWO ON THE RUN!
KA-BLAMM!
THOOOM!
COVER GIRL! YOU NEVER LOOKED SO GOOD!
OR SMELLED THIS BAD! P.U.!!
HOP ON BOARD AND MAKE YOURSELVES USEFUL BY HELPING ME RE-LOAD THOSE MISSILE TUBES!
LET'S RE-LOAD ON THE ROAD! HISS TANKS ARE MOVING IN ALL AROUND US!
TOO LATE! WE'RE TRAPPED! SCARLETT WAS RIGHT, A REAL FIRE-FIGHT IS TOTALLY UNFORGIVING!
CALM DOWN, COVER GIRL... KEEP FIRING. TAKE 'EM OUT ONE AT A TIME. DON'T WORRY ABOUT THE MISSILES, WE'LL KEEP LOADIN'...
THERE'S TOO MANY OF 'EM, ROCK 'N ROLL! WE CAN'T NAIL THEM ALL! THE WOLVERINE HAS HAD IT!
LOOK LIKE TOO MANY TO YOU, AIRBORNE OL' PARD?
NOT BY A LONG SHOT, WILD BILL!

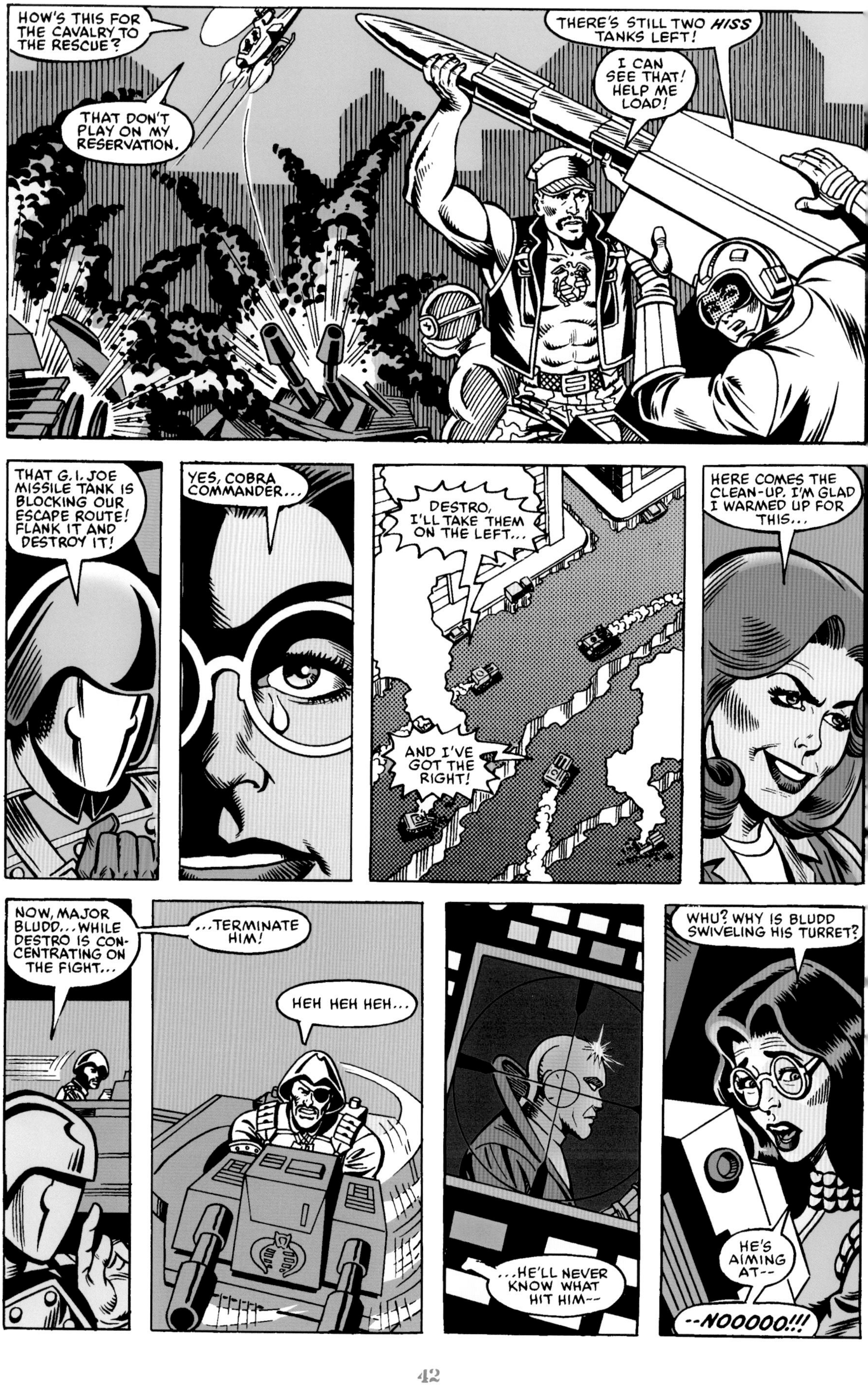
HOW'S THIS FOR THE CAVALRY TO THE RESCUE?
THAT DON'T PLAY ON MY RESERVATION.
THERE'S STILL TWO HISS TANKS LEFT!
I CAN SEE THAT! HELP ME LOAD!
THAT G.I. JOE MISSILE TANK IS BLOCKING OUR ESCAPE ROUTE! FLANK IT AND DESTROY IT!
YES, COBRA COMMANDER...
DESTRO, I'LL TAKE THEM ON THE LEFT...
AND I'VE GOT THE RIGHT!
HERE COMES THE CLEAN-UP. I'M GLAD I WARMED UP FOR THIS...
NOW, MAJOR BLUDD... WHILE DESTRO IS CONCENTRATING ON THE FIGHT...
...TERMINATE HIM!
HEH HEH HEH...
...HE'LL NEVER KNOW WHAT HIT HIM--
WHU? WHY IS BLUDD SWIVELING HIS TURRET?
HE'S AIMING AT--
--NOOOOO!!!

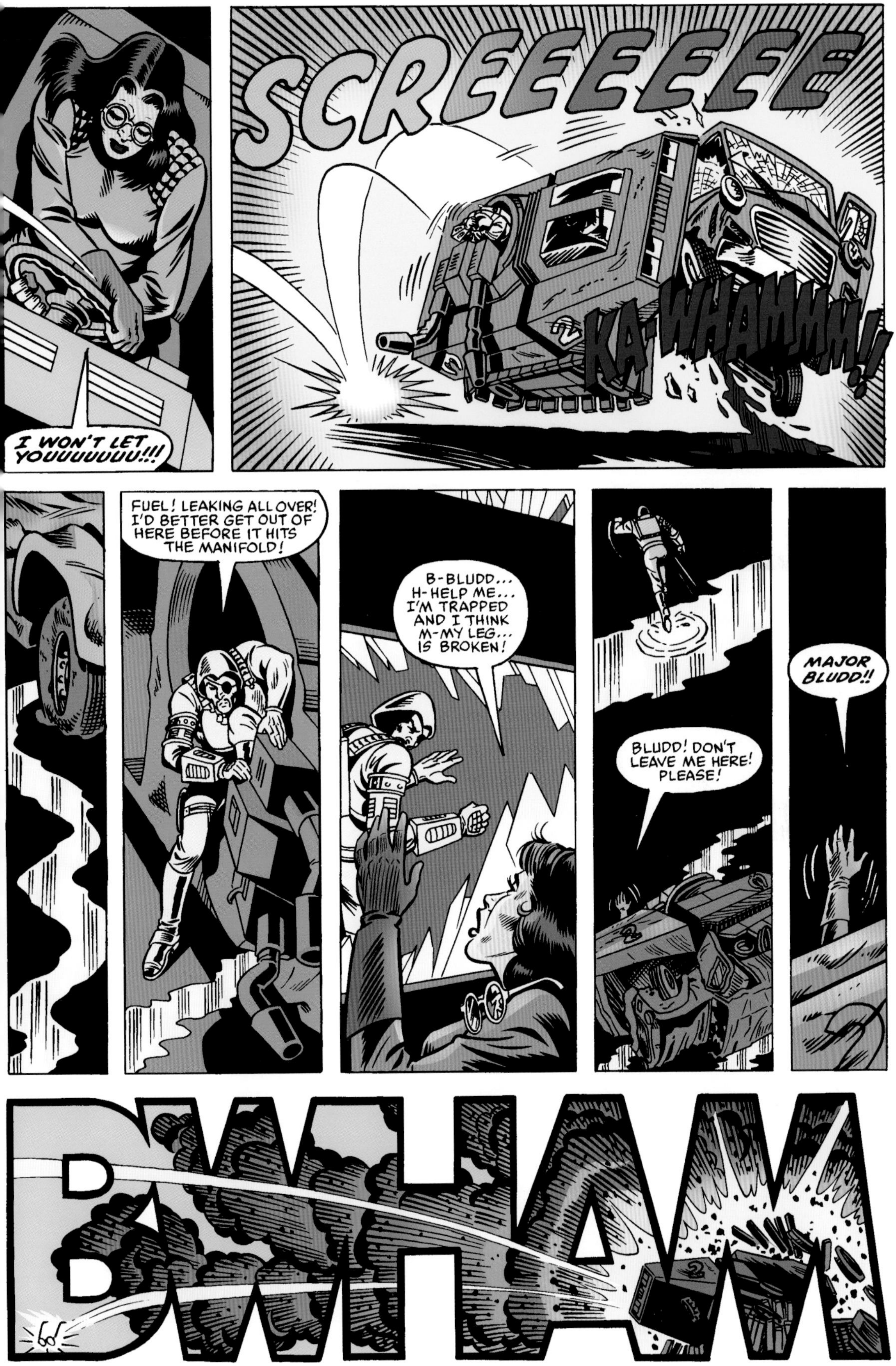
I WON'T LET YOUUUUUUU!!!
SCREEEEEEE
KA-WHAMMM!!
FUEL! LEAKING ALL OVER! I'D BETTER GET OUT OF HERE BEFORE IT HITS THE MANIFOLD!
B-BLUDD... H-HELP ME... I'M TRAPPED AND I THINK M-MY LEG... IS BROKEN!
BLUDD! DON'T LEAVE ME HERE! PLEASE!
MAJOR BLUDD!!
BWHAM

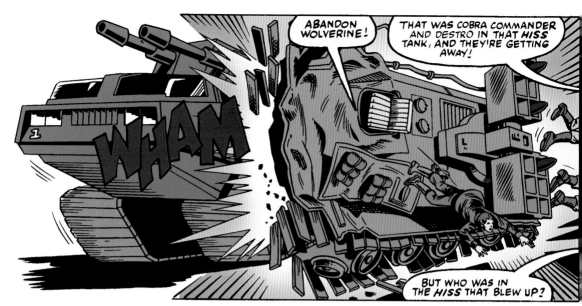

ABANDON WOLVERINE!

THAT WAS COBRA COMMANDER AND DESTRO IN THAT *HISS* TANK, AND THEY'RE GETTING AWAY!

WHAM

BUT WHO WAS IN THE *HISS* THAT BLEW UP?

LOOKS LIKE OUR BOYS TOOK QUITE A PASTING HERE, HAWK! SHOULD WE STOP AND--

NEGATIVE! WE STAY ON THAT *HISS* TANK UNTIL WE RUN IT TO GROUND!

DON'T WORRY ABOUT US, HAWK! WE'LL COMMANDEER THE NEXT SET OF WHEELS THAT ROLLS BY!

COBRA COMMANDER! WAIT FOR ME! IT'S DR. VENOM!

THAT TRAITOR, SCAR-FACE ALMOST-- SAY... WHAT'S WRONG WITH DESTRO?

DESTRO!

SOMEBODY HAS TO MAN THE GUN TURRET...

... DESTRO!

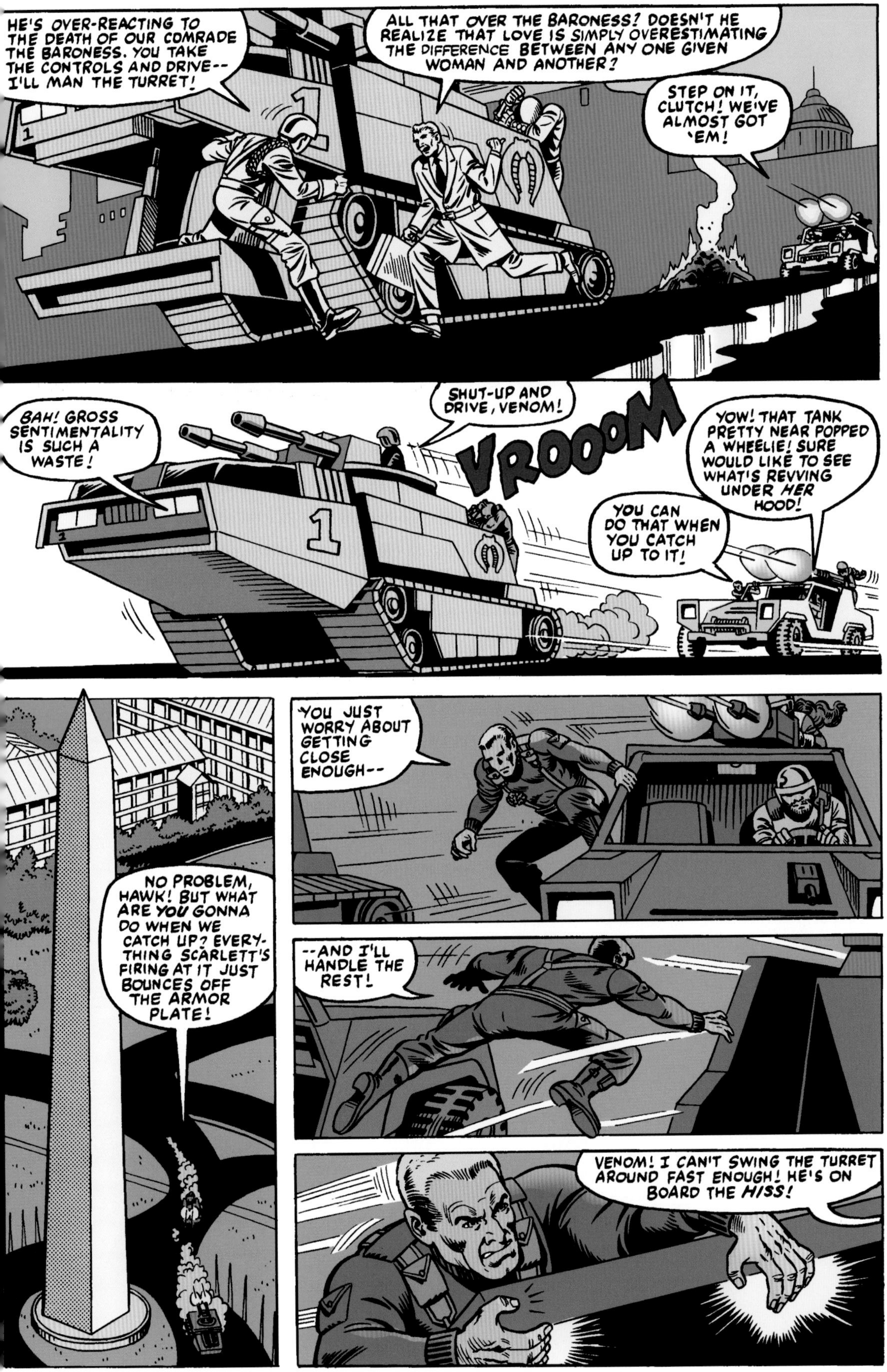
HE'S OVER-REACTING TO THE DEATH OF OUR COMRADE THE BARONESS. YOU TAKE THE CONTROLS AND DRIVE-- I'LL MAN THE TURRET!
ALL THAT OVER THE BARONESS? DOESN'T HE REALIZE THAT LOVE IS SIMPLY OVERESTIMATING THE DIFFERENCE BETWEEN ANY ONE GIVEN WOMAN AND ANOTHER?
STEP ON IT, CLUTCH! WE'VE ALMOST GOT 'EM!
BAH! GROSS SENTIMENTALITY IS SUCH A WASTE!
SHUT-UP AND DRIVE, VENOM!
VROOOM
YOW! THAT TANK PRETTY NEAR POPPED A WHEELIE! SURE WOULD LIKE TO SEE WHAT'S REVVING UNDER HER HOOD!
YOU CAN DO THAT WHEN YOU CATCH UP TO IT!
NO PROBLEM, HAWK! BUT WHAT ARE YOU GONNA DO WHEN WE CATCH UP? EVERY-THING SCARLETT'S FIRING AT IT JUST BOUNCES OFF THE ARMOR PLATE!
YOU JUST WORRY ABOUT GETTING CLOSE ENOUGH--
--AND I'LL HANDLE THE REST!
VENOM! I CAN'T SWING THE TURRET AROUND FAST ENOUGH! HE'S ON BOARD THE HISS!

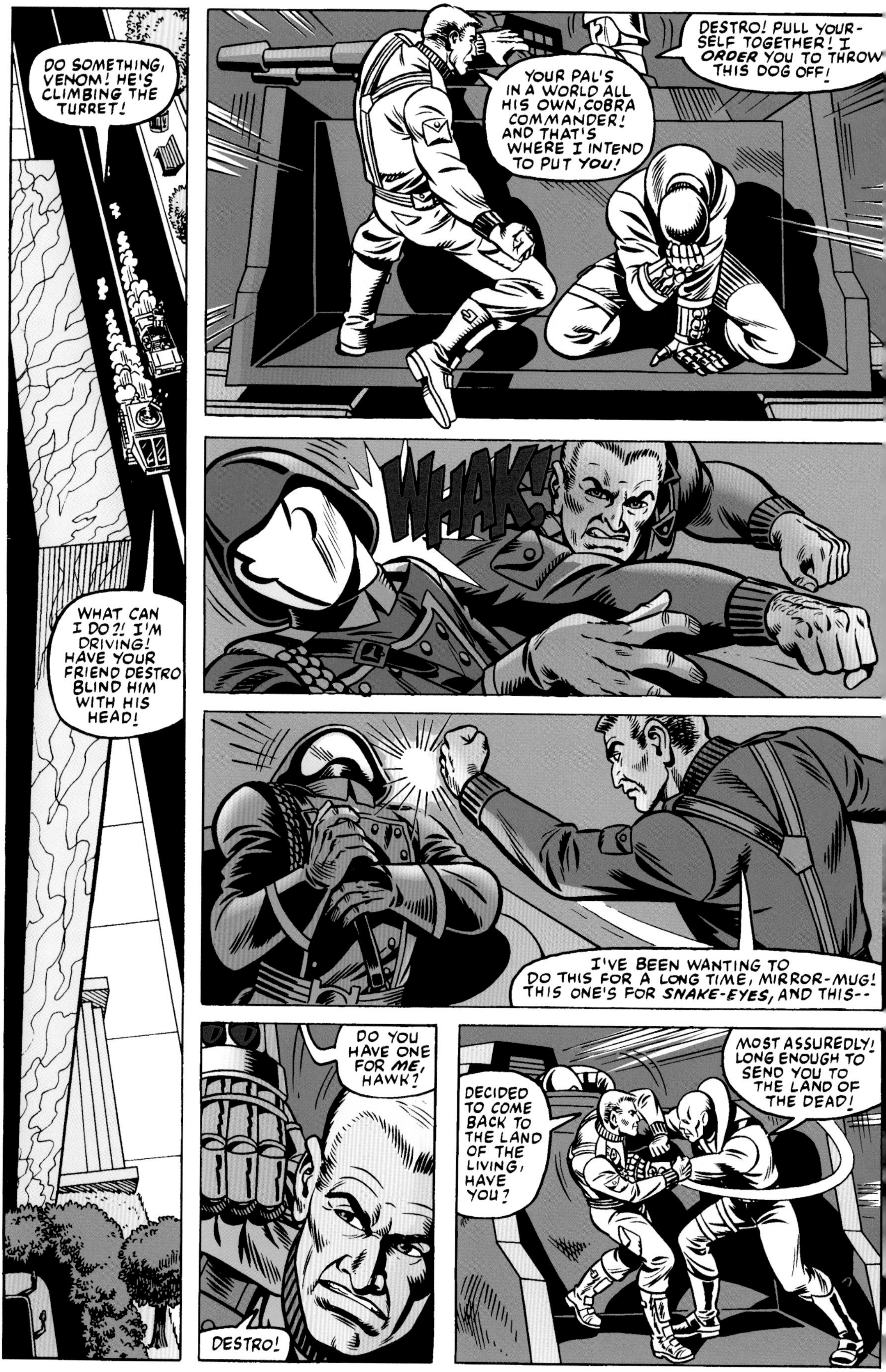
DO SOMETHING, VENOM! HE'S CLIMBING THE TURRET!
WHAT CAN I DO?! I'M DRIVING! HAVE YOUR FRIEND DESTRO BLIND HIM WITH HIS HEAD!
YOUR PAL'S IN A WORLD ALL HIS OWN, COBRA COMMANDER! AND THAT'S WHERE I INTEND TO PUT YOU!
DESTRO! PULL YOURSELF TOGETHER! I ORDER YOU TO THROW THIS DOG OFF!
WHAK!
I'VE BEEN WANTING TO DO THIS FOR A LONG TIME, MIRROR-MUG! THIS ONE'S FOR SNAKE-EYES, AND THIS--
DO YOU HAVE ONE FOR ME, HAWK?
DESTRO!
DECIDED TO COME BACK TO THE LAND OF THE LIVING, HAVE YOU?
MOST ASSUREDLY! LONG ENOUGH TO SEND YOU TO THE LAND OF THE DEAD!

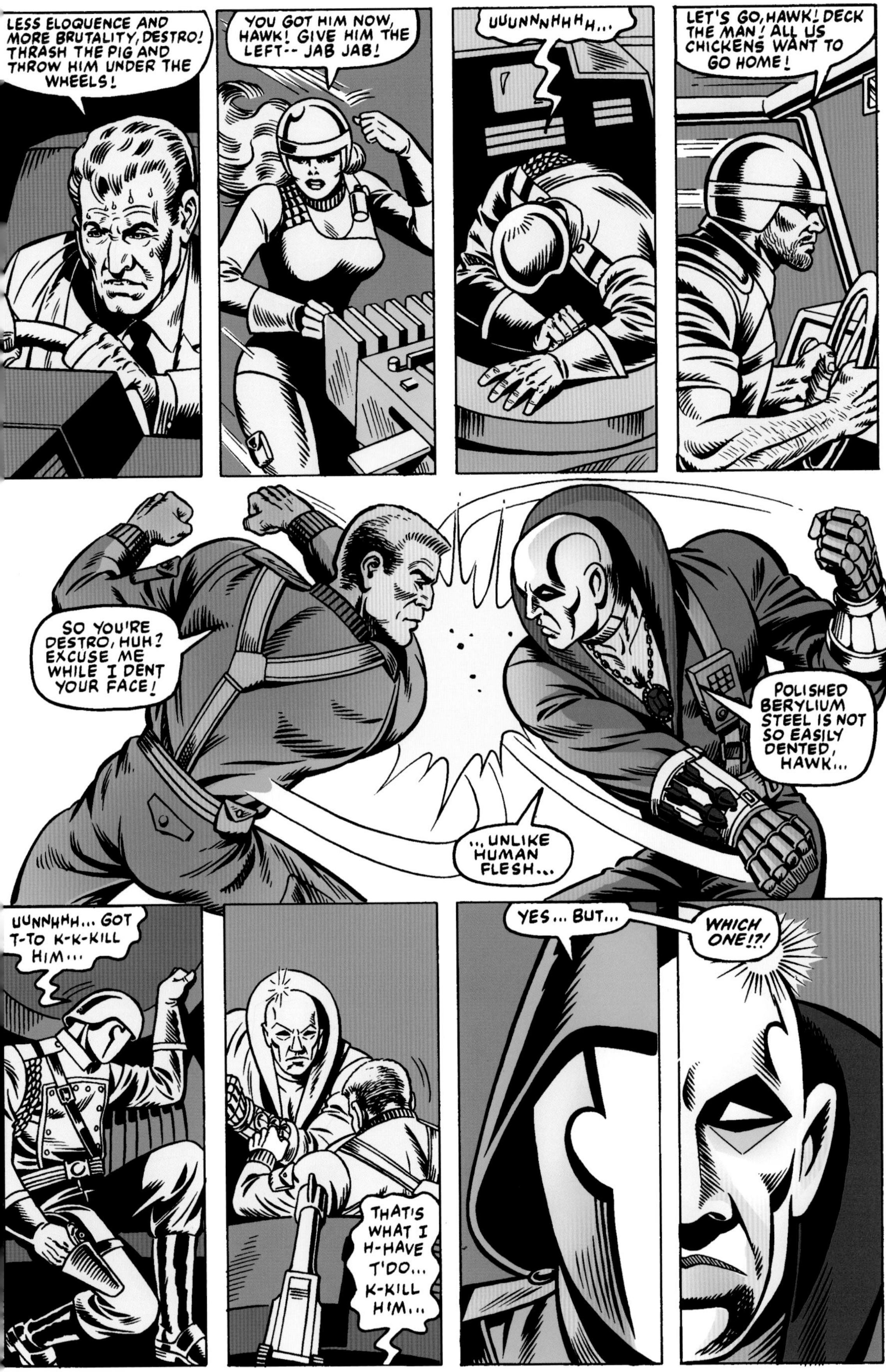
LESS ELOQUENCE AND MORE BRUTALITY, DESTRO! THRASH THE PIG AND THROW HIM UNDER THE WHEELS!
YOU GOT HIM NOW, HAWK! GIVE HIM THE LEFT-- JAB JAB!
UUUNNNHHHHH...
LET'S GO, HAWK! DECK THE MAN! ALL US CHICKENS WANT TO GO HOME!
SO YOU'RE DESTRO, HUH? EXCUSE ME WHILE I DENT YOUR FACE!
POLISHED BERYLIUM STEEL IS NOT SO EASILY DENTED, HAWK...
...UNLIKE HUMAN FLESH...
UUNNHHH... GOT T-TO K-K-KILL HIM...
THAT'S WHAT I H-HAVE T'DO... K-KILL HIM...
YES... BUT...
WHICH ONE!?!

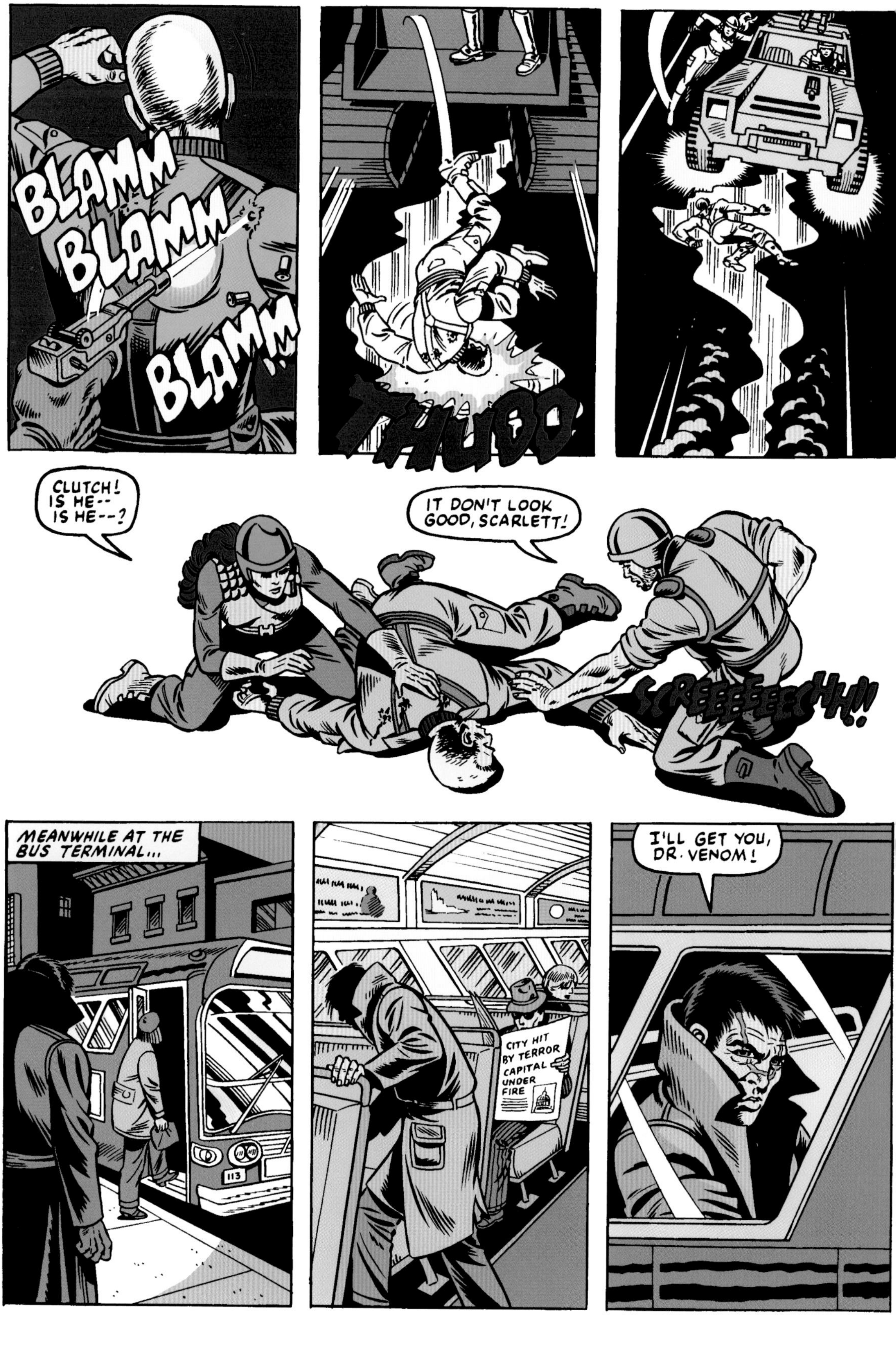
BLAMM
BLAMM
BLAMM!!
THUDD
CLUTCH! IS HE-- IS HE--?
IT DON'T LOOK GOOD, SCARLETT!
SCREEEEEEECHH!!
MEANWHILE AT THE BUS TERMINAL...
113
CITY HIT BY TERROR
CAPITAL UNDER FIRE
I'LL GET YOU, DR. VENOM!

MARVEL® COMICS

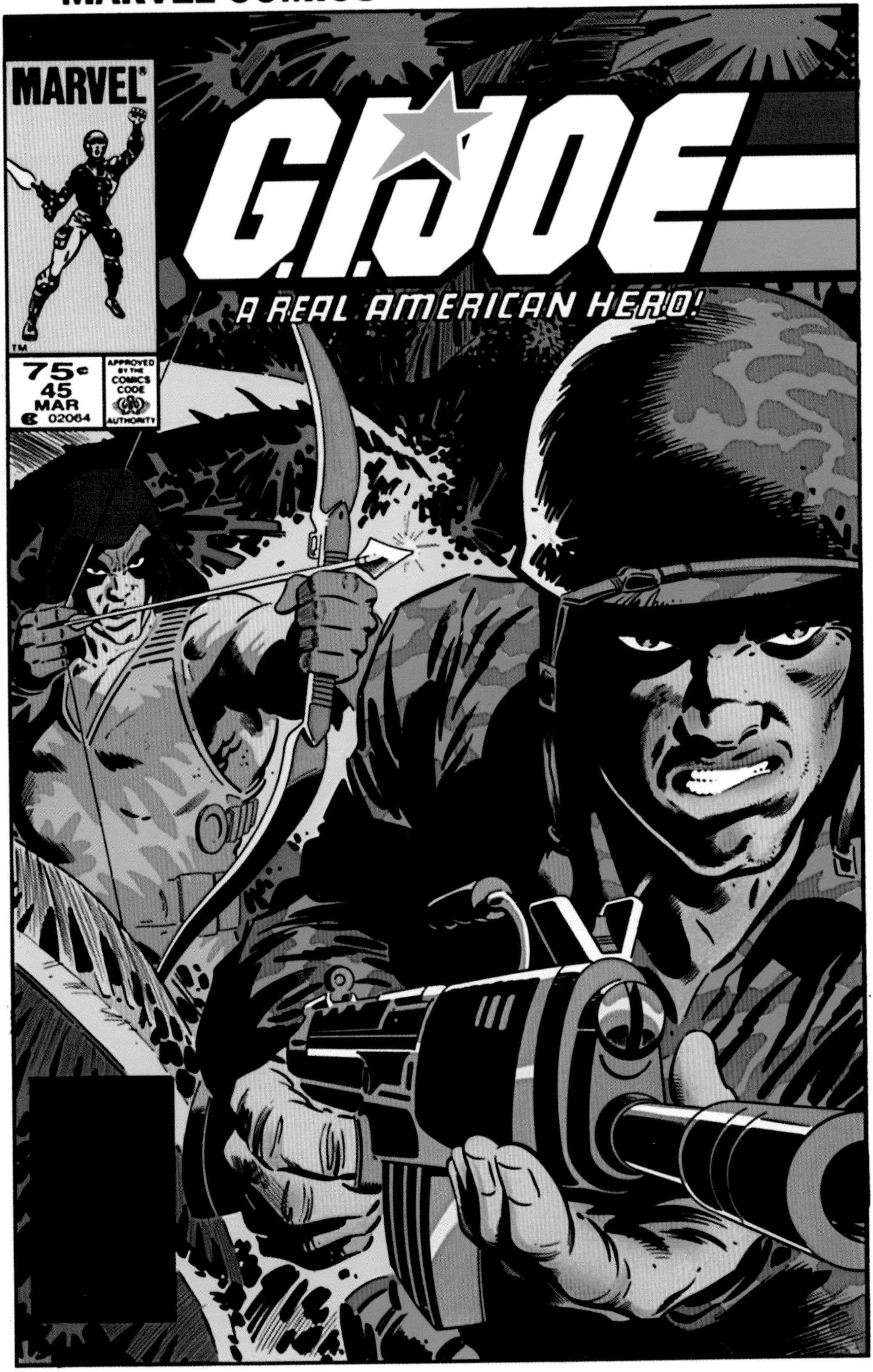

MARVEL®
G.I. JOE
A REAL AMERICAN HERO!
75¢
45
MAR
02064
APPROVED BY THE COMICS CODE AUTHORITY

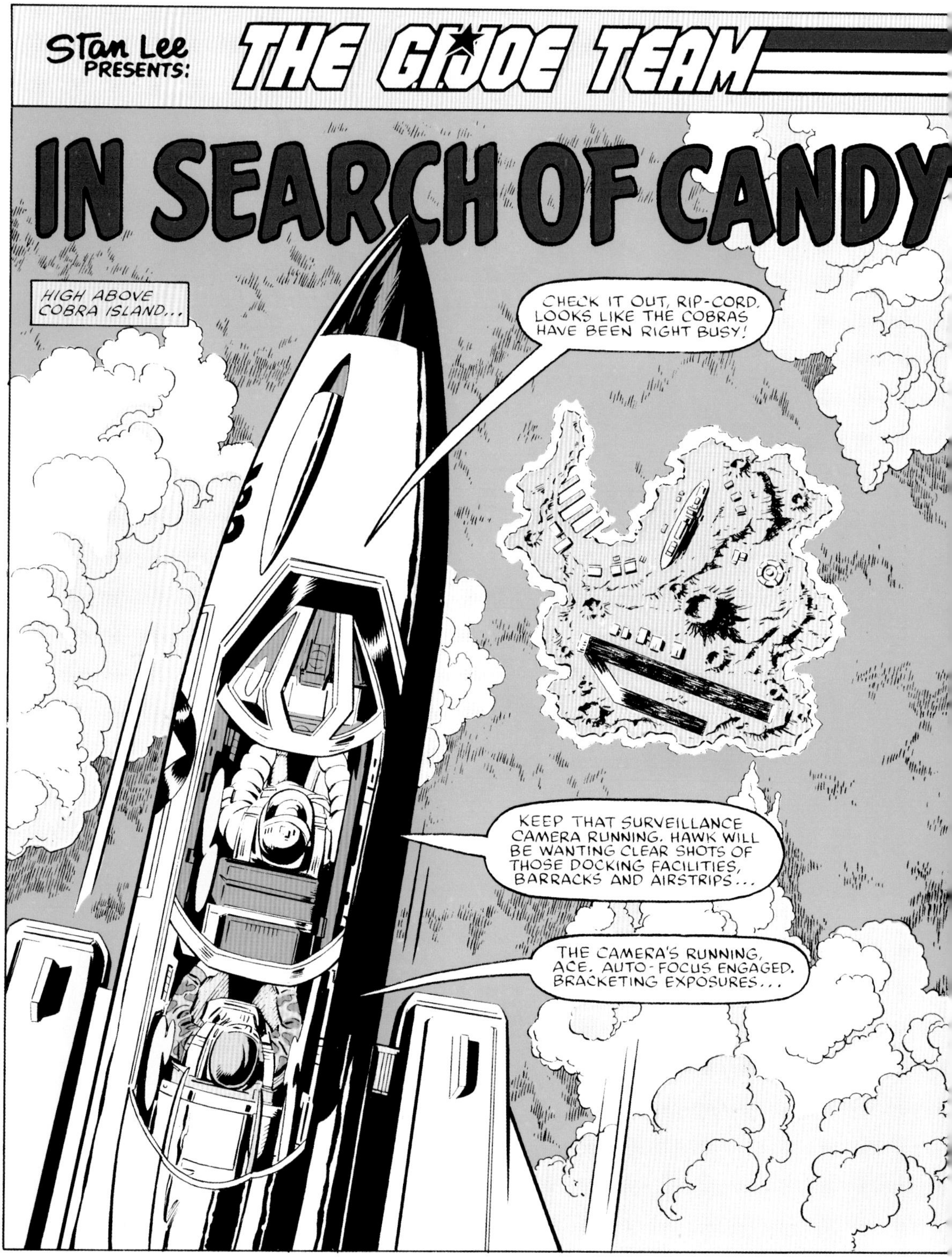
Stan Lee PRESENTS:
THE G.I. JOE TEAM
IN SEARCH OF CANDY
HIGH ABOVE COBRA ISLAND...
CHECK IT OUT, RIP-CORD. LOOKS LIKE THE COBRAS HAVE BEEN RIGHT BUSY!
KEEP THAT SURVEILLANCE CAMERA RUNNING. HAWK WILL BE WANTING CLEAR SHOTS OF THOSE DOCKING FACILITIES, BARRACKS AND AIRSTRIPS...
THE CAMERA'S RUNNING, ACE. AUTO-FOCUS ENGAGED. BRACKETING EXPOSURES...

LARRY HAMA SCRIPT · ROD WHIGHAM PENCILS · ANDY MUSHYNSKY INKS · JOE ROSEN LETTERING · GEORGE ROUSSOS COLORS · DENNIS O'NEIL EDITOR · JIM SHOOTER EDITOR IN CHIEF

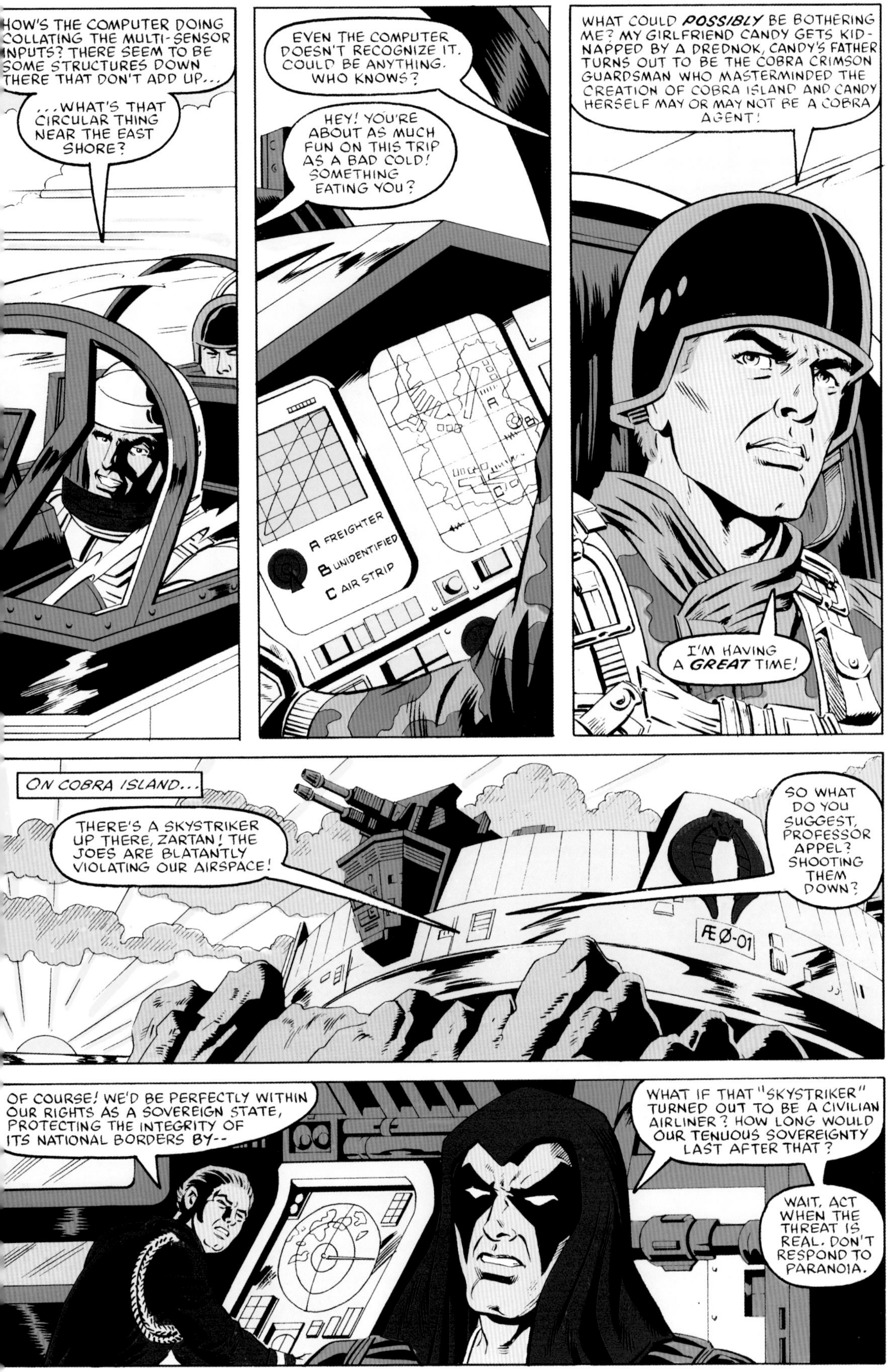
HOW'S THE COMPUTER DOING COLLATING THE MULTI-SENSOR INPUTS? THERE SEEM TO BE SOME STRUCTURES DOWN THERE THAT DON'T ADD UP...
...WHAT'S THAT CIRCULAR THING NEAR THE EAST SHORE?
EVEN THE COMPUTER DOESN'T RECOGNIZE IT. COULD BE ANYTHING. WHO KNOWS?
HEY! YOU'RE ABOUT AS MUCH FUN ON THIS TRIP AS A BAD COLD! SOMETHING EATING YOU?
A FREIGHTER
B UNIDENTIFIED
C AIR STRIP
WHAT COULD POSSIBLY BE BOTHERING ME? MY GIRLFRIEND CANDY GETS KID-NAPPED BY A DREDNOK, CANDY'S FATHER TURNS OUT TO BE THE COBRA CRIMSON GUARDSMAN WHO MASTERMINDED THE CREATION OF COBRA ISLAND AND CANDY HERSELF MAY OR MAY NOT BE A COBRA AGENT!
I'M HAVING A GREAT TIME!
ON COBRA ISLAND...
THERE'S A SKYSTRIKER UP THERE, ZARTAN! THE JOES ARE BLATANTLY VIOLATING OUR AIRSPACE!
SO WHAT DO YOU SUGGEST, PROFESSOR APPEL? SHOOTING THEM DOWN?
ÆØ-01
OF COURSE! WE'D BE PERFECTLY WITHIN OUR RIGHTS AS A SOVEREIGN STATE, PROTECTING THE INTEGRITY OF ITS NATIONAL BORDERS BY--
WHAT IF THAT "SKYSTRIKER" TURNED OUT TO BE A CIVILIAN AIRLINER? HOW LONG WOULD OUR TENUOUS SOVEREIGNTY LAST AFTER THAT?
WAIT. ACT WHEN THE THREAT IS REAL. DON'T RESPOND TO PARANOIA.

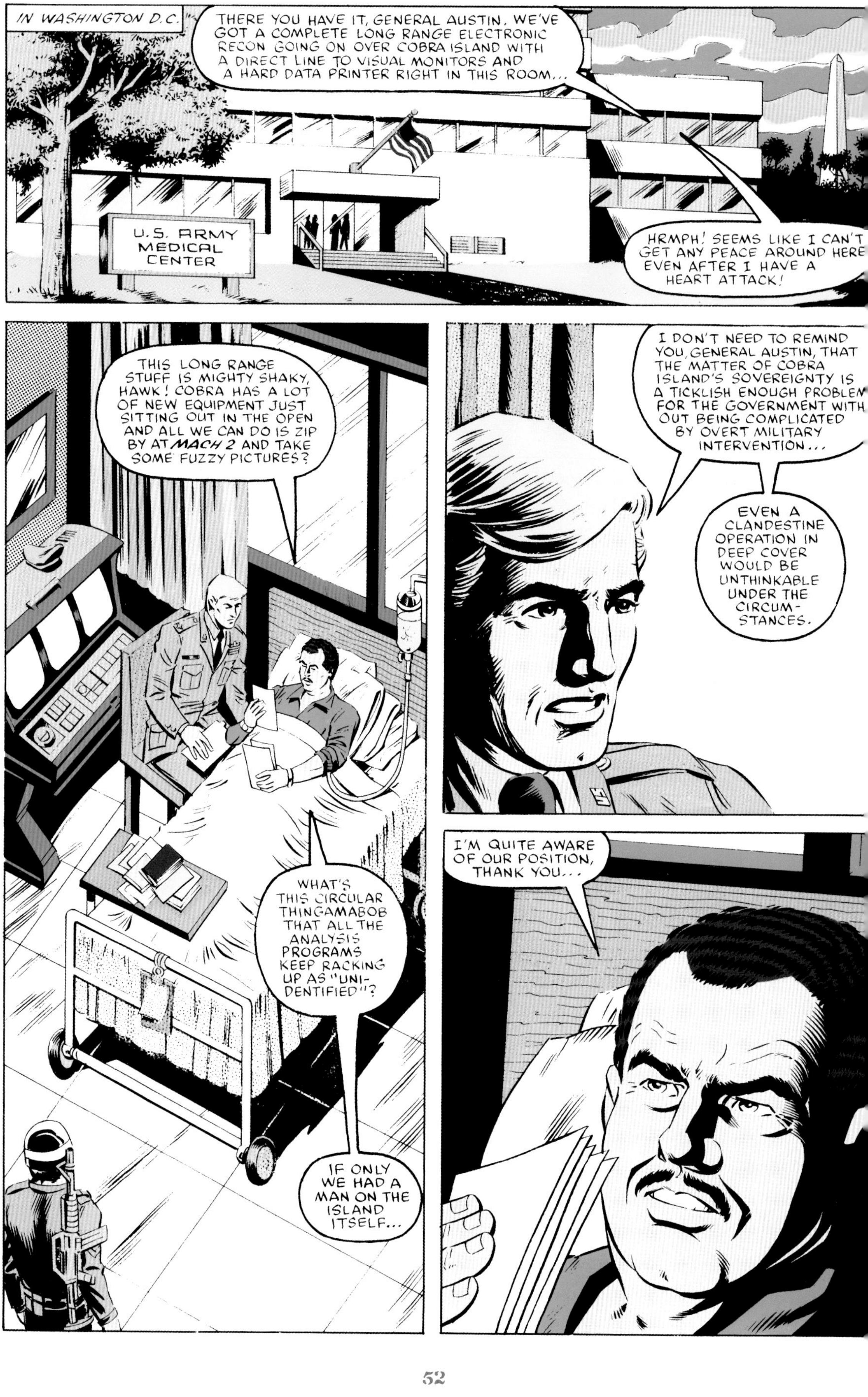
IN WASHINGTON D.C.
THERE YOU HAVE IT, GENERAL AUSTIN. WE'VE GOT A COMPLETE LONG RANGE ELECTRONIC RECON GOING ON OVER COBRA ISLAND WITH A DIRECT LINE TO VISUAL MONITORS AND A HARD DATA PRINTER RIGHT IN THIS ROOM...
U.S. ARMY MEDICAL CENTER
HRMPH! SEEMS LIKE I CAN'T GET ANY PEACE AROUND HERE EVEN AFTER I HAVE A HEART ATTACK!
THIS LONG RANGE STUFF IS MIGHTY SHAKY, HAWK! COBRA HAS A LOT OF NEW EQUIPMENT JUST SITTING OUT IN THE OPEN AND ALL WE CAN DO IS ZIP BY AT MACH 2 AND TAKE SOME FUZZY PICTURES?
WHAT'S THIS CIRCULAR THINGAMABOB THAT ALL THE ANALYSIS PROGRAMS KEEP RACKING UP AS "UNIDENTIFIED"?
IF ONLY WE HAD A MAN ON THE ISLAND ITSELF...
I DON'T NEED TO REMIND YOU, GENERAL AUSTIN, THAT THE MATTER OF COBRA ISLAND'S SOVEREIGNTY IS A TICKLISH ENOUGH PROBLEM FOR THE GOVERNMENT WITHOUT BEING COMPLICATED BY OVERT MILITARY INTERVENTION...
EVEN A CLANDESTINE OPERATION IN DEEP COVER WOULD BE UNTHINKABLE UNDER THE CIRCUMSTANCES.
I'M QUITE AWARE OF OUR POSITION, THANK YOU...

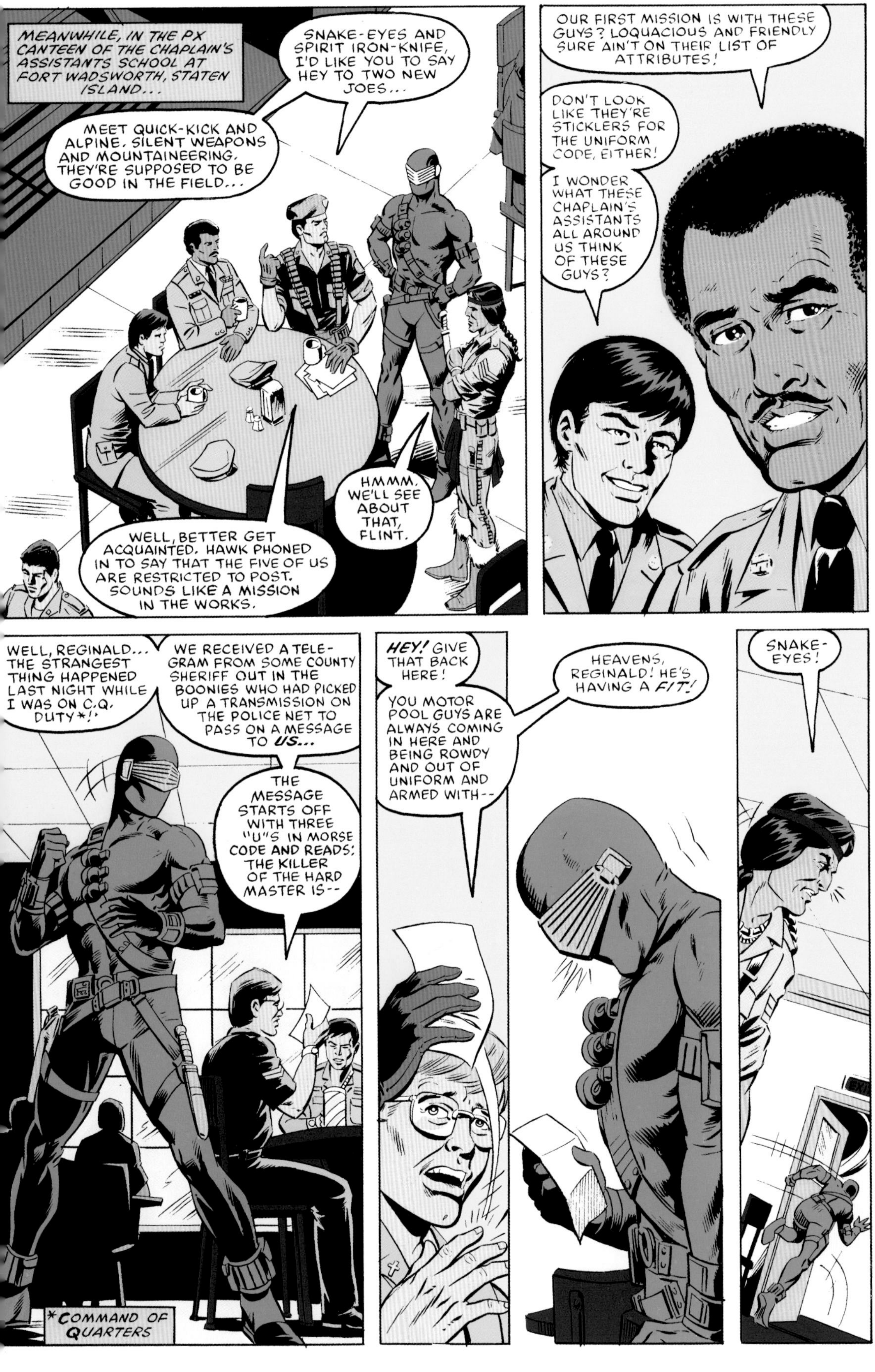
MEANWHILE, IN THE PX CANTEEN OF THE CHAPLAIN'S ASSISTANTS SCHOOL AT FORT WADSWORTH, STATEN ISLAND...
SNAKE-EYES AND SPIRIT IRON-KNIFE, I'D LIKE YOU TO SAY HEY TO TWO NEW JOES...
MEET QUICK-KICK AND ALPINE. SILENT WEAPONS AND MOUNTAINEERING. THEY'RE SUPPOSED TO BE GOOD IN THE FIELD...
WELL, BETTER GET ACQUAINTED. HAWK PHONED IN TO SAY THAT THE FIVE OF US ARE RESTRICTED TO POST. SOUNDS LIKE A MISSION IN THE WORKS.
HMMM. WE'LL SEE ABOUT THAT, FLINT.
OUR FIRST MISSION IS WITH THESE GUYS? LOQUACIOUS AND FRIENDLY SURE AIN'T ON THEIR LIST OF ATTRIBUTES!
DON'T LOOK LIKE THEY'RE STICKLERS FOR THE UNIFORM CODE, EITHER!
I WONDER WHAT THESE CHAPLAIN'S ASSISTANTS ALL AROUND US THINK OF THESE GUYS?
WELL, REGINALD... THE STRANGEST THING HAPPENED LAST NIGHT WHILE I WAS ON C.Q. DUTY*!
WE RECEIVED A TELEGRAM FROM SOME COUNTY SHERIFF OUT IN THE BOONIES WHO HAD PICKED UP A TRANSMISSION ON THE POLICE NET TO PASS ON A MESSAGE TO US...
THE MESSAGE STARTS OFF WITH THREE "U"S IN MORSE CODE AND READS: THE KILLER OF THE HARD MASTER IS--
*COMMAND OF QUARTERS
HEY! GIVE THAT BACK HERE!
YOU MOTOR POOL GUYS ARE ALWAYS COMING IN HERE AND BEING ROWDY AND OUT OF UNIFORM AND ARMED WITH--
HEAVENS, REGINALD! HE'S HAVING A FIT!
SNAKE-EYES!

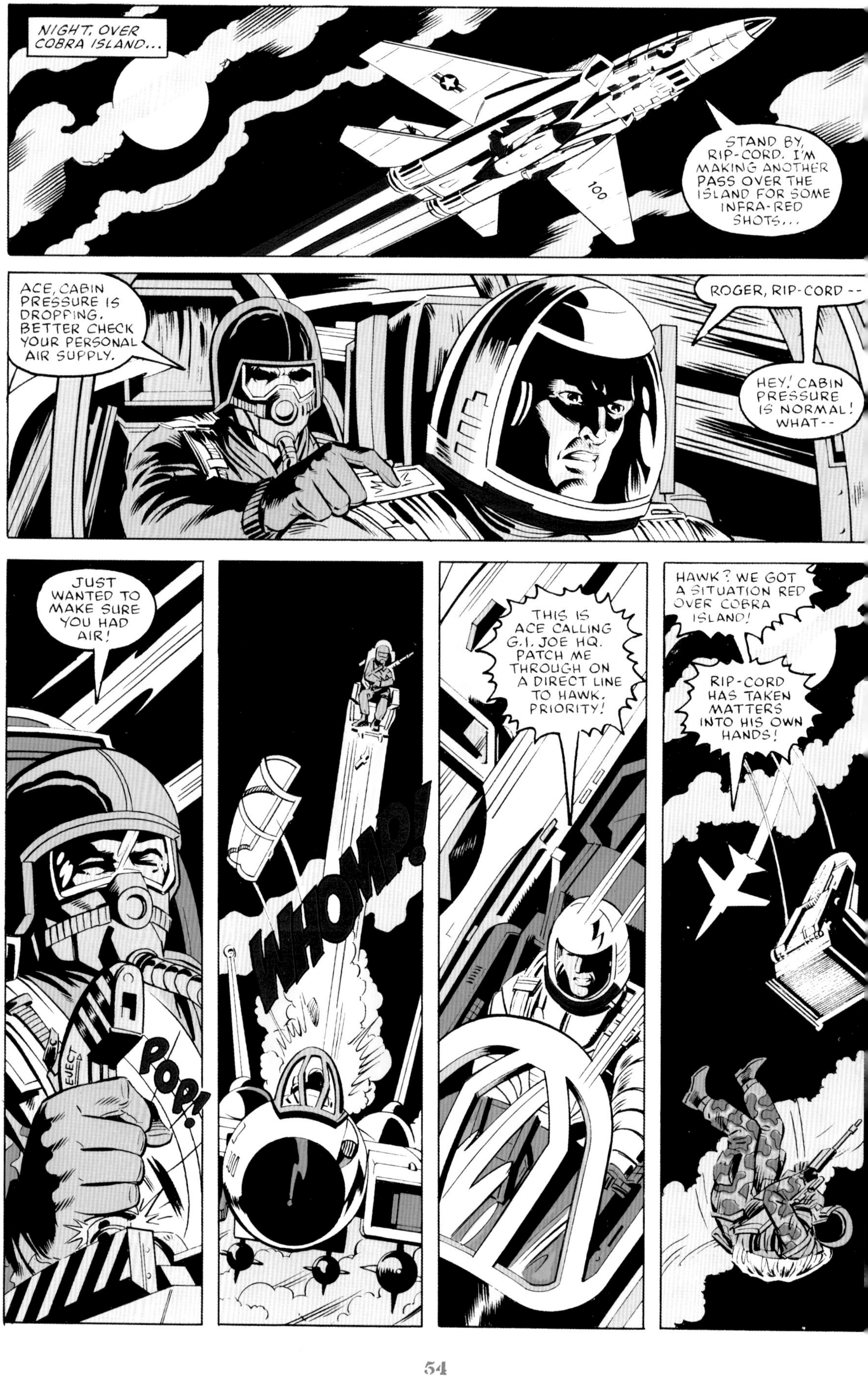
NIGHT, OVER COBRA ISLAND...
STAND BY, RIP-CORD. I'M MAKING ANOTHER PASS OVER THE ISLAND FOR SOME INFRA-RED SHOTS...
100
ACE, CABIN PRESSURE IS DROPPING. BETTER CHECK YOUR PERSONAL AIR SUPPLY.
ROGER, RIP-CORD --
HEY! CABIN PRESSURE IS NORMAL! WHAT--
JUST WANTED TO MAKE SURE YOU HAD AIR!
EJECT
POP!
WHOMP!
THIS IS ACE CALLING G.I. JOE HQ. PATCH ME THROUGH ON A DIRECT LINE TO HAWK. PRIORITY!
HAWK? WE GOT A SITUATION RED OVER COBRA ISLAND!
RIP-CORD HAS TAKEN MATTERS INTO HIS OWN HANDS!

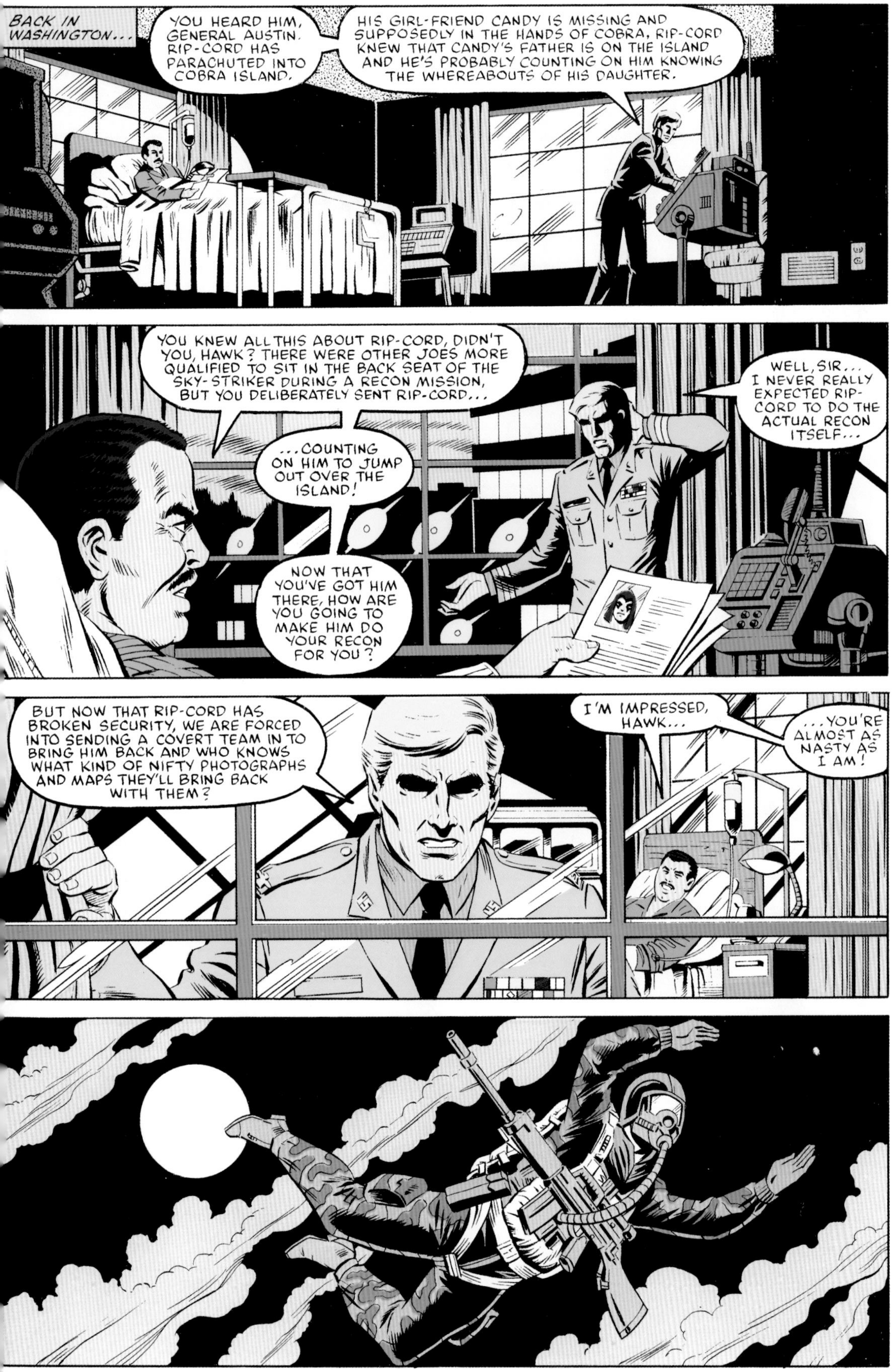
BACK IN WASHINGTON...
YOU HEARD HIM, GENERAL AUSTIN. RIP-CORD HAS PARACHUTED INTO COBRA ISLAND.
HIS GIRL-FRIEND CANDY IS MISSING AND SUPPOSEDLY IN THE HANDS OF COBRA. RIP-CORD KNEW THAT CANDY'S FATHER IS ON THE ISLAND AND HE'S PROBABLY COUNTING ON HIM KNOWING THE WHEREABOUTS OF HIS DAUGHTER.
YOU KNEW ALL THIS ABOUT RIP-CORD, DIDN'T YOU, HAWK? THERE WERE OTHER JOES MORE QUALIFIED TO SIT IN THE BACK SEAT OF THE SKY-STRIKER DURING A RECON MISSION, BUT YOU DELIBERATELY SENT RIP-CORD...
...COUNTING ON HIM TO JUMP OUT OVER THE ISLAND!
NOW THAT YOU'VE GOT HIM THERE, HOW ARE YOU GOING TO MAKE HIM DO YOUR RECON FOR YOU?
WELL, SIR... I NEVER REALLY EXPECTED RIP-CORD TO DO THE ACTUAL RECON ITSELF...
BUT NOW THAT RIP-CORD HAS BROKEN SECURITY, WE ARE FORCED INTO SENDING A COVERT TEAM IN TO BRING HIM BACK AND WHO KNOWS WHAT KIND OF NIFTY PHOTOGRAPHS AND MAPS THEY'LL BRING BACK WITH THEM?
I'M IMPRESSED, HAWK...
...YOU'RE ALMOST AS NASTY AS I AM!

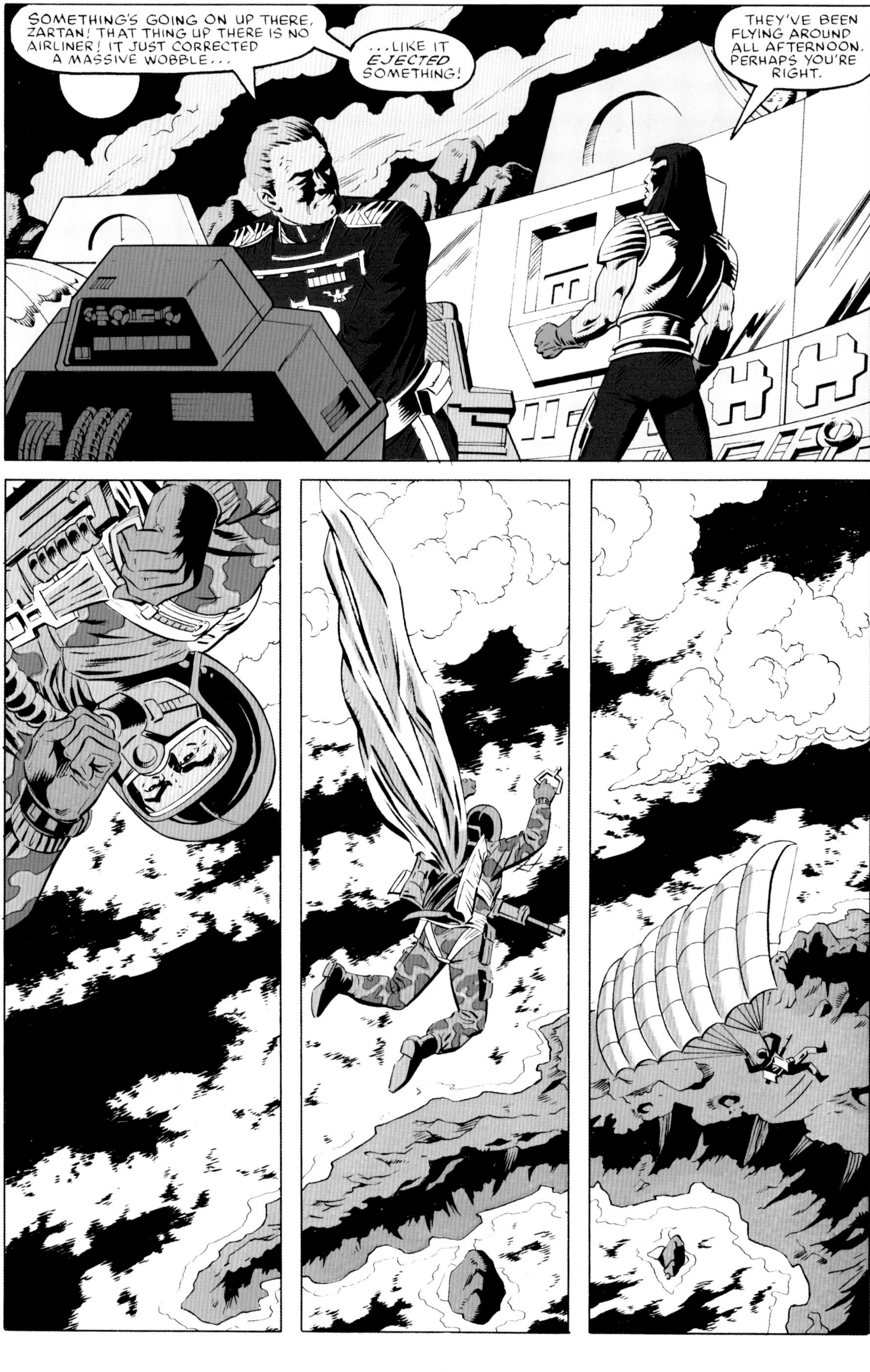
SOMETHING'S GOING ON UP THERE, ZARTAN! THAT THING UP THERE IS NO AIRLINER! IT JUST CORRECTED A MASSIVE WOBBLE...
...LIKE IT EJECTED SOMETHING!
THEY'VE BEEN FLYING AROUND ALL AFTERNOON. PERHAPS YOU'RE RIGHT.

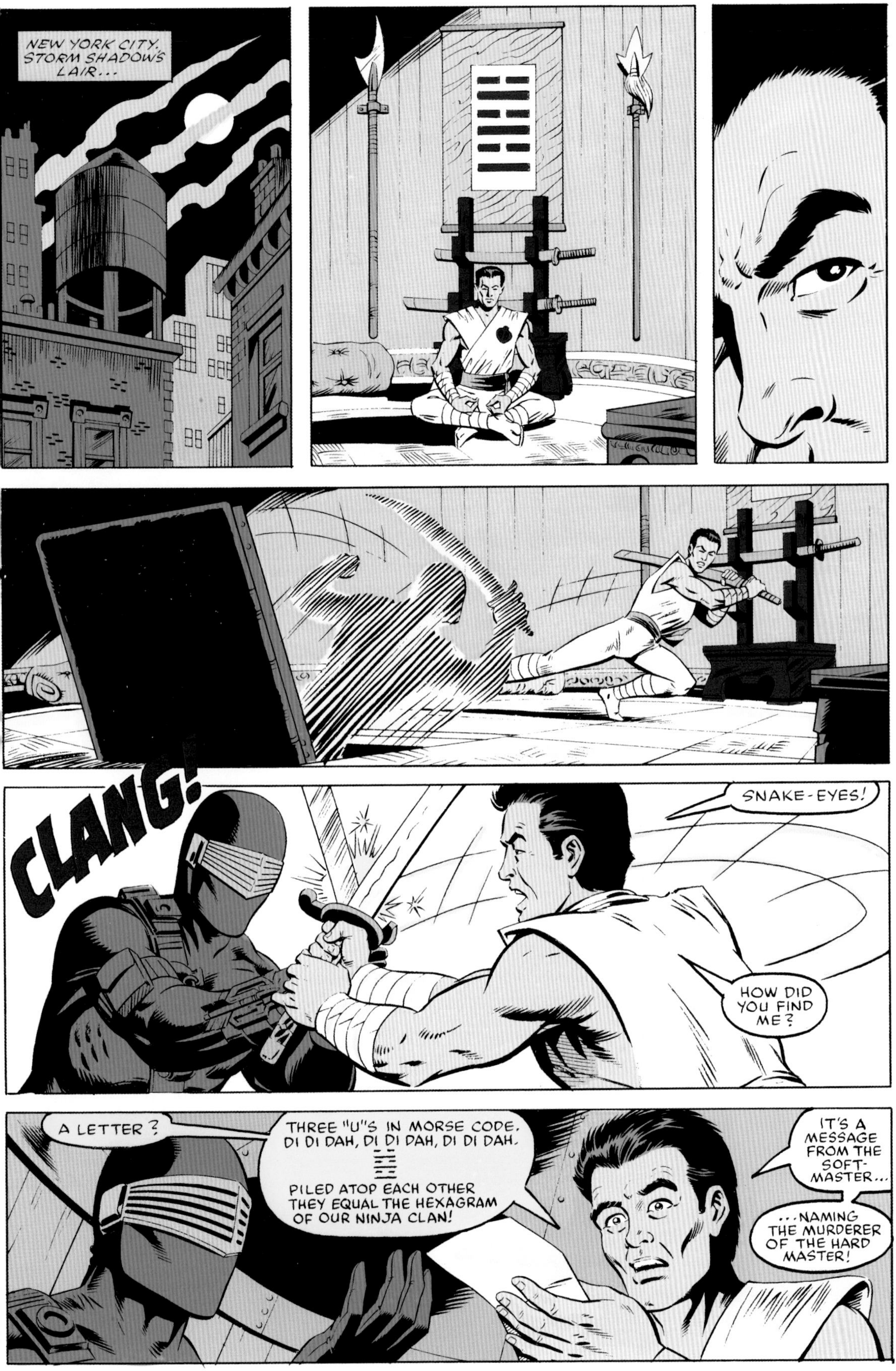
NEW YORK CITY. STORM SHADOW'S LAIR...
CLANG!
SNAKE-EYES!
HOW DID YOU FIND ME?
A LETTER?
THREE "U"S IN MORSE CODE. DI DI DAH, DI DI DAH, DI DI DAH.
PILED ATOP EACH OTHER THEY EQUAL THE HEXAGRAM OF OUR NINJA CLAN!
IT'S A MESSAGE FROM THE SOFT-MASTER...
...NAMING THE MURDERER OF THE HARD MASTER!

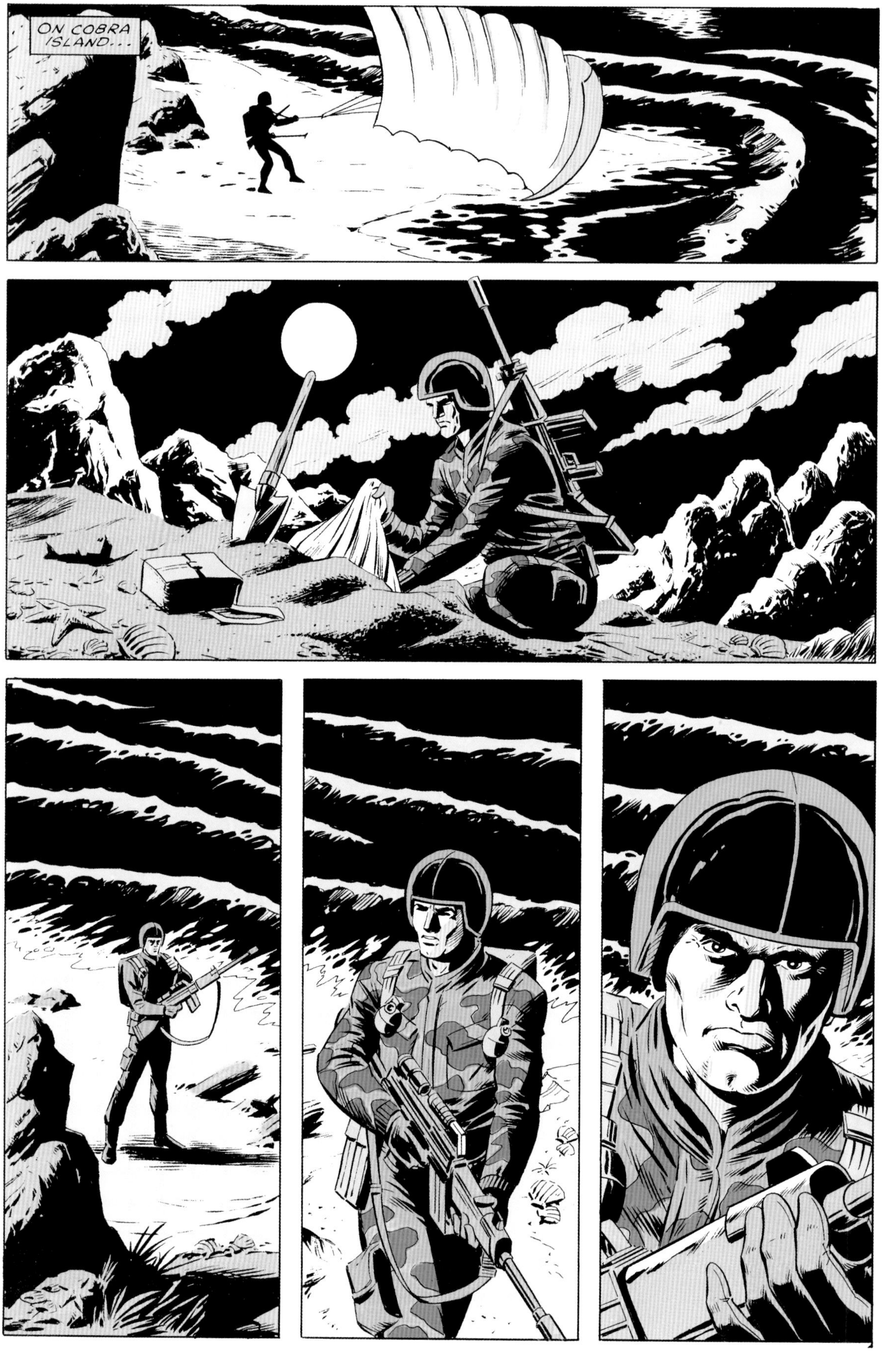
ON COBRA ISLAND...

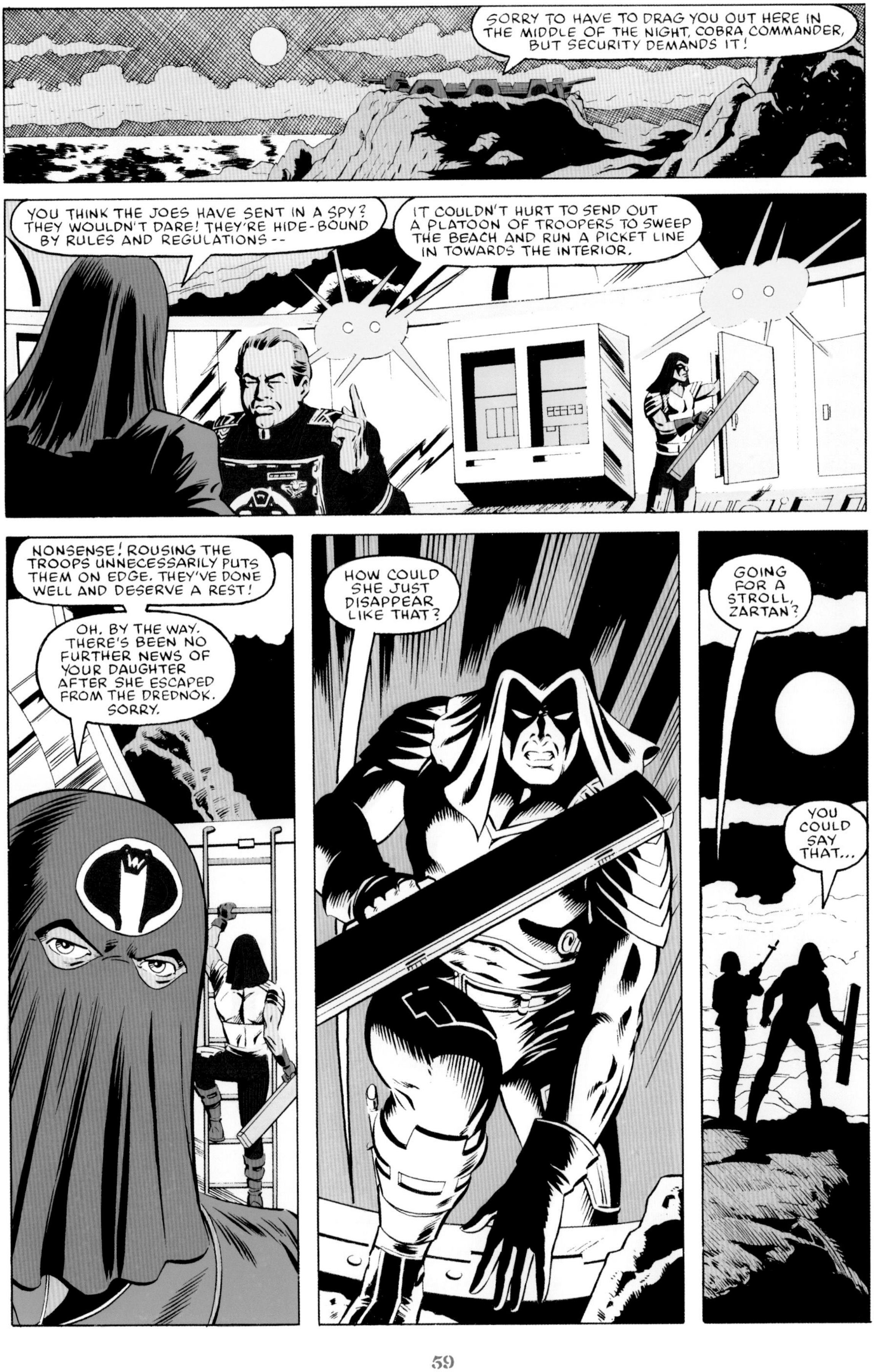
SORRY TO HAVE TO DRAG YOU OUT HERE IN THE MIDDLE OF THE NIGHT, COBRA COMMANDER, BUT SECURITY DEMANDS IT!
YOU THINK THE JOES HAVE SENT IN A SPY? THEY WOULDN'T DARE! THEY'RE HIDE-BOUND BY RULES AND REGULATIONS --
IT COULDN'T HURT TO SEND OUT A PLATOON OF TROOPERS TO SWEEP THE BEACH AND RUN A PICKET LINE IN TOWARDS THE INTERIOR.
NONSENSE! ROUSING THE TROOPS UNNECESSARILY PUTS THEM ON EDGE. THEY'VE DONE WELL AND DESERVE A REST!
OH, BY THE WAY. THERE'S BEEN NO FURTHER NEWS OF YOUR DAUGHTER AFTER SHE ESCAPED FROM THE DREDNOK. SORRY.
HOW COULD SHE JUST DISAPPEAR LIKE THAT?
GOING FOR A STROLL, ZARTAN?
YOU COULD SAY THAT...

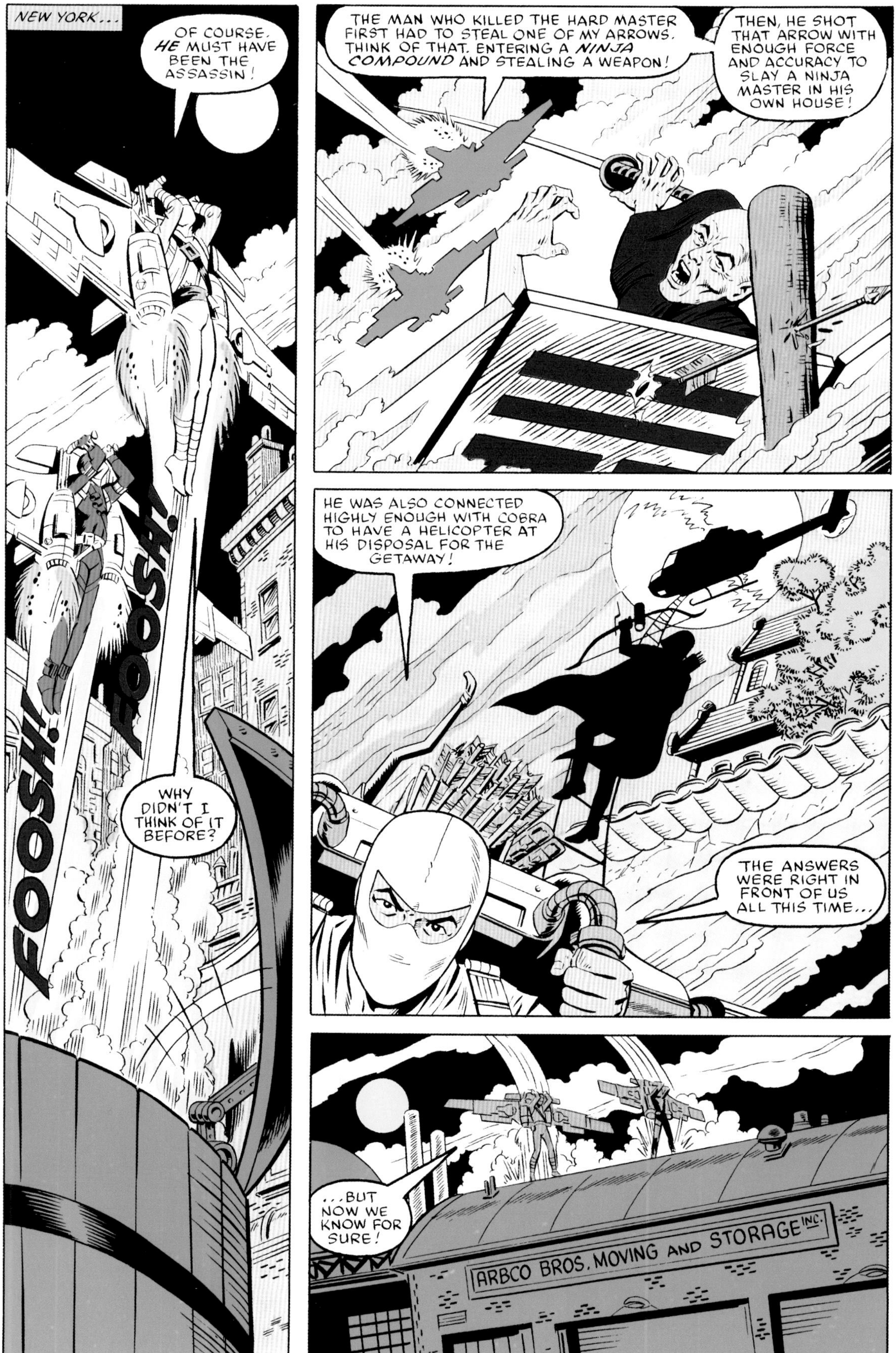
NEW YORK...
OF COURSE. HE MUST HAVE BEEN THE ASSASSIN!
FOOSH!
FOOSH!
WHY DIDN'T I THINK OF IT BEFORE?
THE MAN WHO KILLED THE HARD MASTER FIRST HAD TO STEAL ONE OF MY ARROWS. THINK OF THAT. ENTERING A NINJA COMPOUND AND STEALING A WEAPON!
THEN, HE SHOT THAT ARROW WITH ENOUGH FORCE AND ACCURACY TO SLAY A NINJA MASTER IN HIS OWN HOUSE!
HE WAS ALSO CONNECTED HIGHLY ENOUGH WITH COBRA TO HAVE A HELICOPTER AT HIS DISPOSAL FOR THE GETAWAY!
THE ANSWERS WERE RIGHT IN FRONT OF US ALL THIS TIME...
...BUT NOW WE KNOW FOR SURE!
ARBCO BROS. MOVING AND STORAGE INC.

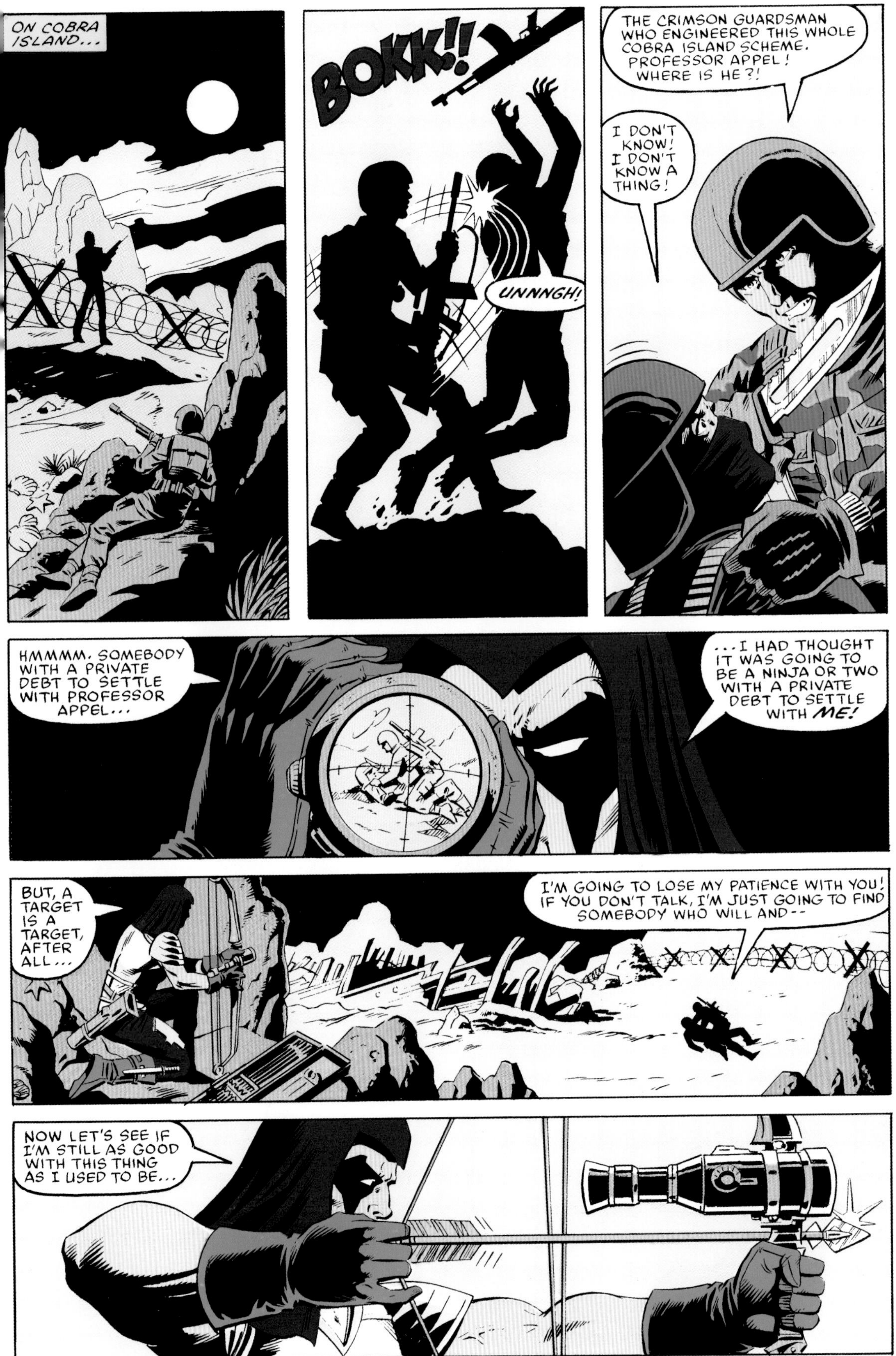

ON COBRA ISLAND...
BOKK!!
UNNNGH!
THE CRIMSON GUARDSMAN WHO ENGINEERED THIS WHOLE COBRA ISLAND SCHEME. PROFESSOR APPEL! WHERE IS HE?!
I DON'T KNOW! I DON'T KNOW A THING!
HMMMM. SOMEBODY WITH A PRIVATE DEBT TO SETTLE WITH PROFESSOR APPEL...
...I HAD THOUGHT IT WAS GOING TO BE A NINJA OR TWO WITH A PRIVATE DEBT TO SETTLE WITH ME!
BUT, A TARGET IS A TARGET, AFTER ALL...
I'M GOING TO LOSE MY PATIENCE WITH YOU! IF YOU DON'T TALK, I'M JUST GOING TO FIND SOMEBODY WHO WILL AND--
NOW LET'S SEE IF I'M STILL AS GOOD WITH THIS THING AS I USED TO BE...

NEW YORK...

WE'LL LEAVE THE *CLAW*S HERE. THEY HAVE NOWHERE NEAR THE RANGE TO REACH MY UNCLE'S KILLER...

...FORTUNATELY I KNOW THE LOCATION OF MOST COBRA SAFE HOUSES IN NEW YORK.

THIS PARTICULAR ONE HOUSES THE BARONESS'S PERSONAL RATTLER ATTACK JET!

JUST THE THING TO FLY US TO *COBRA ISLAND!*

VROOOM

ARBCO BROS. MO

AT McGUIRE FIELD...

WHAT'S UP, FLINT? I THOUGHT SNAKE-EYES WAS SUPPOSED TO GO ON THIS EXCURSION...

SOMETHING CAME UP, WILD-BILL.

IT DON'T SEEM RIGHT. DOING A NIGHT INSERTION WITHOUT OL' SNAKES...

WE CAN HANDLE IT, RIGHT, ALPINE?

YOU SAID IT, QUICK-KICK.

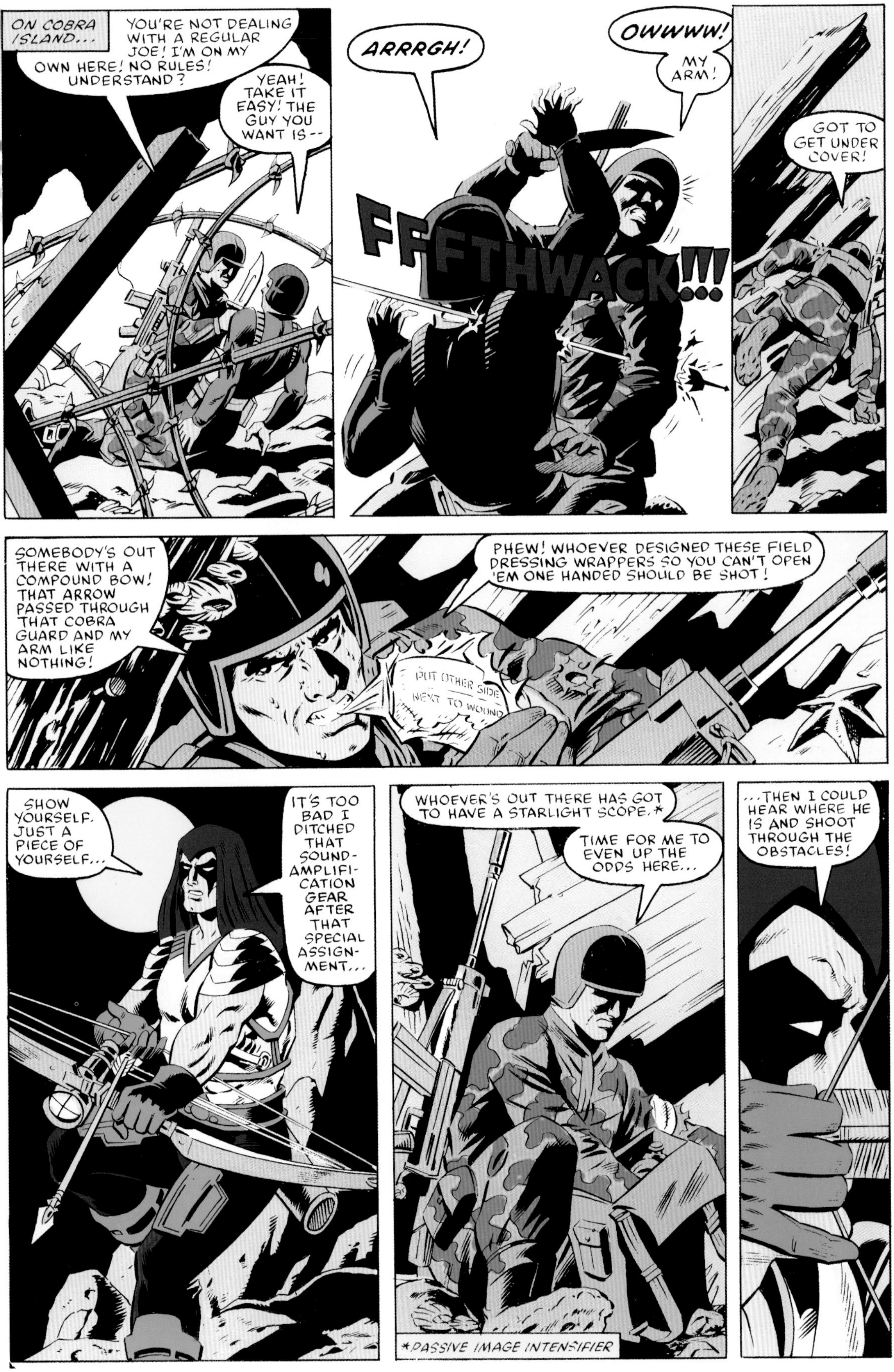
ON COBRA ISLAND...
YOU'RE NOT DEALING WITH A REGULAR JOE! I'M ON MY OWN HERE! NO RULES! UNDERSTAND?
YEAH! TAKE IT EASY! THE GUY YOU WANT IS--
ARRRGH!
FFFTHWACK!!!
OWWWW!
MY ARM!
GOT TO GET UNDER COVER!
SOMEBODY'S OUT THERE WITH A COMPOUND BOW! THAT ARROW PASSED THROUGH THAT COBRA GUARD AND MY ARM LIKE NOTHING!
PHEW! WHOEVER DESIGNED THESE FIELD DRESSING WRAPPERS SO YOU CAN'T OPEN 'EM ONE HANDED SHOULD BE SHOT!
PUT OTHER SIDE NEXT TO WOUND
SHOW YOURSELF. JUST A PIECE OF YOURSELF...
IT'S TOO BAD I DITCHED THAT SOUND-AMPLIFICATION GEAR AFTER THAT SPECIAL ASSIGNMENT...
WHOEVER'S OUT THERE HAS GOT TO HAVE A STARLIGHT SCOPE.*
TIME FOR ME TO EVEN UP THE ODDS HERE...
*PASSIVE IMAGE INTENSIFIER
...THEN I COULD HEAR WHERE HE IS AND SHOOT THROUGH THE OBSTACLES!

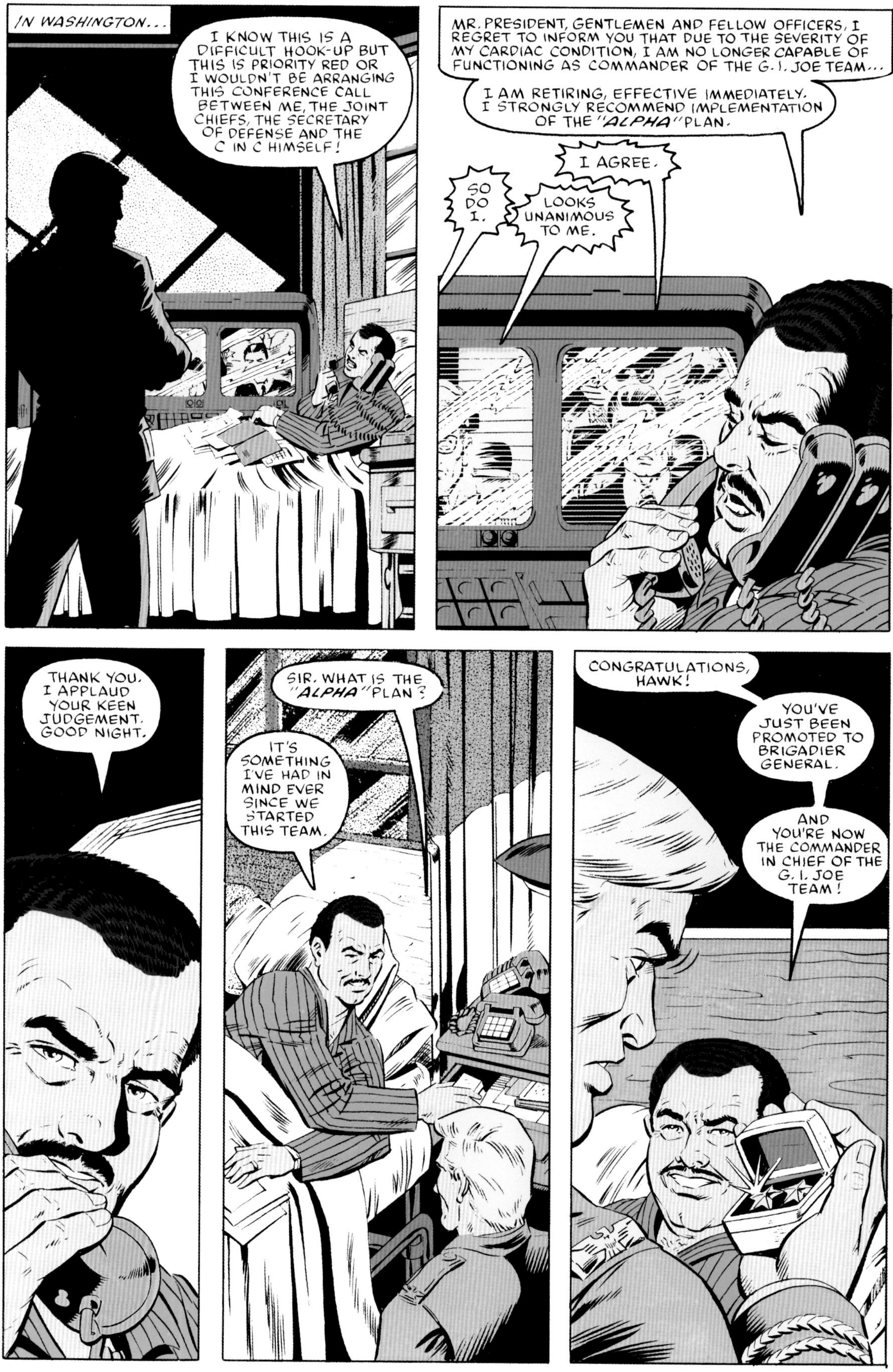
IN WASHINGTON...
I KNOW THIS IS A DIFFICULT HOOK-UP BUT THIS IS PRIORITY RED OR I WOULDN'T BE ARRANGING THIS CONFERENCE CALL BETWEEN ME, THE JOINT CHIEFS, THE SECRETARY OF DEFENSE AND THE C IN C HIMSELF!
MR. PRESIDENT, GENTLEMEN AND FELLOW OFFICERS, I REGRET TO INFORM YOU THAT DUE TO THE SEVERITY OF MY CARDIAC CONDITION, I AM NO LONGER CAPABLE OF FUNCTIONING AS COMMANDER OF THE G.I. JOE TEAM...
I AM RETIRING, EFFECTIVE IMMEDIATELY. I STRONGLY RECOMMEND IMPLEMENTATION OF THE "ALPHA" PLAN.
I AGREE.
SO DO I.
LOOKS UNANIMOUS TO ME.
THANK YOU. I APPLAUD YOUR KEEN JUDGEMENT. GOOD NIGHT.
SIR. WHAT IS THE "ALPHA" PLAN?
IT'S SOMETHING I'VE HAD IN MIND EVER SINCE WE STARTED THIS TEAM.
CONGRATULATIONS, HAWK!
YOU'VE JUST BEEN PROMOTED TO BRIGADIER GENERAL.
AND YOU'RE NOW THE COMMANDER IN CHIEF OF THE G.I. JOE TEAM!

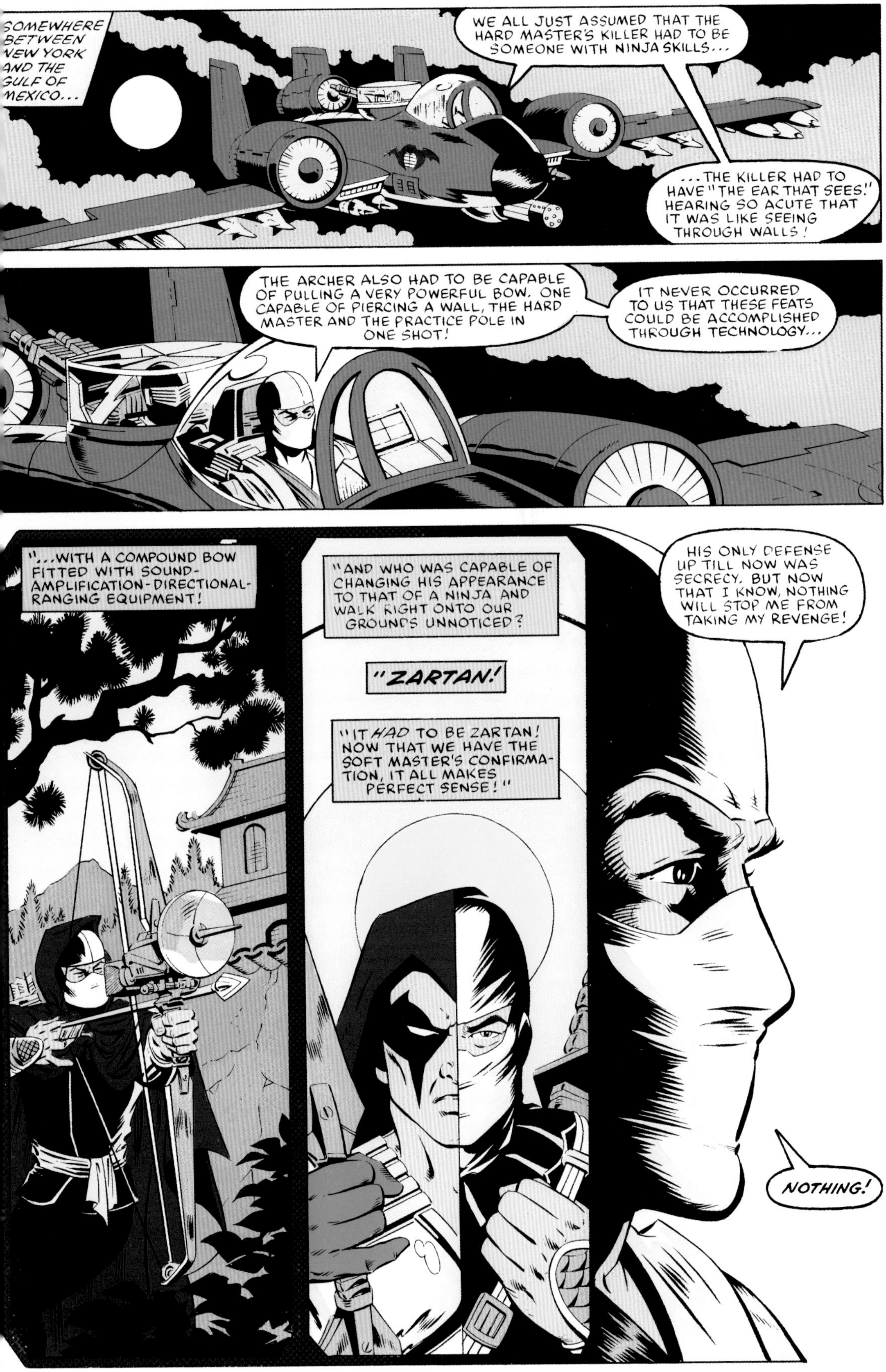
SOMEWHERE BETWEEN NEW YORK AND THE GULF OF MEXICO...
WE ALL JUST ASSUMED THAT THE HARD MASTER'S KILLER HAD TO BE SOMEONE WITH NINJA SKILLS...
...THE KILLER HAD TO HAVE "THE EAR THAT SEES!" HEARING SO ACUTE THAT IT WAS LIKE SEEING THROUGH WALLS!
THE ARCHER ALSO HAD TO BE CAPABLE OF PULLING A VERY POWERFUL BOW. ONE CAPABLE OF PIERCING A WALL, THE HARD MASTER AND THE PRACTICE POLE IN ONE SHOT!
IT NEVER OCCURRED TO US THAT THESE FEATS COULD BE ACCOMPLISHED THROUGH TECHNOLOGY...
"...WITH A COMPOUND BOW FITTED WITH SOUND-AMPLIFICATION-DIRECTIONAL-RANGING EQUIPMENT!
"AND WHO WAS CAPABLE OF CHANGING HIS APPEARANCE TO THAT OF A NINJA AND WALK RIGHT ONTO OUR GROUNDS UNNOTICED?
"ZARTAN!
"IT HAD TO BE ZARTAN! NOW THAT WE HAVE THE SOFT MASTER'S CONFIRMATION, IT ALL MAKES PERFECT SENSE!"
HIS ONLY DEFENSE UP TILL NOW WAS SECRECY. BUT NOW THAT I KNOW, NOTHING WILL STOP ME FROM TAKING MY REVENGE!
NOTHING!

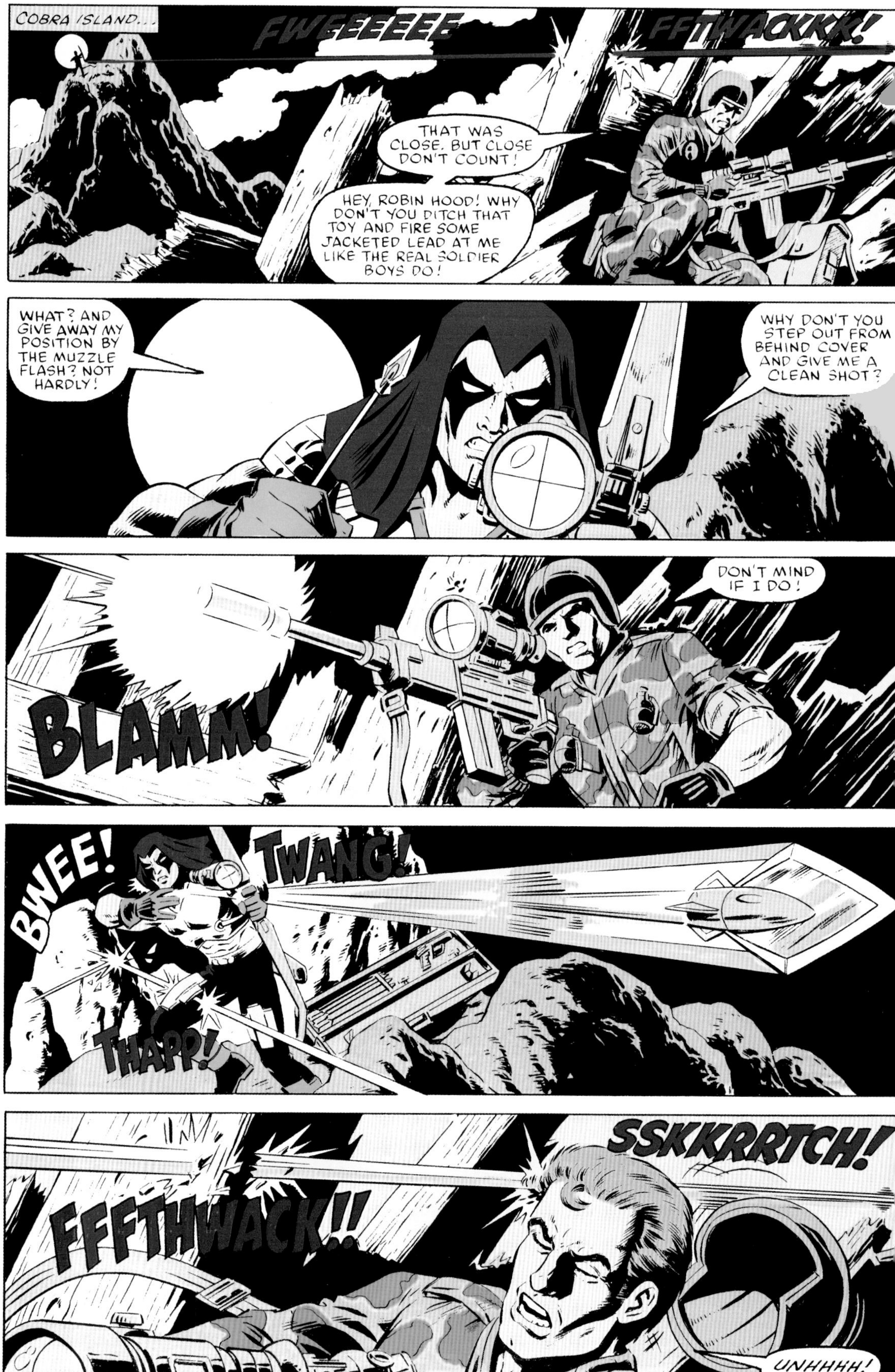
COBRA ISLAND...
FWEEEEEE
FFTWACKKK!
THAT WAS CLOSE. BUT CLOSE DON'T COUNT!
HEY, ROBIN HOOD! WHY DON'T YOU DITCH THAT TOY AND FIRE SOME JACKETED LEAD AT ME LIKE THE REAL SOLDIER BOYS DO!
WHAT? AND GIVE AWAY MY POSITION BY THE MUZZLE FLASH? NOT HARDLY!
WHY DON'T YOU STEP OUT FROM BEHIND COVER AND GIVE ME A CLEAN SHOT?
DON'T MIND IF I DO!
BLAMM!
BWEE!
TWANG!
THAPP!
SSKKRRTCH!
FFFTHWACK!!
UNHHHH!

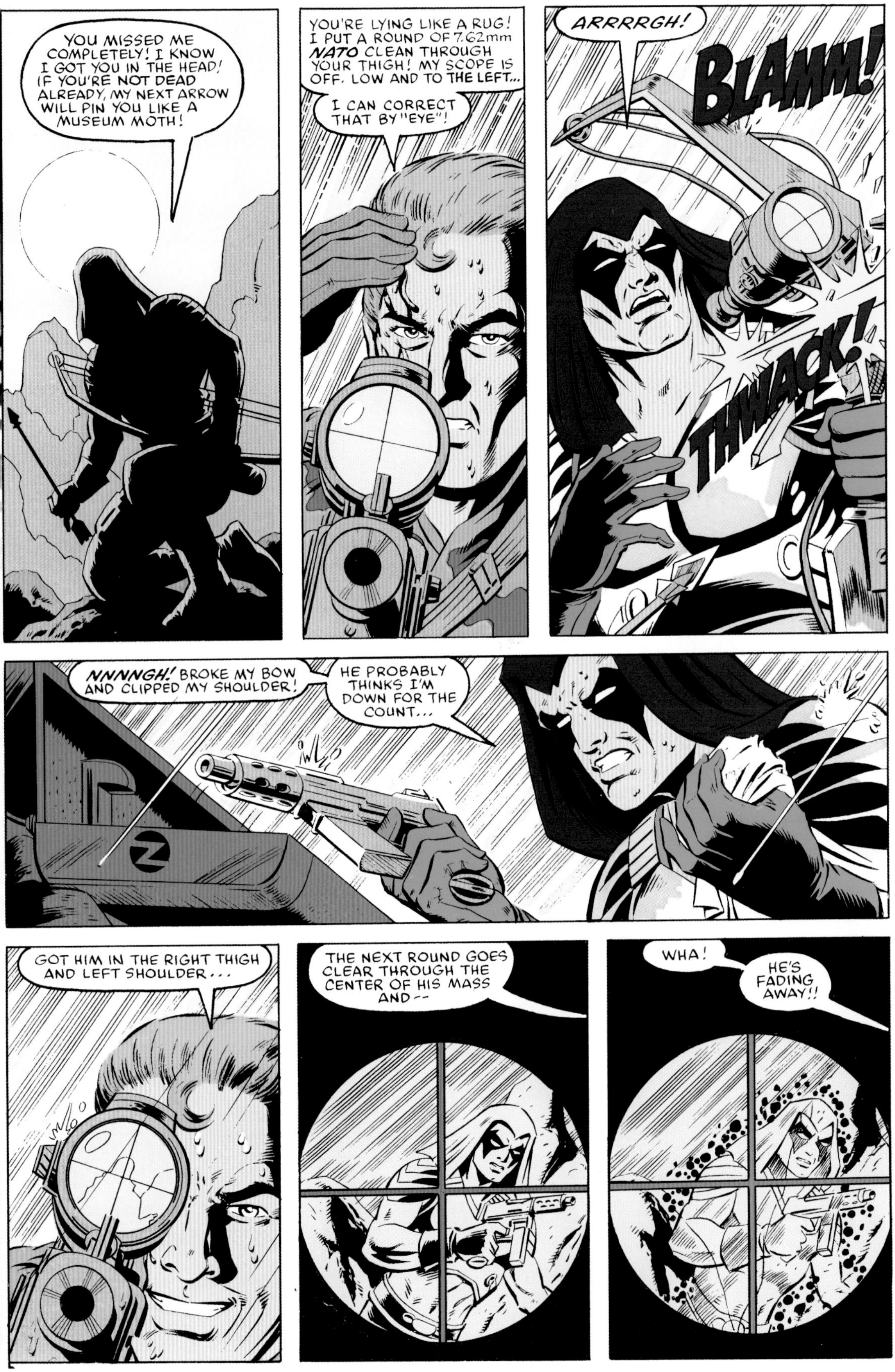

YOU MISSED ME COMPLETELY! I KNOW I GOT YOU IN THE HEAD! IF YOU'RE NOT DEAD ALREADY, MY NEXT ARROW WILL PIN YOU LIKE A MUSEUM MOTH!
YOU'RE LYING LIKE A RUG! I PUT A ROUND OF 7.62mm NATO CLEAN THROUGH YOUR THIGH! MY SCOPE IS OFF. LOW AND TO THE LEFT...
I CAN CORRECT THAT BY "EYE"!
ARRRRGH!
BLAMM!
THWACK!
NNNNGH! BROKE MY BOW AND CLIPPED MY SHOULDER!
HE PROBABLY THINKS I'M DOWN FOR THE COUNT...
GOT HIM IN THE RIGHT THIGH AND LEFT SHOULDER...
THE NEXT ROUND GOES CLEAR THROUGH THE CENTER OF HIS MASS AND--
WHA!
HE'S FADING AWAY!!

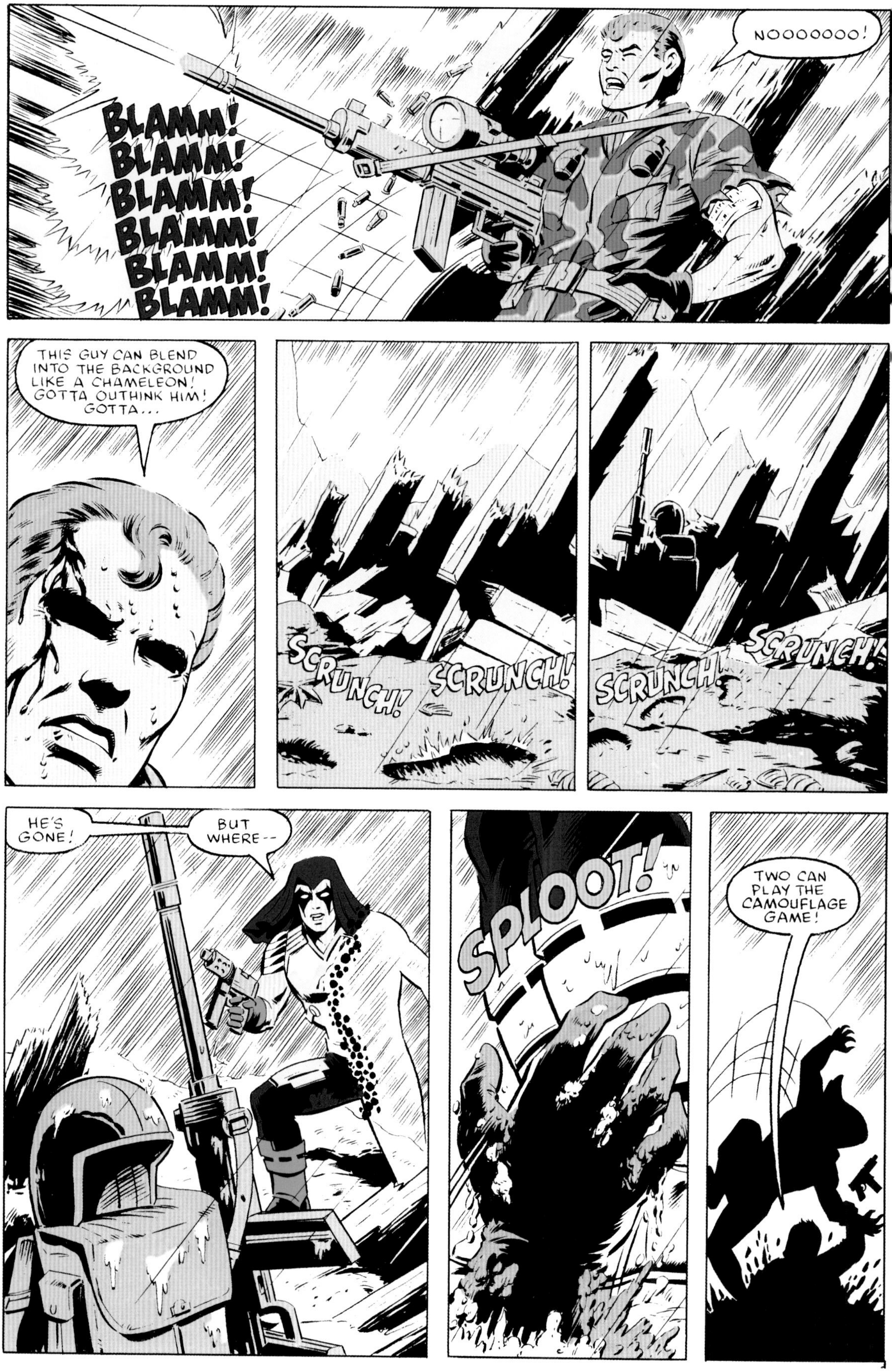

NOOOOOOO!
BLAMM! BLAMM! BLAMM! BLAMM! BLAMM! BLAMM!
THIS GUY CAN BLEND INTO THE BACKGROUND LIKE A CHAMELEON! GOTTA OUTTHINK HIM! GOTTA...
SCRUNCH!
SCRUNCH!
SCRUNCH!
SCRUNCH!
HE'S GONE!
BUT WHERE--
SPLOOT!
TWO CAN PLAY THE CAMOUFLAGE GAME!

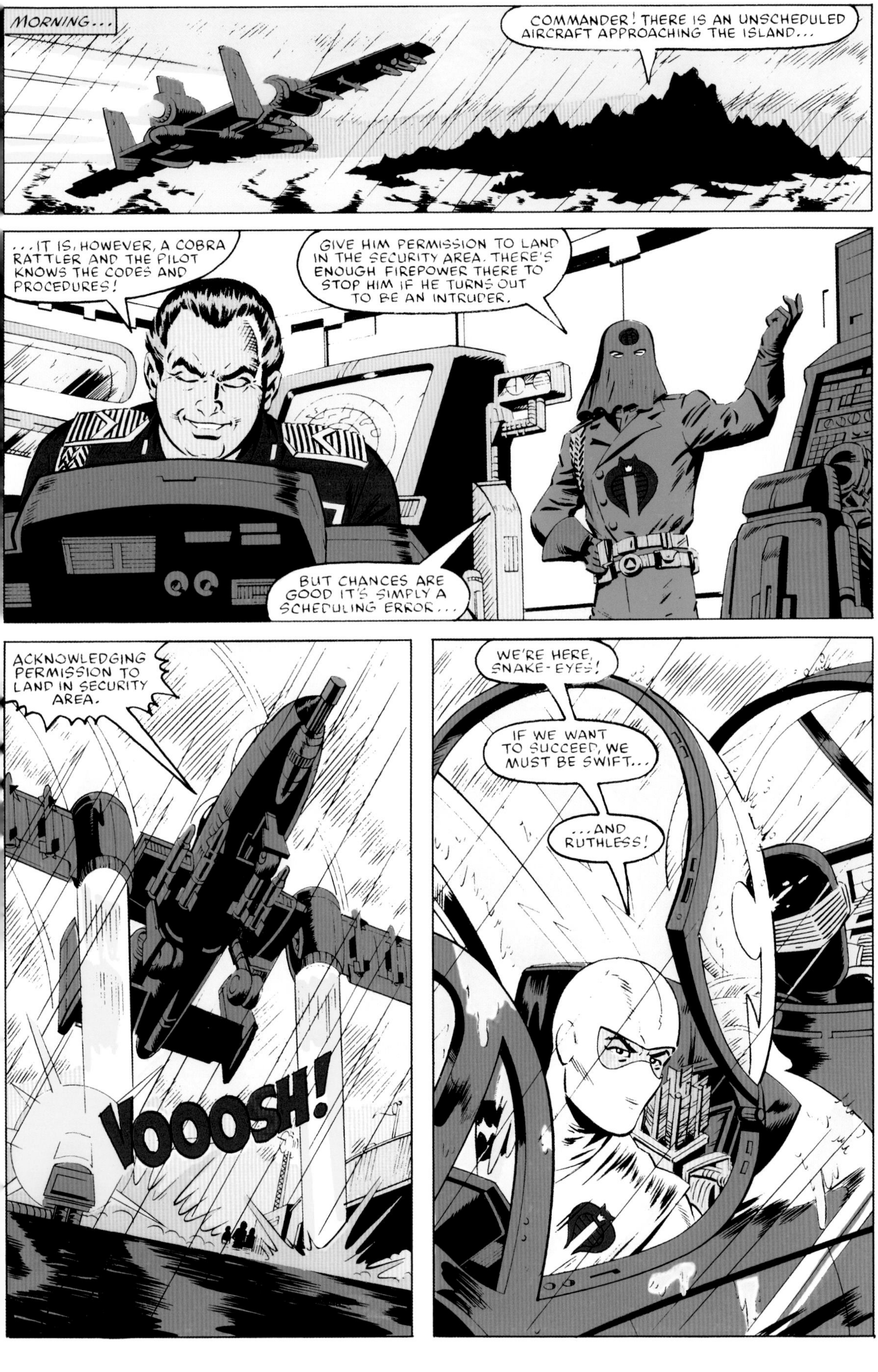
MORNING...
COMMANDER! THERE IS AN UNSCHEDULED AIRCRAFT APPROACHING THE ISLAND...
...IT IS, HOWEVER, A COBRA RATTLER AND THE PILOT KNOWS THE CODES AND PROCEDURES!
GIVE HIM PERMISSION TO LAND IN THE SECURITY AREA. THERE'S ENOUGH FIREPOWER THERE TO STOP HIM IF HE TURNS OUT TO BE AN INTRUDER.
BUT CHANCES ARE GOOD IT'S SIMPLY A SCHEDULING ERROR...
ACKNOWLEDGING PERMISSION TO LAND IN SECURITY AREA.
VOOOSH!
WE'RE HERE, SNAKE-EYES!
IF WE WANT TO SUCCEED, WE MUST BE SWIFT...
...AND RUTHLESS!

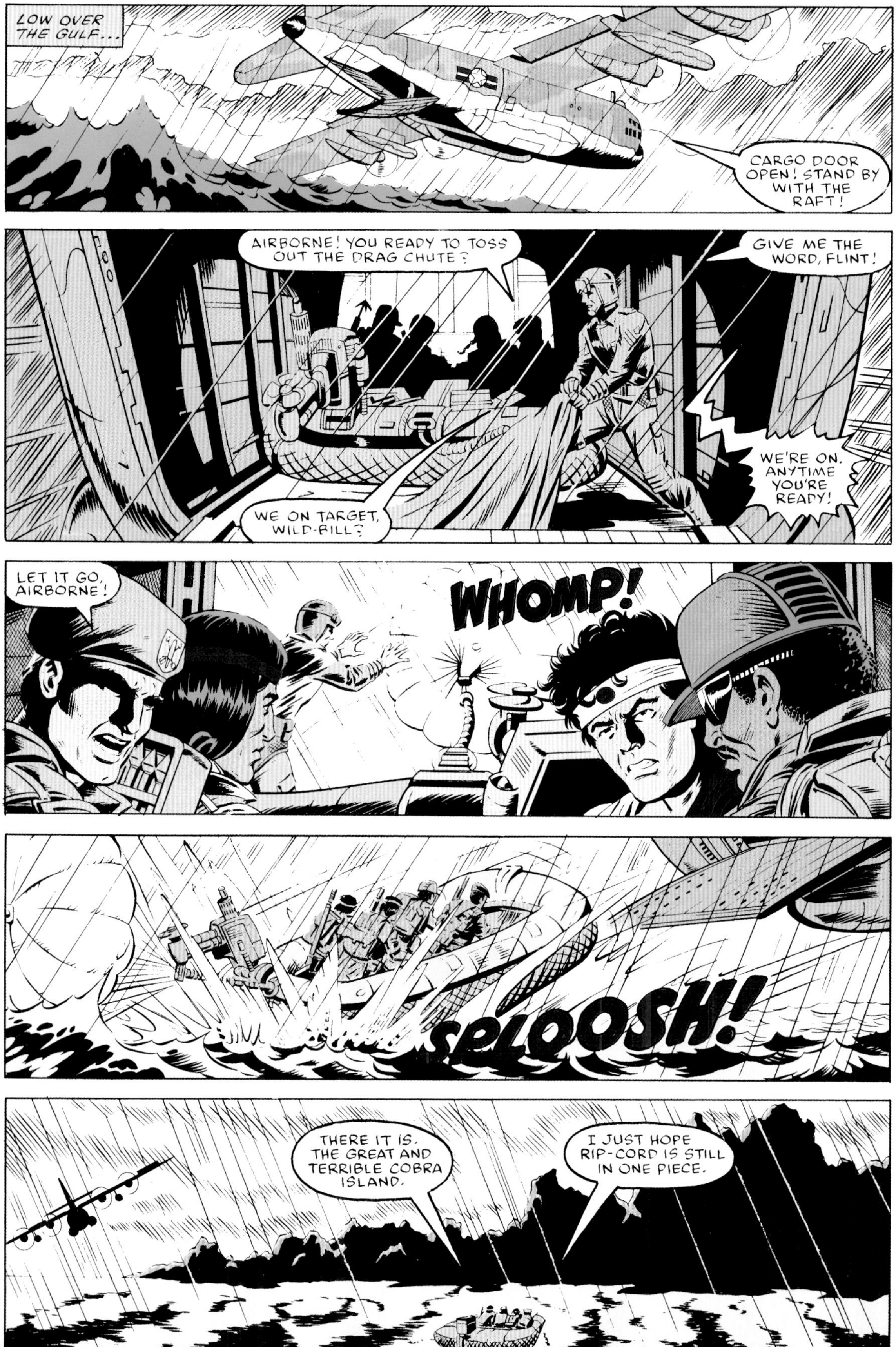
LOW OVER THE GULF...
CARGO DOOR OPEN! STAND BY WITH THE RAFT!
AIRBORNE! YOU READY TO TOSS OUT THE DRAG CHUTE?
GIVE ME THE WORD, FLINT!
WE ON TARGET, WILD-BILL?
WE'RE ON. ANYTIME YOU'RE READY!
LET IT GO, AIRBORNE!
WHOMP!
SPLOOSH!
THERE IT IS. THE GREAT AND TERRIBLE COBRA ISLAND.
I JUST HOPE RIP-CORD IS STILL IN ONE PIECE.

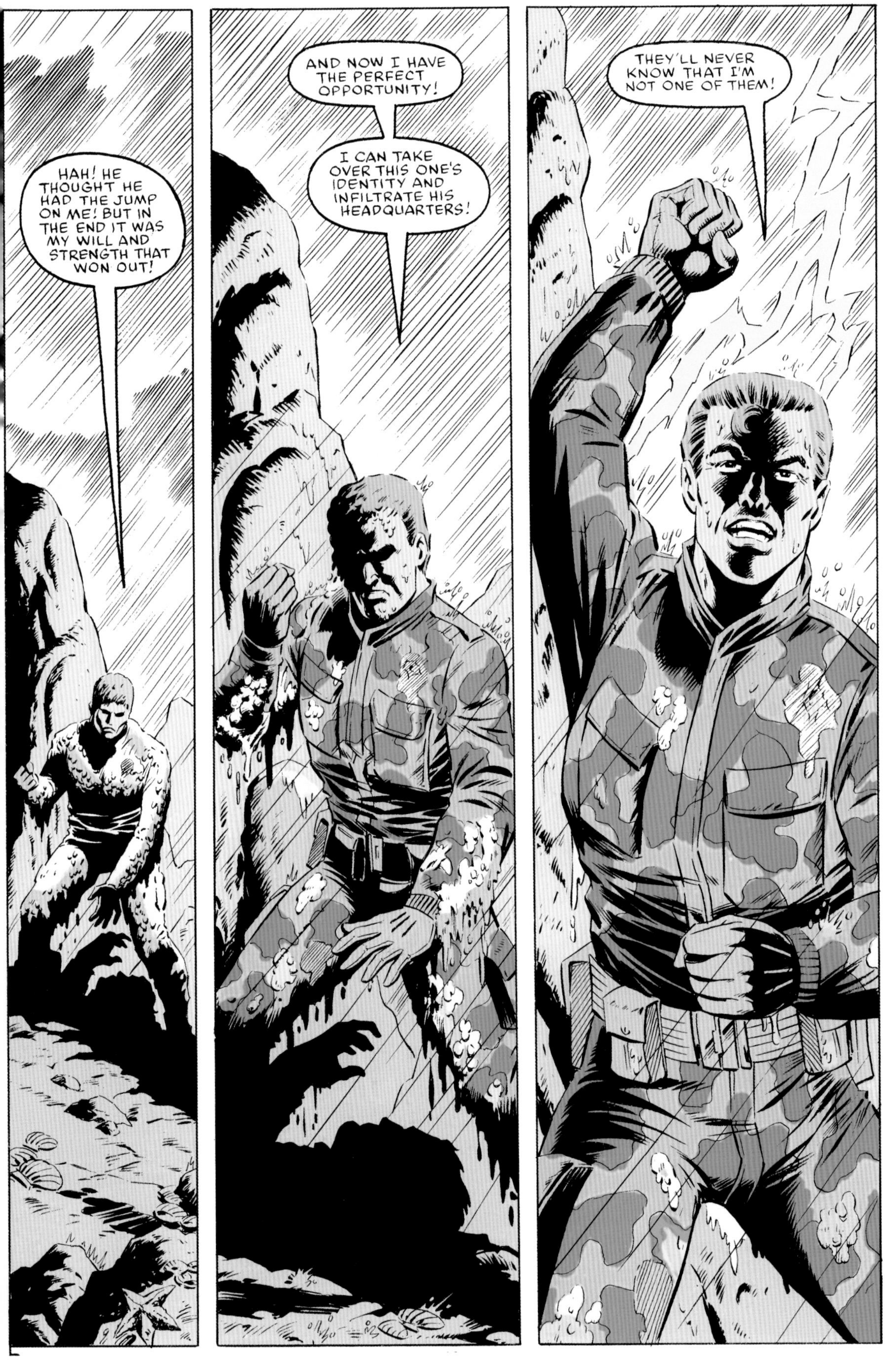
HAH! HE THOUGHT HE HAD THE JUMP ON ME! BUT IN THE END IT WAS MY WILL AND STRENGTH THAT WON OUT!
AND NOW I HAVE THE PERFECT OPPORTUNITY!
I CAN TAKE OVER THIS ONE'S IDENTITY AND INFILTRATE HIS HEADQUARTERS!
THEY'LL NEVER KNOW THAT I'M NOT ONE OF THEM!

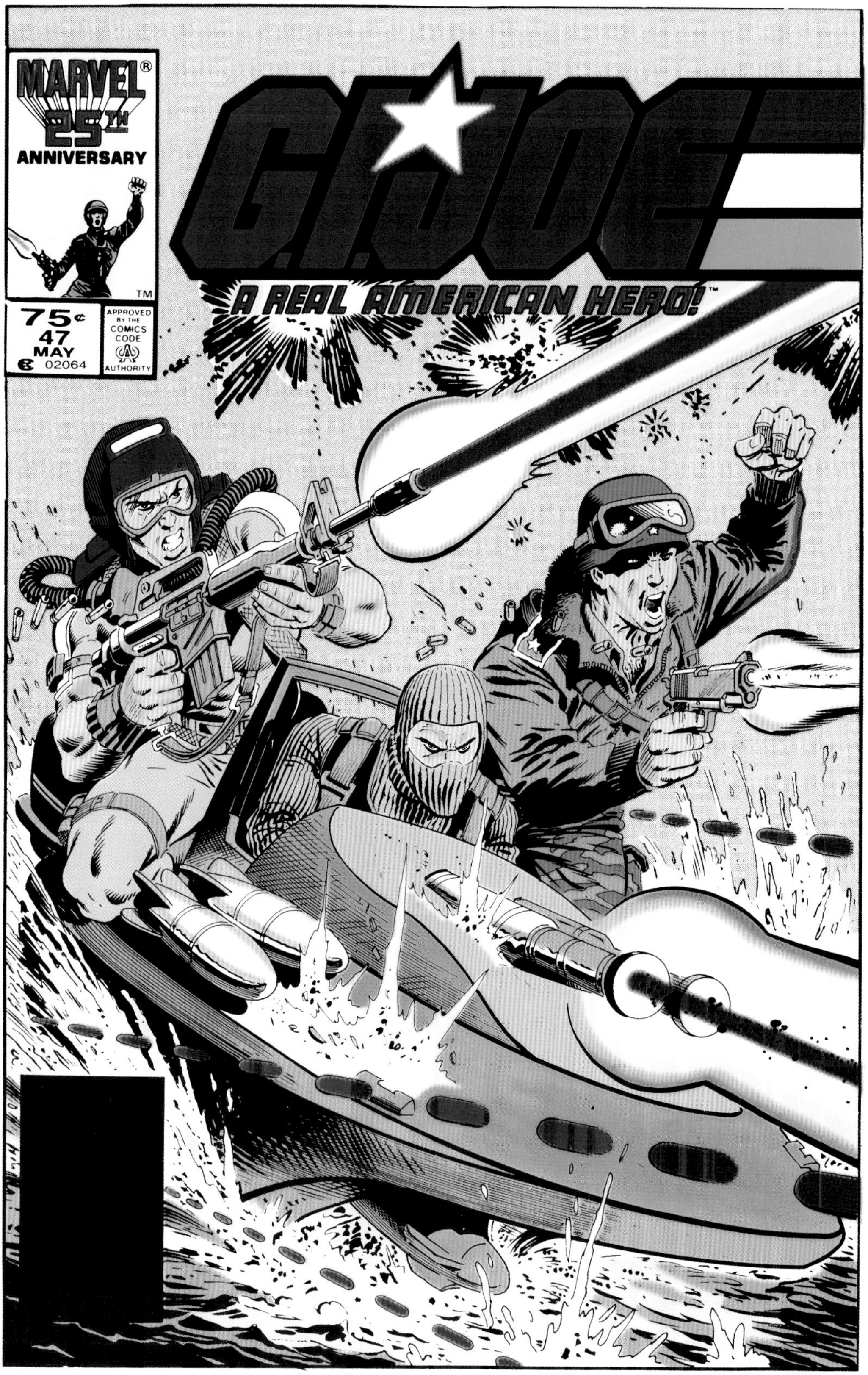
MARVEL®
25TH
ANNIVERSARY
G.I. JOE
A REAL AMERICAN HERO!™
TM
75¢
47
MAY
02064
APPROVED BY THE COMICS CODE AUTHORITY

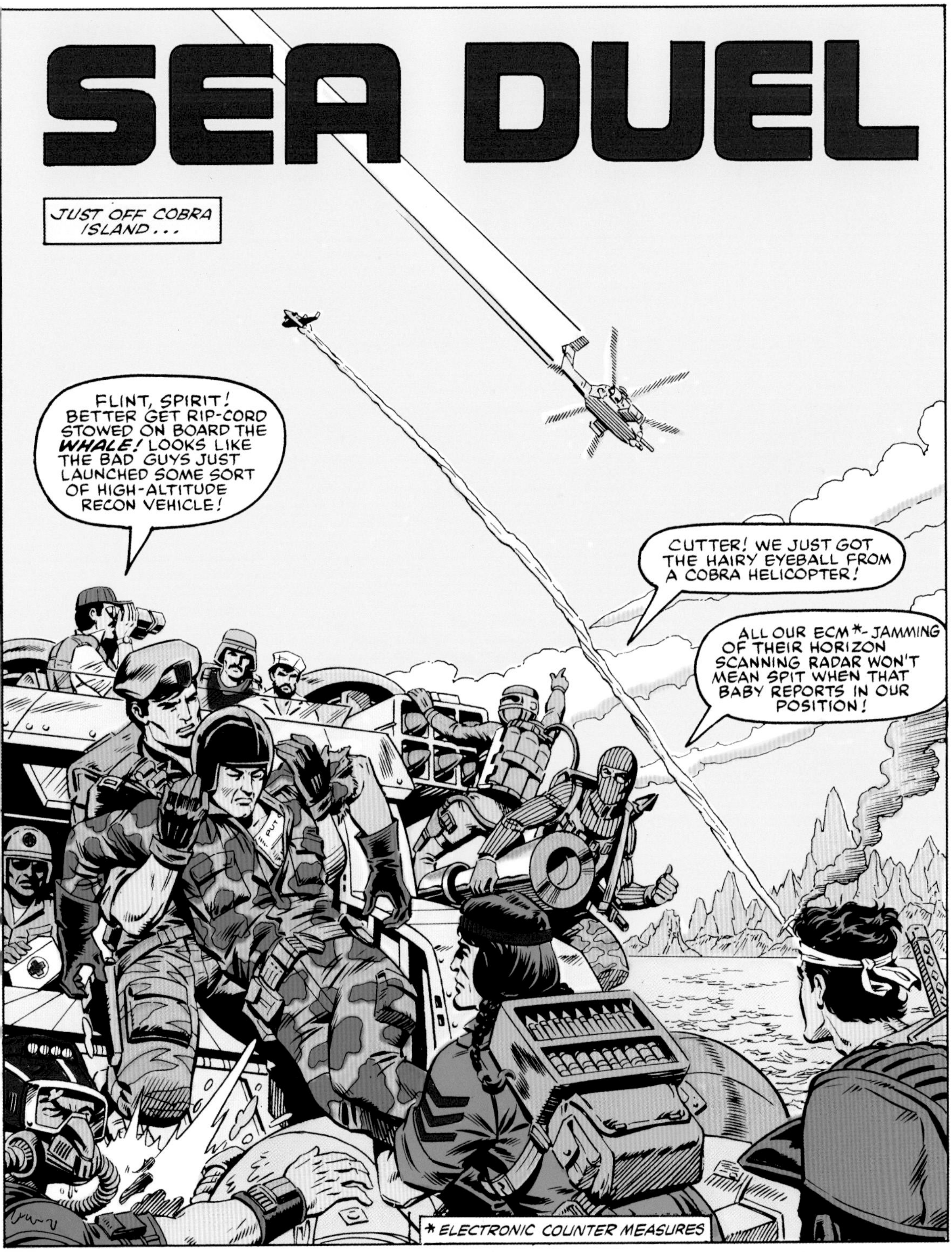
SEA DUEL
JUST OFF COBRA ISLAND...
FLINT, SPIRIT! BETTER GET RIP-CORD STOWED ON BOARD THE WHALE! LOOKS LIKE THE BAD GUYS JUST LAUNCHED SOME SORT OF HIGH-ALTITUDE RECON VEHICLE!
CUTTER! WE JUST GOT THE HAIRY EYEBALL FROM A COBRA HELICOPTER!
ALL OUR ECM*- JAMMING OF THEIR HORIZON SCANNING RADAR WON'T MEAN SPIT WHEN THAT BABY REPORTS IN OUR POSITION!
*ELECTRONIC COUNTER MEASURES

LARRY HAMA SCRIPT · ROD WHIGHAM PENCILS · ANDY MUSHYNSKY INKS · GEORGE ROUSSOS COLORS · JOE ROSEN LETTERING · DENNY O'NEIL EDITOR · JIM SHOOTER ED IN CHIEF

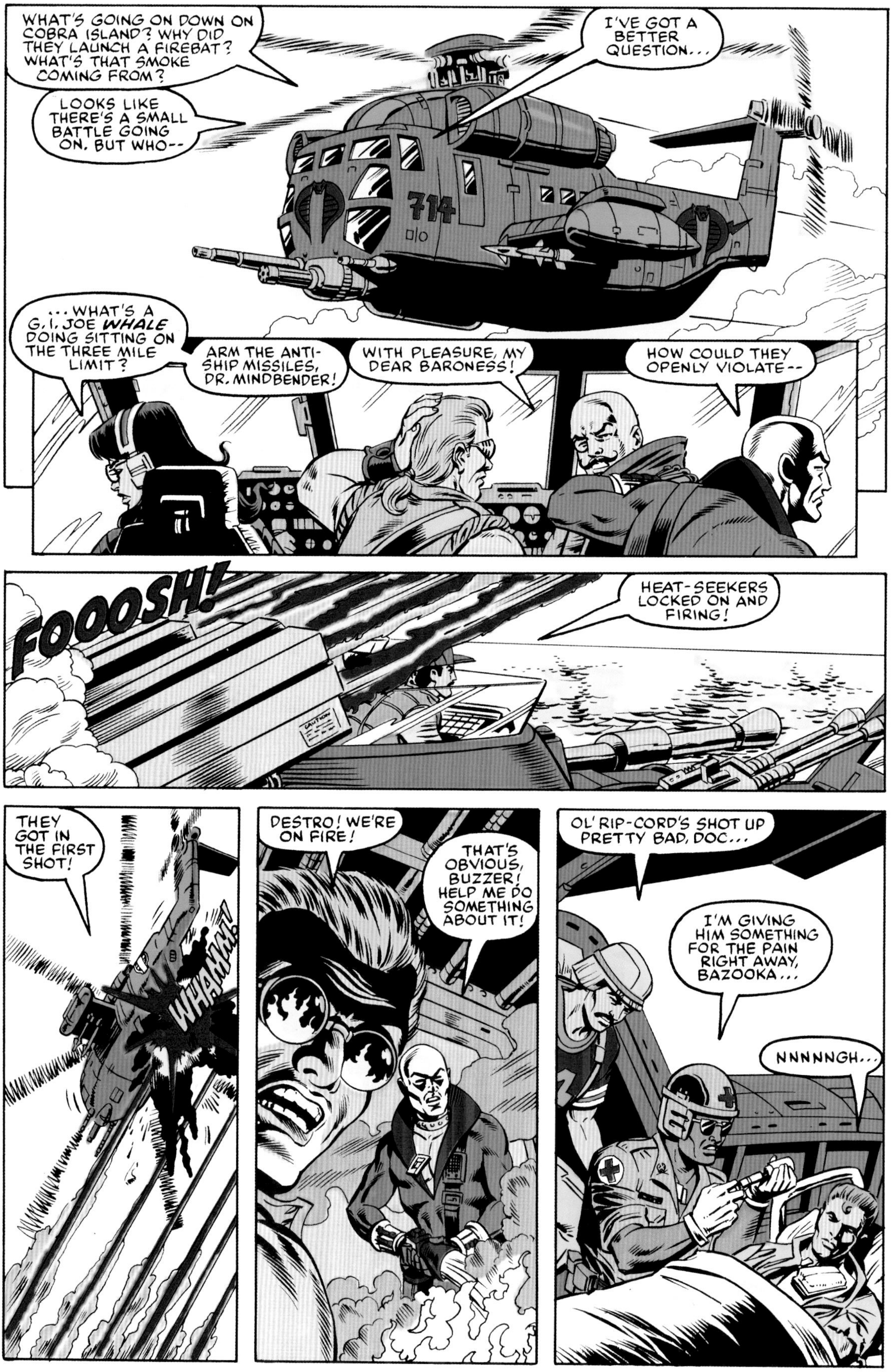
WHAT'S GOING ON DOWN ON COBRA ISLAND? WHY DID THEY LAUNCH A FIREBAT? WHAT'S THAT SMOKE COMING FROM?
I'VE GOT A BETTER QUESTION...
LOOKS LIKE THERE'S A SMALL BATTLE GOING ON. BUT WHO--
...WHAT'S A G.I. JOE *WHALE* DOING SITTING ON THE THREE MILE LIMIT?
ARM THE ANTI-SHIP MISSILES, DR. MINDBENDER!
WITH PLEASURE, MY DEAR BARONESS!
HOW COULD THEY OPENLY VIOLATE--
FOOOSH!
HEAT-SEEKERS LOCKED ON AND FIRING!
THEY GOT IN THE FIRST SHOT!
WHAMM!
DESTRO! WE'RE ON FIRE!
THAT'S OBVIOUS, BUZZER! HELP ME DO SOMETHING ABOUT IT!
OL' RIP-CORD'S SHOT UP PRETTY BAD, DOC...
I'M GIVING HIM SOMETHING FOR THE PAIN RIGHT AWAY, BAZOOKA...
NNNNNGH...

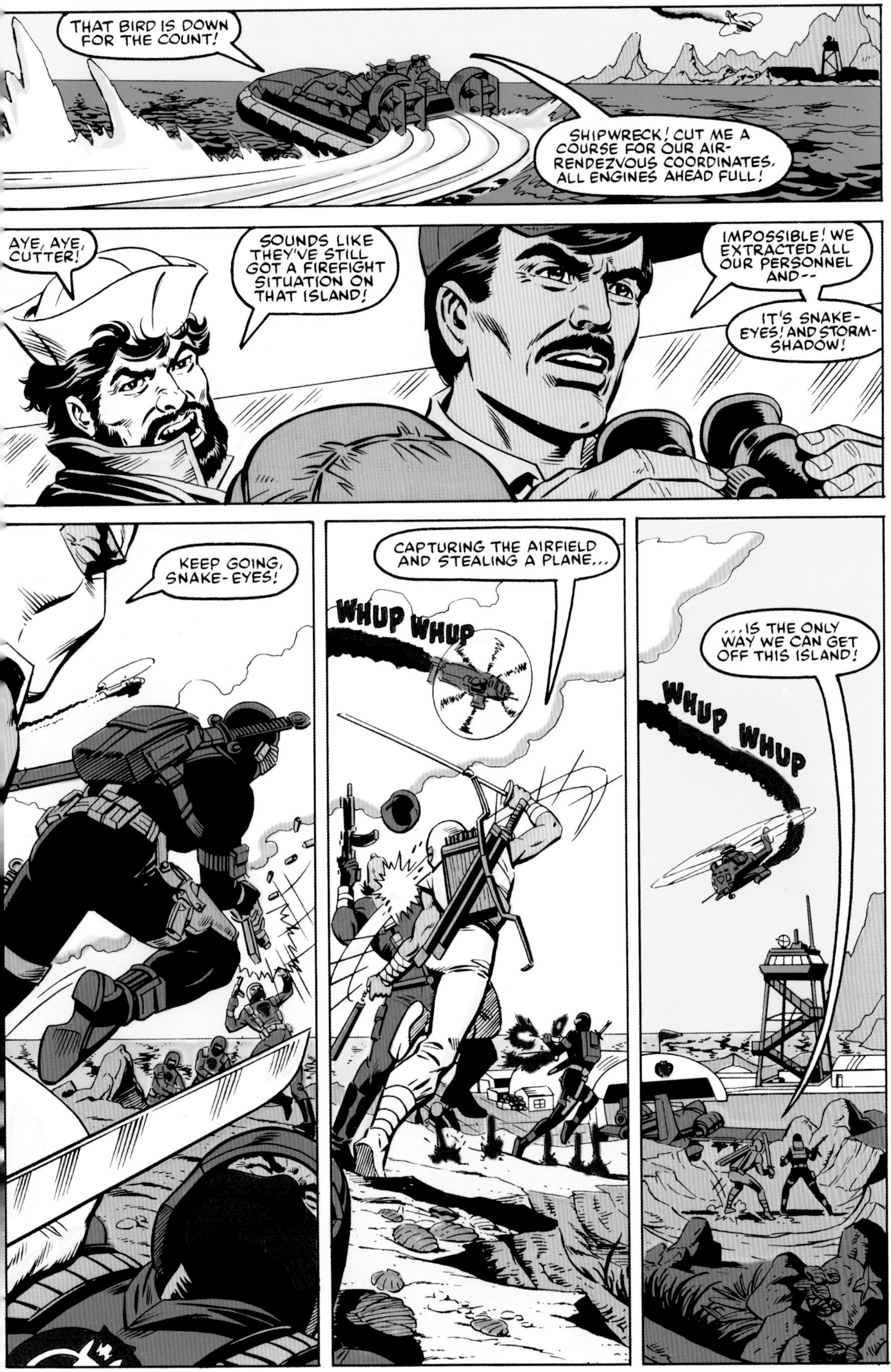
THAT BIRD IS DOWN FOR THE COUNT!
SHIPWRECK! CUT ME A COURSE FOR OUR AIR-RENDEZVOUS COORDINATES. ALL ENGINES AHEAD FULL!
AYE, AYE, CUTTER!
SOUNDS LIKE THEY'VE STILL GOT A FIREFIGHT SITUATION ON THAT ISLAND!
IMPOSSIBLE! WE EXTRACTED ALL OUR PERSONNEL AND--
IT'S SNAKE-EYES! AND STORM-SHADOW!
KEEP GOING, SNAKE-EYES!
CAPTURING THE AIRFIELD AND STEALING A PLANE...
WHUP WHUP
...IS THE ONLY WAY WE CAN GET OFF THIS ISLAND!
WHUP WHUP

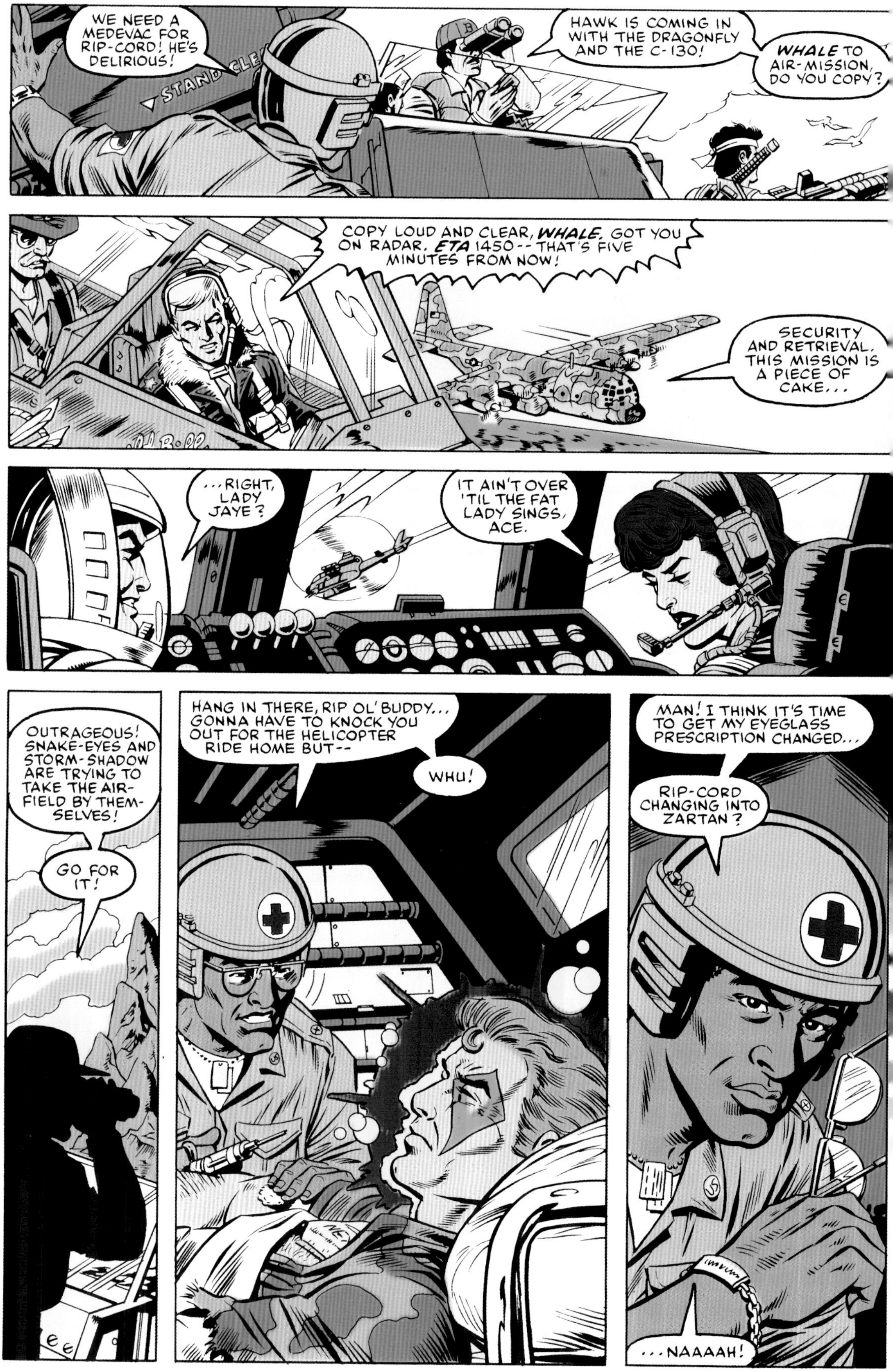
WE NEED A MEDEVAC FOR RIP-CORD! HE'S DELIRIOUS!
STAND CLE
HAWK IS COMING IN WITH THE DRAGONFLY AND THE C-130!
WHALE TO AIR-MISSION, DO YOU COPY?
COPY LOUD AND CLEAR, WHALE. GOT YOU ON RADAR. ETA 1450--THAT'S FIVE MINUTES FROM NOW!
SECURITY AND RETRIEVAL. THIS MISSION IS A PIECE OF CAKE...
...RIGHT, LADY JAYE?
IT AIN'T OVER 'TIL THE FAT LADY SINGS, ACE.
OUTRAGEOUS! SNAKE-EYES AND STORM-SHADOW ARE TRYING TO TAKE THE AIR-FIELD BY THEM-SELVES!
GO FOR IT!
HANG IN THERE, RIP OL' BUDDY... GONNA HAVE TO KNOCK YOU OUT FOR THE HELICOPTER RIDE HOME BUT--
WHU!
MAN! I THINK IT'S TIME TO GET MY EYEGLASS PRESCRIPTION CHANGED...
RIP-CORD CHANGING INTO ZARTAN?
...NAAAAH!

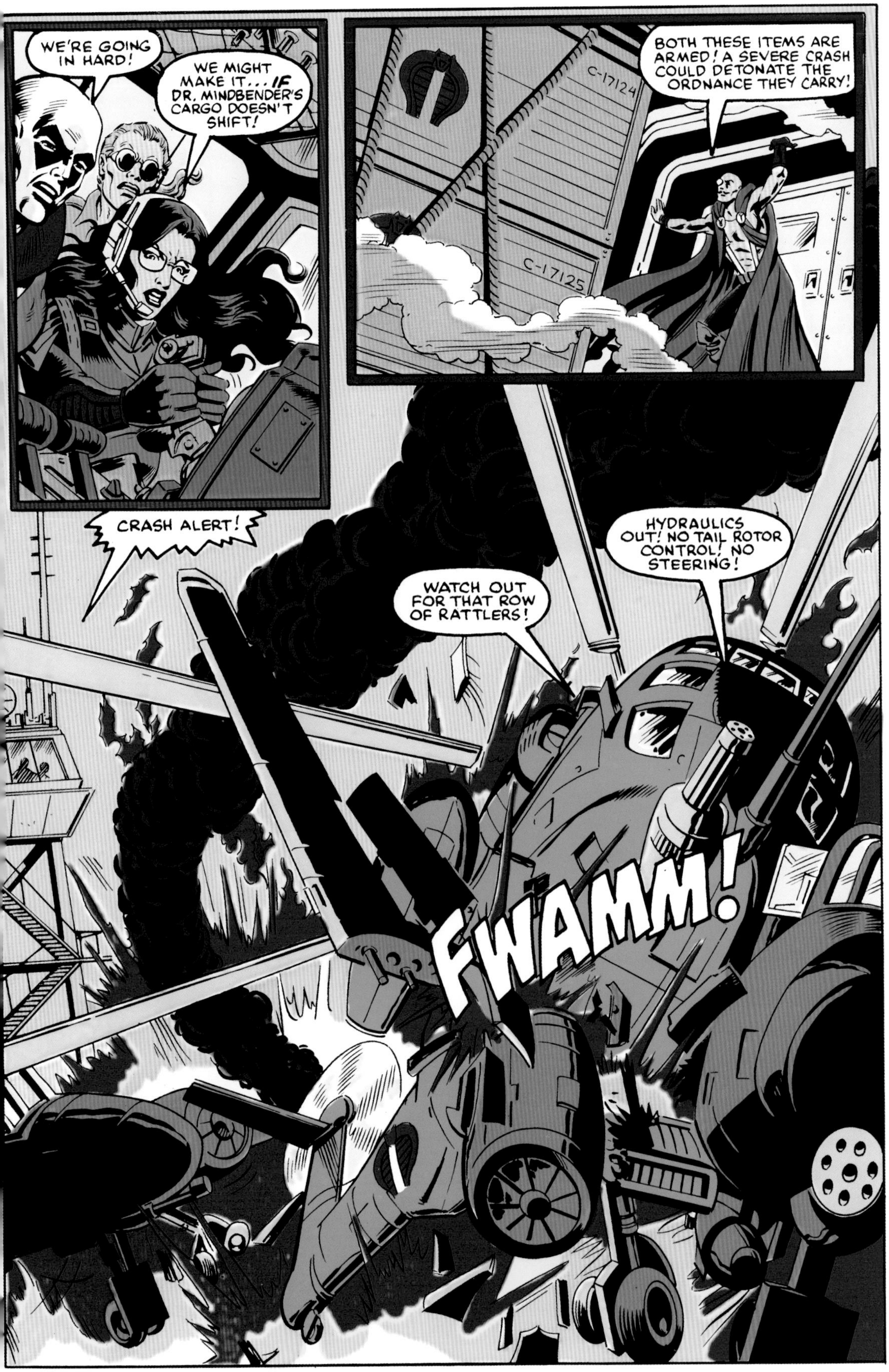
WE'RE GOING IN HARD!
WE MIGHT MAKE IT... IF DR. MINDBENDER'S CARGO DOESN'T SHIFT!
BOTH THESE ITEMS ARE ARMED! A SEVERE CRASH COULD DETONATE THE ORDNANCE THEY CARRY!
C-17124
C-17125
CRASH ALERT!
HYDRAULICS OUT! NO TAIL ROTOR CONTROL! NO STEERING!
WATCH OUT FOR THAT ROW OF RATTLERS!
FWAMM!

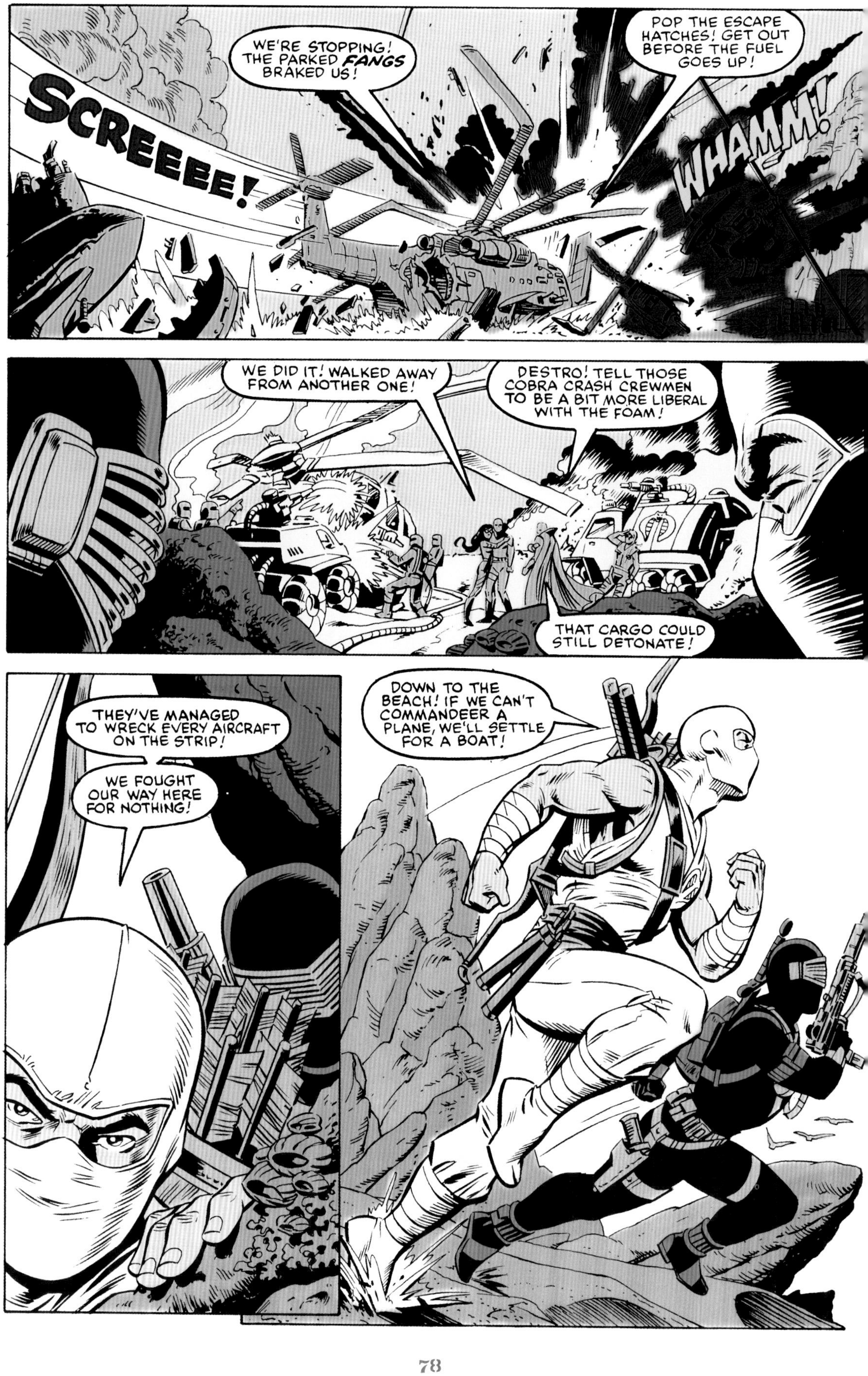
SCREEEEE!
WE'RE STOPPING! THE PARKED FANGS BRAKED US!
POP THE ESCAPE HATCHES! GET OUT BEFORE THE FUEL GOES UP!
WHAMM!
WE DID IT! WALKED AWAY FROM ANOTHER ONE!
DESTRO! TELL THOSE COBRA CRASH CREWMEN TO BE A BIT MORE LIBERAL WITH THE FOAM!
THAT CARGO COULD STILL DETONATE!
THEY'VE MANAGED TO WRECK EVERY AIRCRAFT ON THE STRIP!
WE FOUGHT OUR WAY HERE FOR NOTHING!
DOWN TO THE BEACH! IF WE CAN'T COMMANDEER A PLANE, WE'LL SETTLE FOR A BOAT!

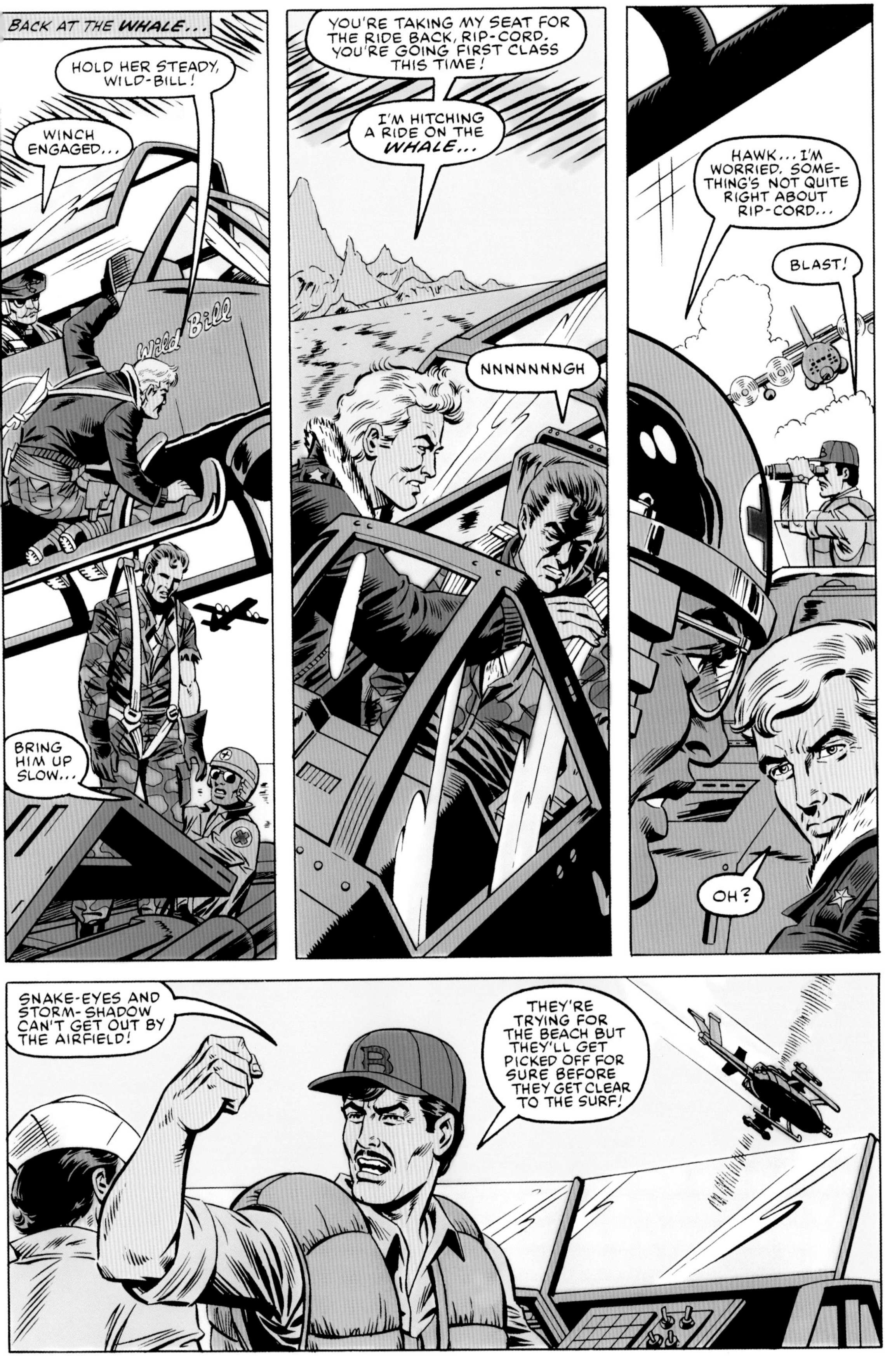
BACK AT THE WHALE...
HOLD HER STEADY, WILD-BILL!
WINCH ENGAGED...
Wild Bill
BRING HIM UP SLOW...
YOU'RE TAKING MY SEAT FOR THE RIDE BACK, RIP-CORD. YOU'RE GOING FIRST CLASS THIS TIME!
I'M HITCHING A RIDE ON THE WHALE...
NNNNNNNGH
HAWK... I'M WORRIED. SOMETHING'S NOT QUITE RIGHT ABOUT RIP-CORD...
BLAST!
OH?
SNAKE-EYES AND STORM-SHADOW CAN'T GET OUT BY THE AIRFIELD!
THEY'RE TRYING FOR THE BEACH BUT THEY'LL GET PICKED OFF FOR SURE BEFORE THEY GET CLEAR TO THE SURF!

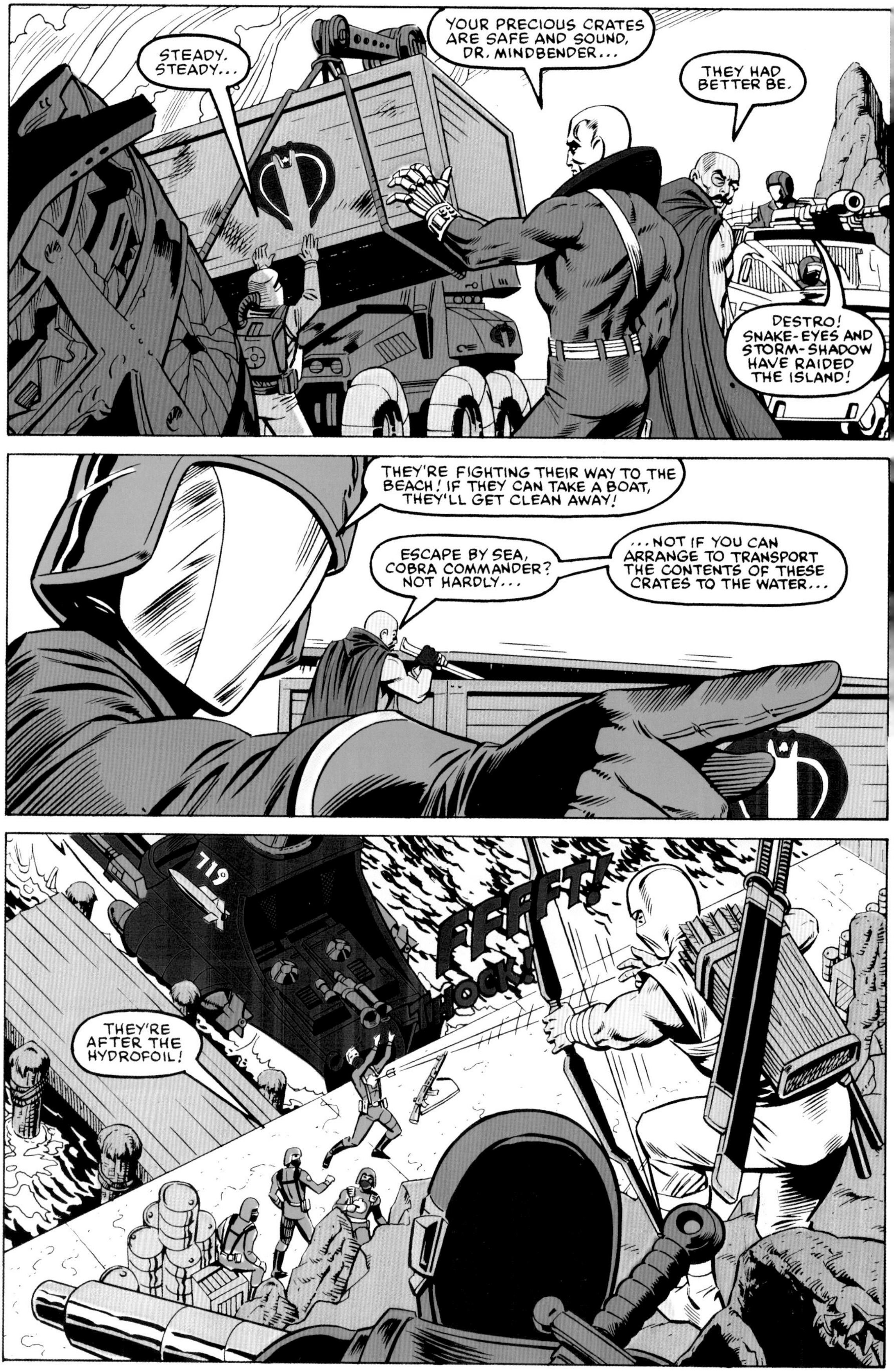
STEADY. STEADY...
YOUR PRECIOUS CRATES ARE SAFE AND SOUND, DR. MINDBENDER...
THEY HAD BETTER BE.
DESTRO! SNAKE-EYES AND STORM-SHADOW HAVE RAIDED THE ISLAND!
THEY'RE FIGHTING THEIR WAY TO THE BEACH! IF THEY CAN TAKE A BOAT, THEY'LL GET CLEAN AWAY!
ESCAPE BY SEA, COBRA COMMANDER? NOT HARDLY...
...NOT IF YOU CAN ARRANGE TO TRANSPORT THE CONTENTS OF THESE CRATES TO THE WATER...
FFFFT!
THOCK!
THEY'RE AFTER THE HYDROFOIL!

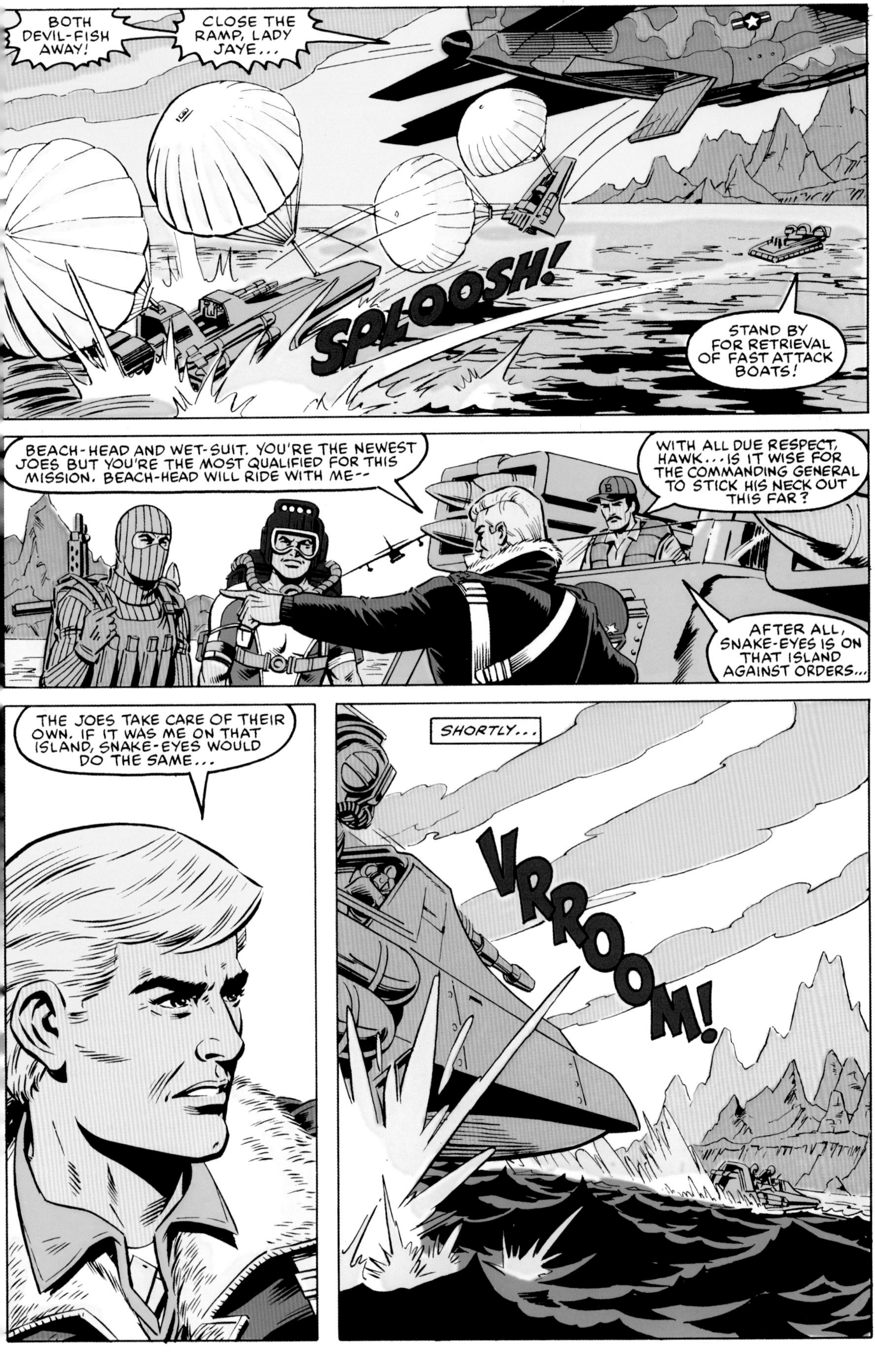
BOTH DEVIL-FISH AWAY!
CLOSE THE RAMP, LADY JAYE...
SPLOOSH!
STAND BY FOR RETRIEVAL OF FAST ATTACK BOATS!
BEACH-HEAD AND WET-SUIT. YOU'RE THE NEWEST JOES BUT YOU'RE THE MOST QUALIFIED FOR THIS MISSION. BEACH-HEAD WILL RIDE WITH ME--
WITH ALL DUE RESPECT, HAWK... IS IT WISE FOR THE COMMANDING GENERAL TO STICK HIS NECK OUT THIS FAR?
AFTER ALL, SNAKE-EYES IS ON THAT ISLAND AGAINST ORDERS...
THE JOES TAKE CARE OF THEIR OWN. IF IT WAS ME ON THAT ISLAND, SNAKE-EYES WOULD DO THE SAME...
SHORTLY...
VRROOM!

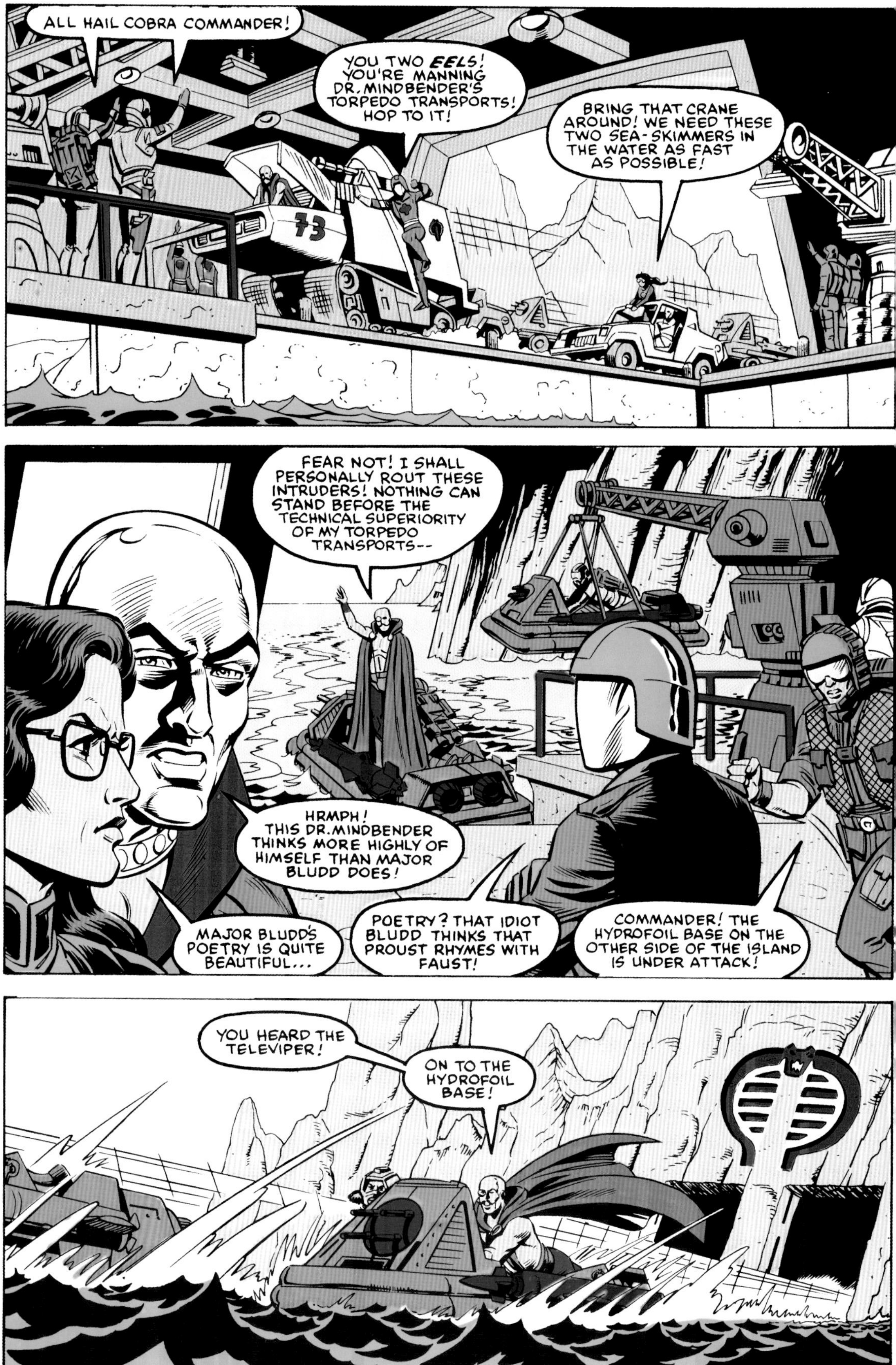
ALL HAIL COBRA COMMANDER!
YOU TWO EELS! YOU'RE MANNING DR. MINDBENDER'S TORPEDO TRANSPORTS! HOP TO IT!
BRING THAT CRANE AROUND! WE NEED THESE TWO SEA-SKIMMERS IN THE WATER AS FAST AS POSSIBLE!
73
FEAR NOT! I SHALL PERSONALLY ROUT THESE INTRUDERS! NOTHING CAN STAND BEFORE THE TECHNICAL SUPERIORITY OF MY TORPEDO TRANSPORTS--
HRMPH! THIS DR. MINDBENDER THINKS MORE HIGHLY OF HIMSELF THAN MAJOR BLUDD DOES!
MAJOR BLUDD'S POETRY IS QUITE BEAUTIFUL...
POETRY? THAT IDIOT BLUDD THINKS THAT PROUST RHYMES WITH FAUST!
COMMANDER! THE HYDROFOIL BASE ON THE OTHER SIDE OF THE ISLAND IS UNDER ATTACK!
YOU HEARD THE TELEVIPER!
ON TO THE HYDROFOIL BASE!

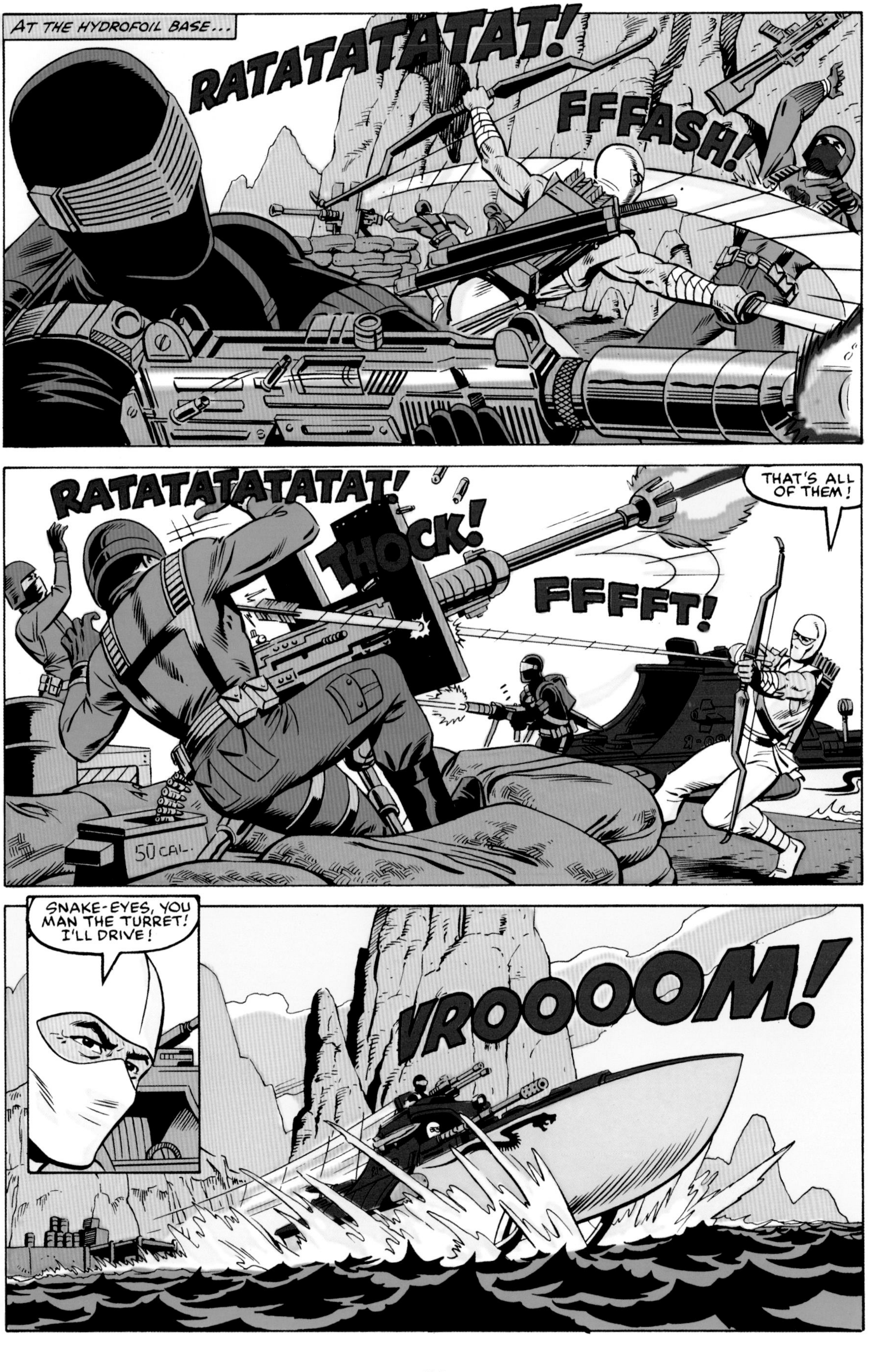
AT THE HYDROFOIL BASE...
RATATATATAT!
FFFASH!
RATATATATATAT!
THOCK!
FFFFT!
THAT'S ALL OF THEM!
50 CAL.
SNAKE-EYES, YOU MAN THE TURRET! I'LL DRIVE!
VROOOOM!

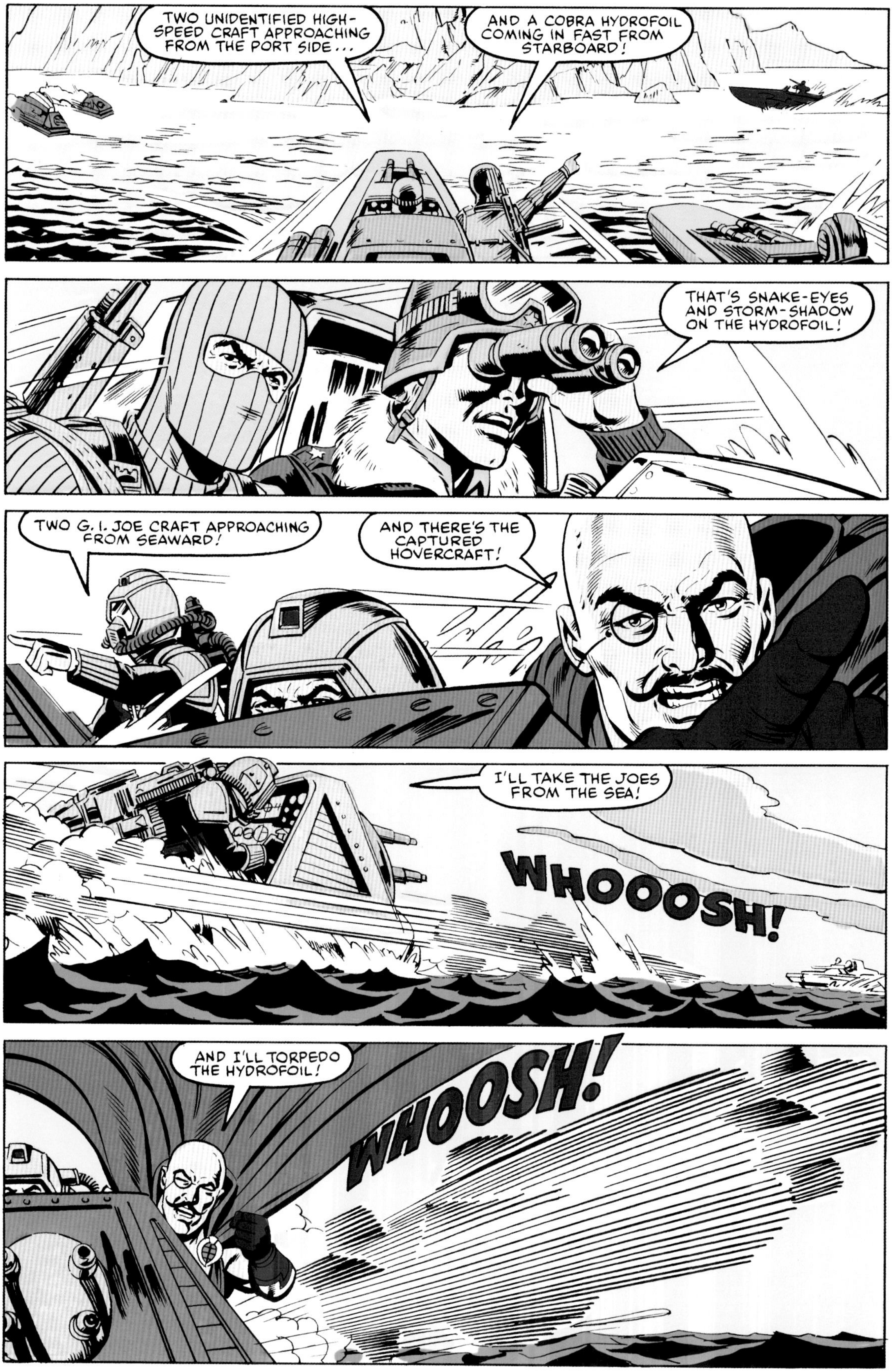
TWO UNIDENTIFIED HIGH-SPEED CRAFT APPROACHING FROM THE PORT SIDE...
AND A COBRA HYDROFOIL COMING IN FAST FROM STARBOARD!
THAT'S SNAKE-EYES AND STORM-SHADOW ON THE HYDROFOIL!
TWO G.I. JOE CRAFT APPROACHING FROM SEAWARD!
AND THERE'S THE CAPTURED HOVERCRAFT!
I'LL TAKE THE JOES FROM THE SEA!
WHOOOOSH!
AND I'LL TORPEDO THE HYDROFOIL!
WHOOSH!

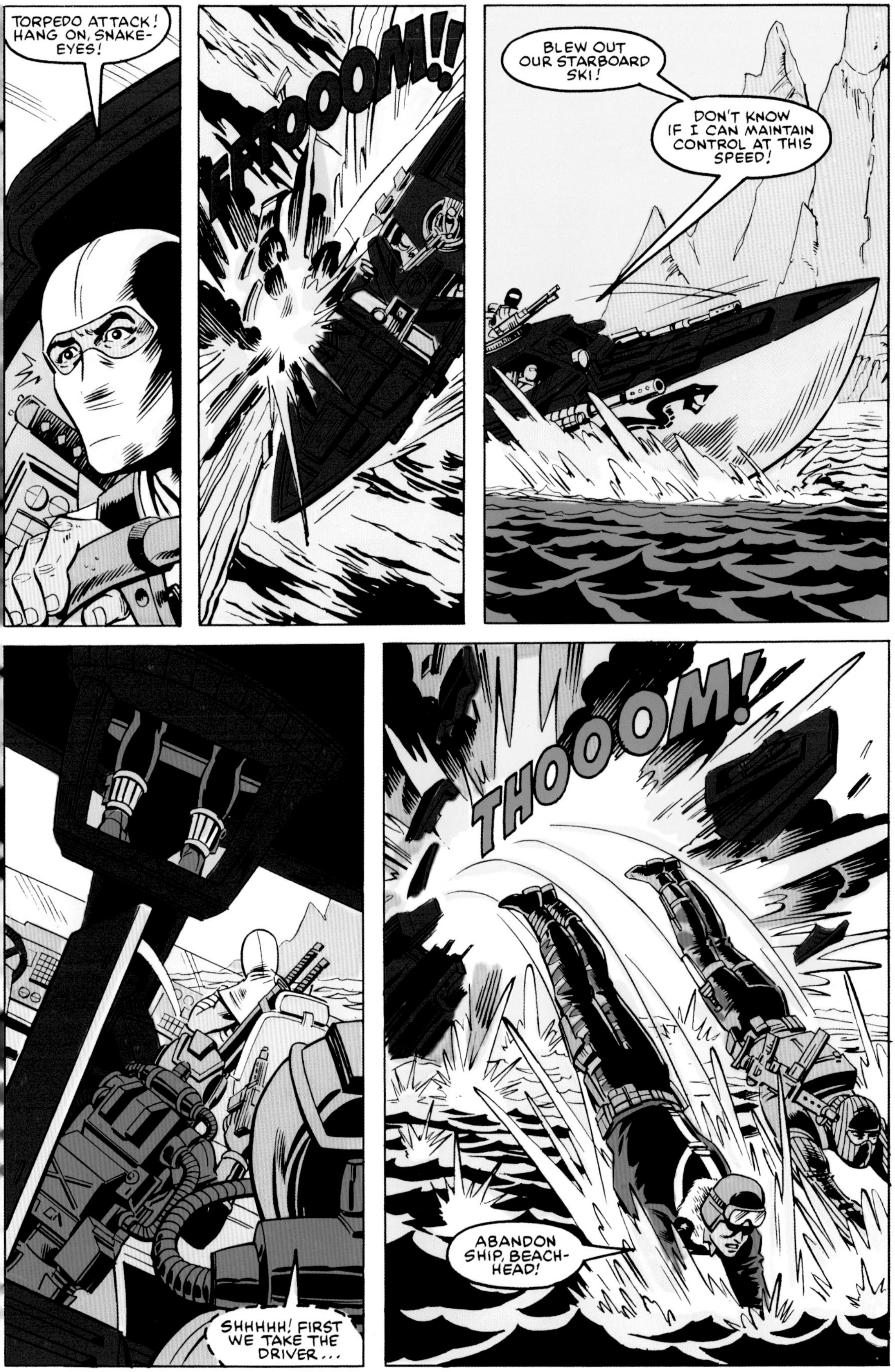
TORPEDO ATTACK! HANG ON, SNAKE-EYES!
THOOOOM!!
BLEW OUT OUR STARBOARD SKI!
DON'T KNOW IF I CAN MAINTAIN CONTROL AT THIS SPEED!
SHHHHH! FIRST WE TAKE THE DRIVER...
THOOOM!
ABANDON SHIP, BEACH-HEAD!

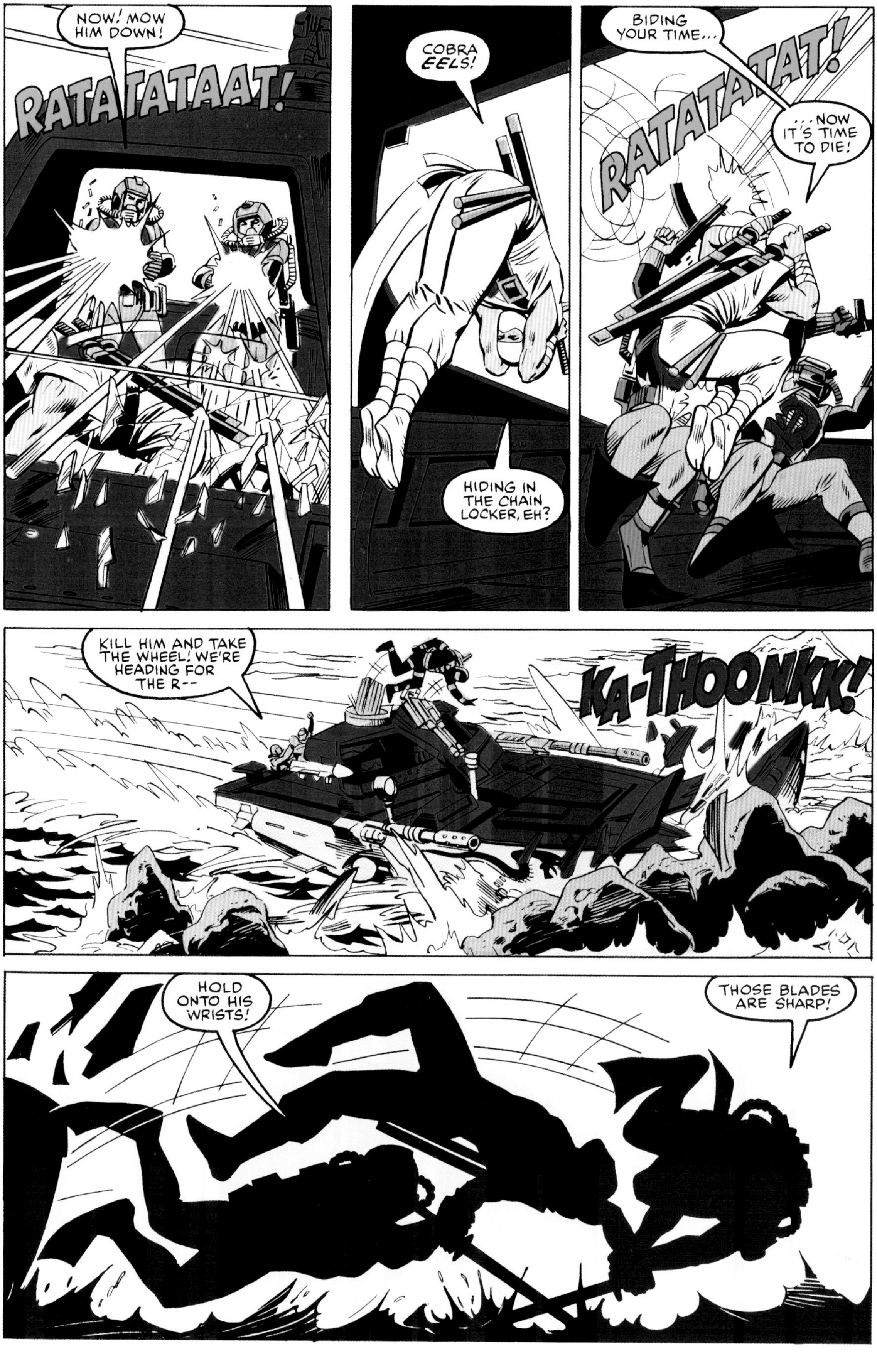
NOW! MOW HIM DOWN!
RATATATAAT!
COBRA EELS!
HIDING IN THE CHAIN LOCKER, EH?
BIDING YOUR TIME...
RATATATAT!
...NOW IT'S TIME TO DIE!
KILL HIM AND TAKE THE WHEEL! WE'RE HEADING FOR THE R--
KA-THOONKK!
HOLD ONTO HIS WRISTS!
THOSE BLADES ARE SHARP!

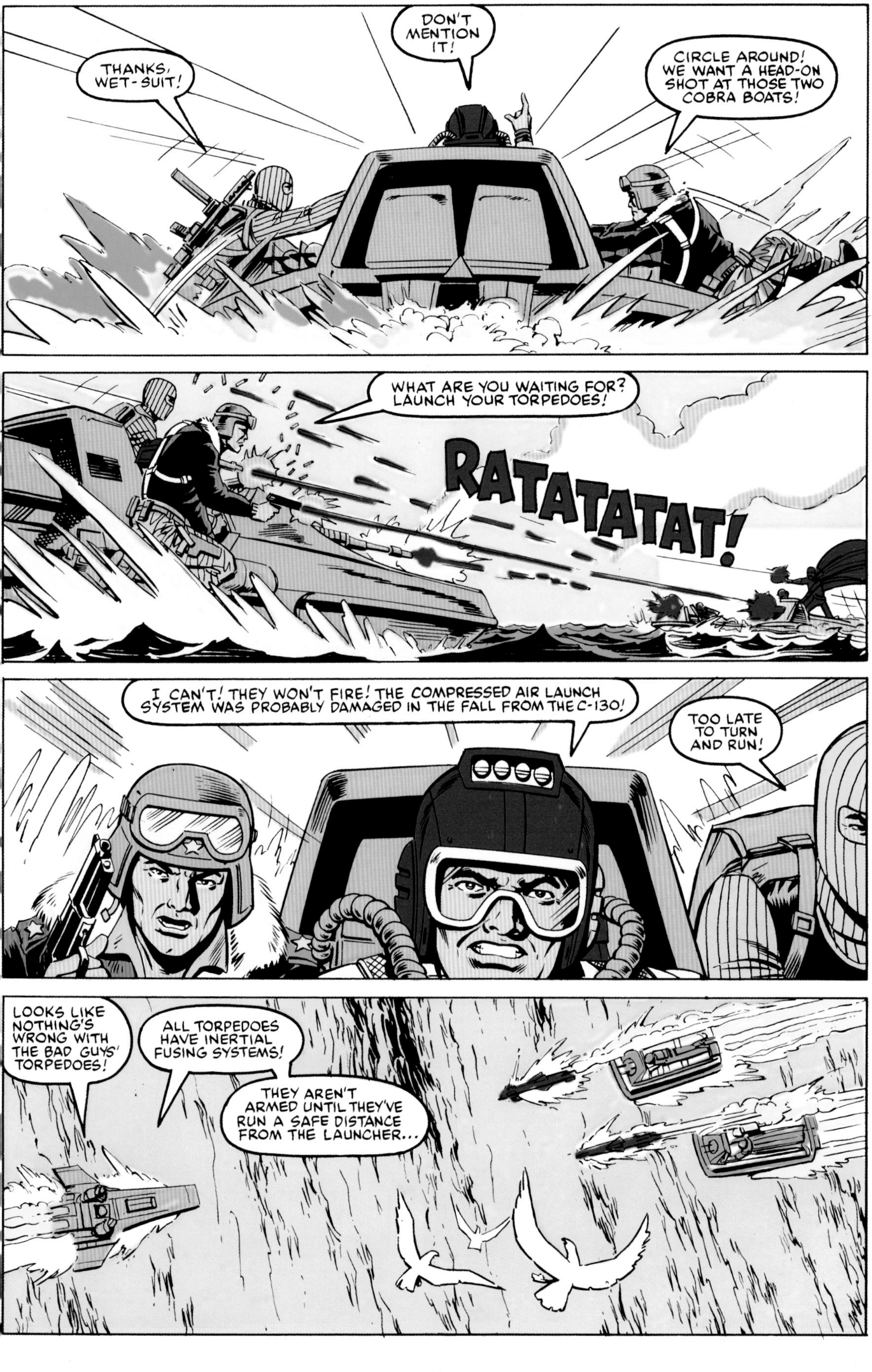
THANKS, WET-SUIT!
DON'T MENTION IT!
CIRCLE AROUND! WE WANT A HEAD-ON SHOT AT THOSE TWO COBRA BOATS!
WHAT ARE YOU WAITING FOR? LAUNCH YOUR TORPEDOES!
RATATATAT!
I CAN'T! THEY WON'T FIRE! THE COMPRESSED AIR LAUNCH SYSTEM WAS PROBABLY DAMAGED IN THE FALL FROM THE C-130!
TOO LATE TO TURN AND RUN!
LOOKS LIKE NOTHING'S WRONG WITH THE BAD GUYS' TORPEDOES!
ALL TORPEDOES HAVE INERTIAL FUSING SYSTEMS!
THEY AREN'T ARMED UNTIL THEY'VE RUN A SAFE DISTANCE FROM THE LAUNCHER...

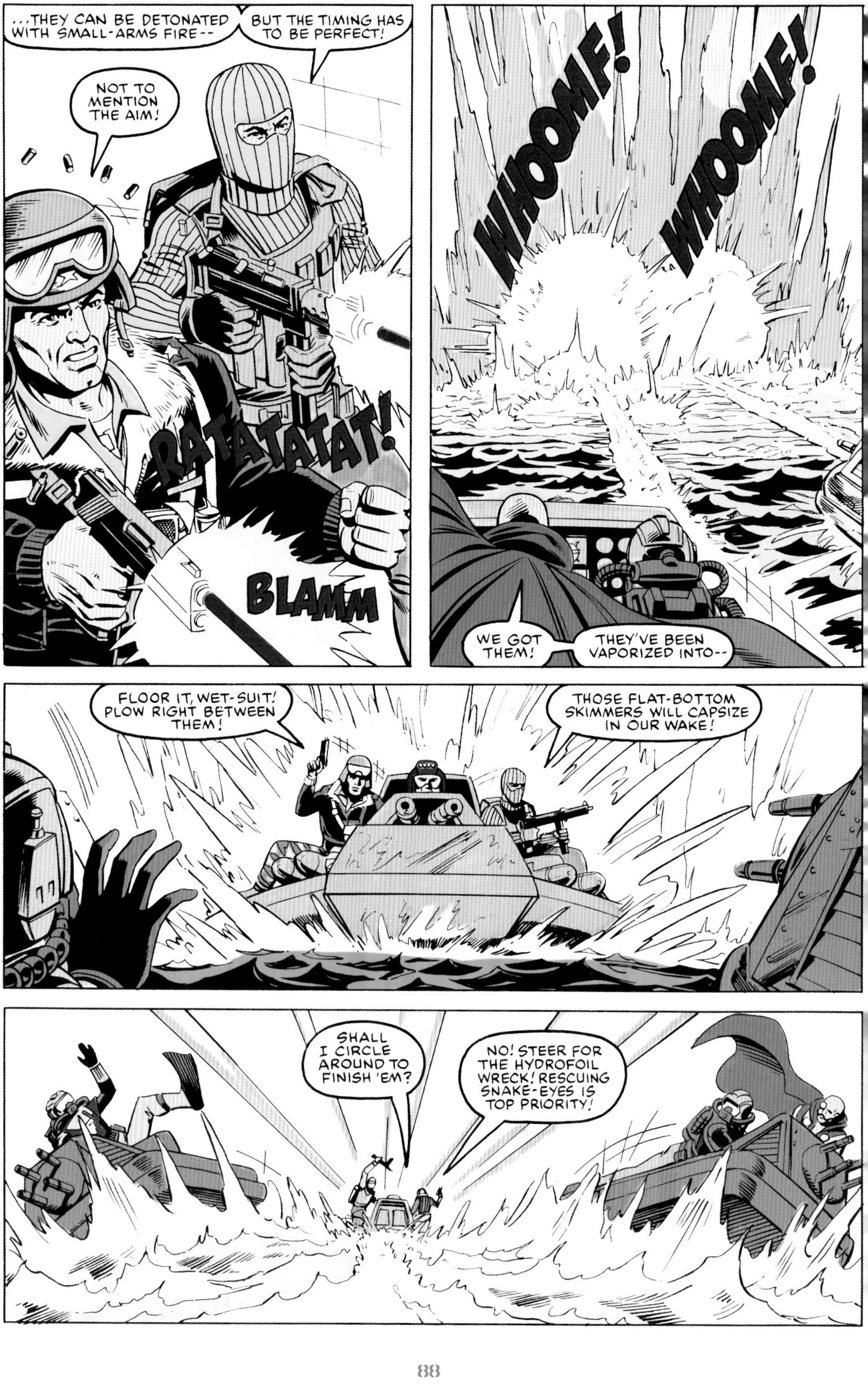
...THEY CAN BE DETONATED WITH SMALL-ARMS FIRE--
BUT THE TIMING HAS TO BE PERFECT!
NOT TO MENTION THE AIM!
RATATATAT!
BLAMM
WHOOMF!
WHOOMF!
WE GOT THEM!
THEY'VE BEEN VAPORIZED INTO--
FLOOR IT, WET-SUIT! PLOW RIGHT BETWEEN THEM!
THOSE FLAT-BOTTOM SKIMMERS WILL CAPSIZE IN OUR WAKE!
SHALL I CIRCLE AROUND TO FINISH 'EM?
NO! STEER FOR THE HYDROFOIL WRECK! RESCUING SNAKE-EYES IS TOP PRIORITY!

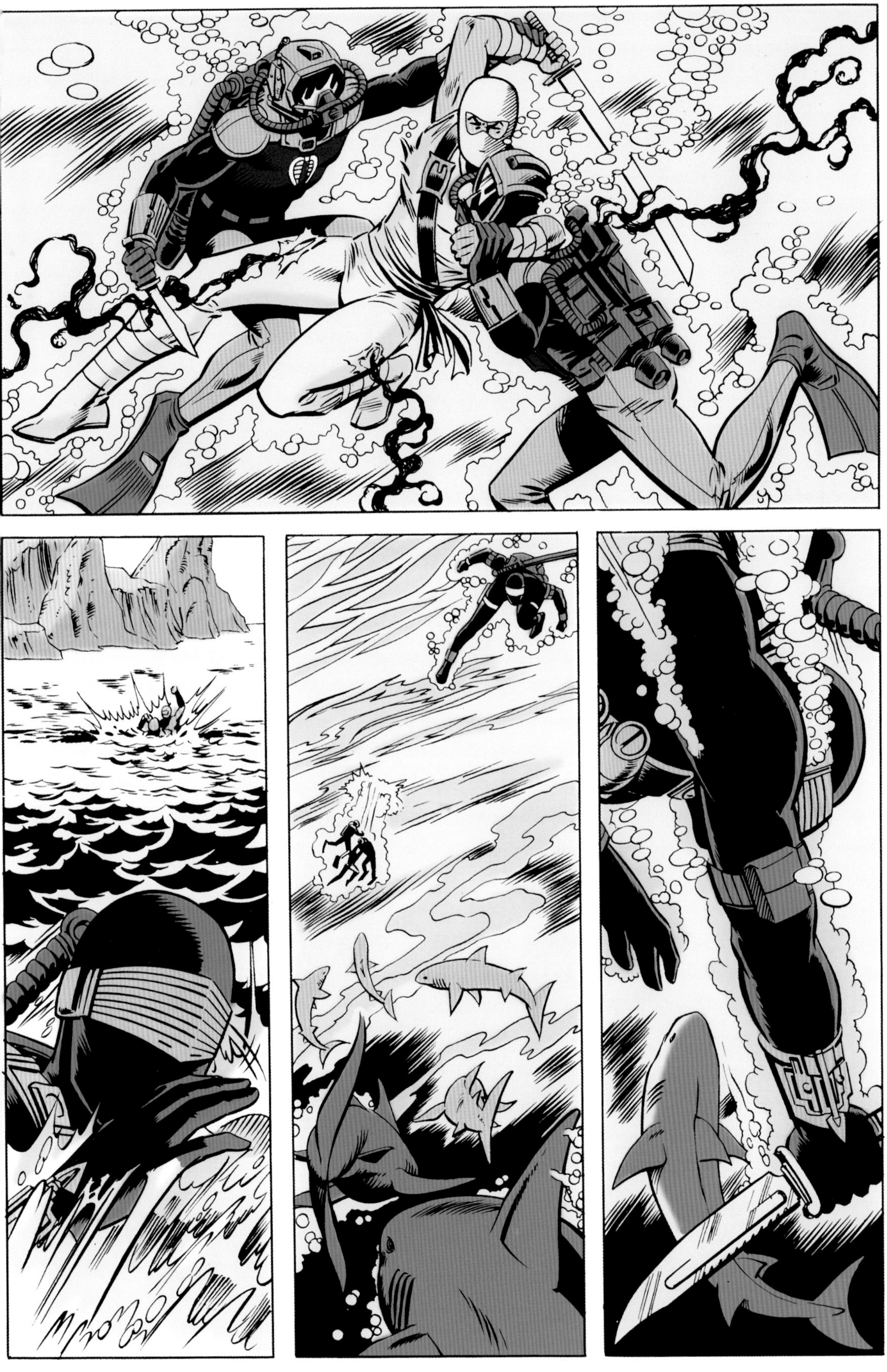

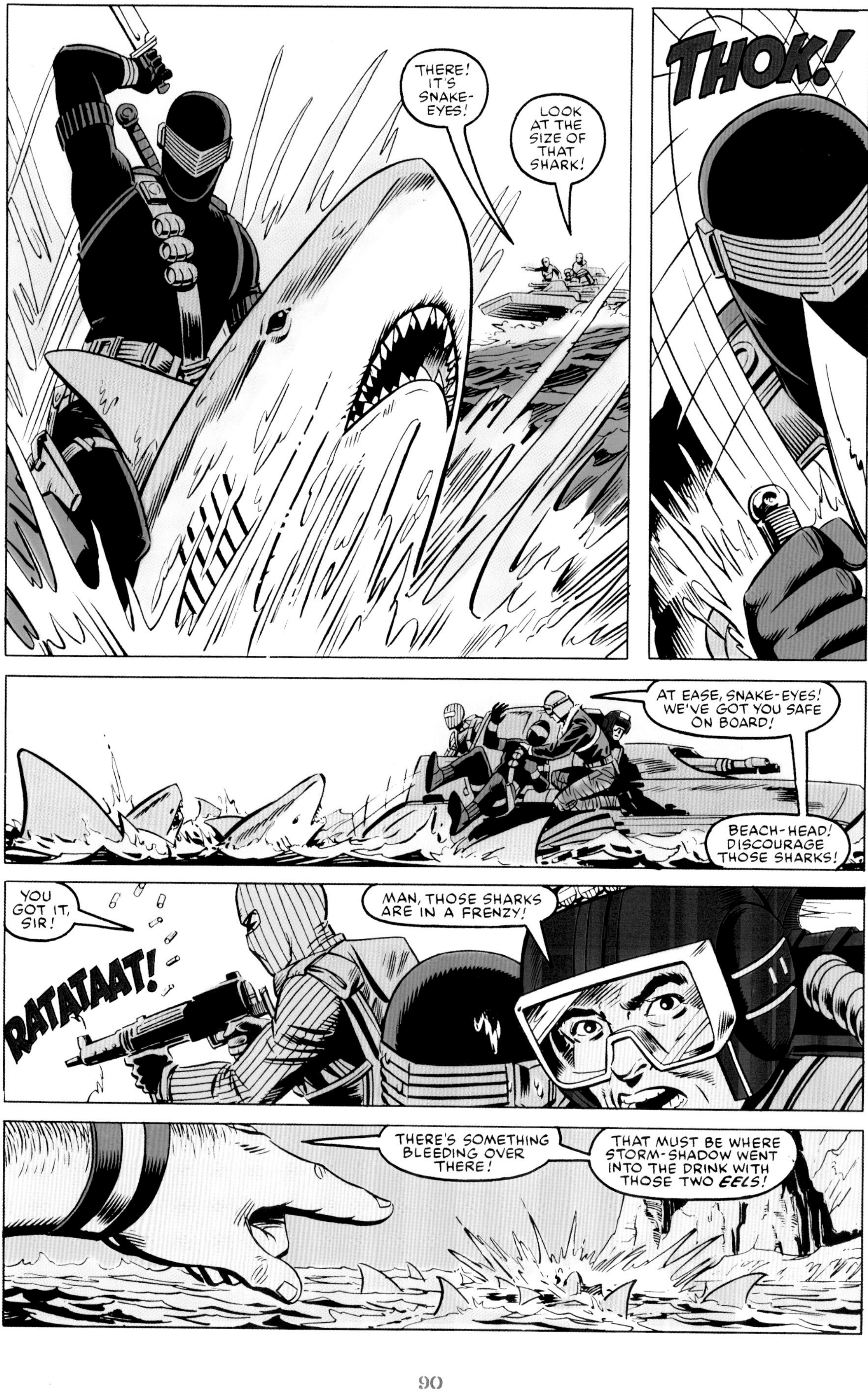
THERE! IT'S SNAKE-EYES!
LOOK AT THE SIZE OF THAT SHARK!
THOK!
AT EASE, SNAKE-EYES! WE'VE GOT YOU SAFE ON BOARD!
BEACH-HEAD! DISCOURAGE THOSE SHARKS!
YOU GOT IT, SIR!
RATATAAT!
MAN, THOSE SHARKS ARE IN A FRENZY!
THERE'S SOMETHING BLEEDING OVER THERE!
THAT MUST BE WHERE STORM-SHADOW WENT INTO THE DRINK WITH THOSE TWO EELS!

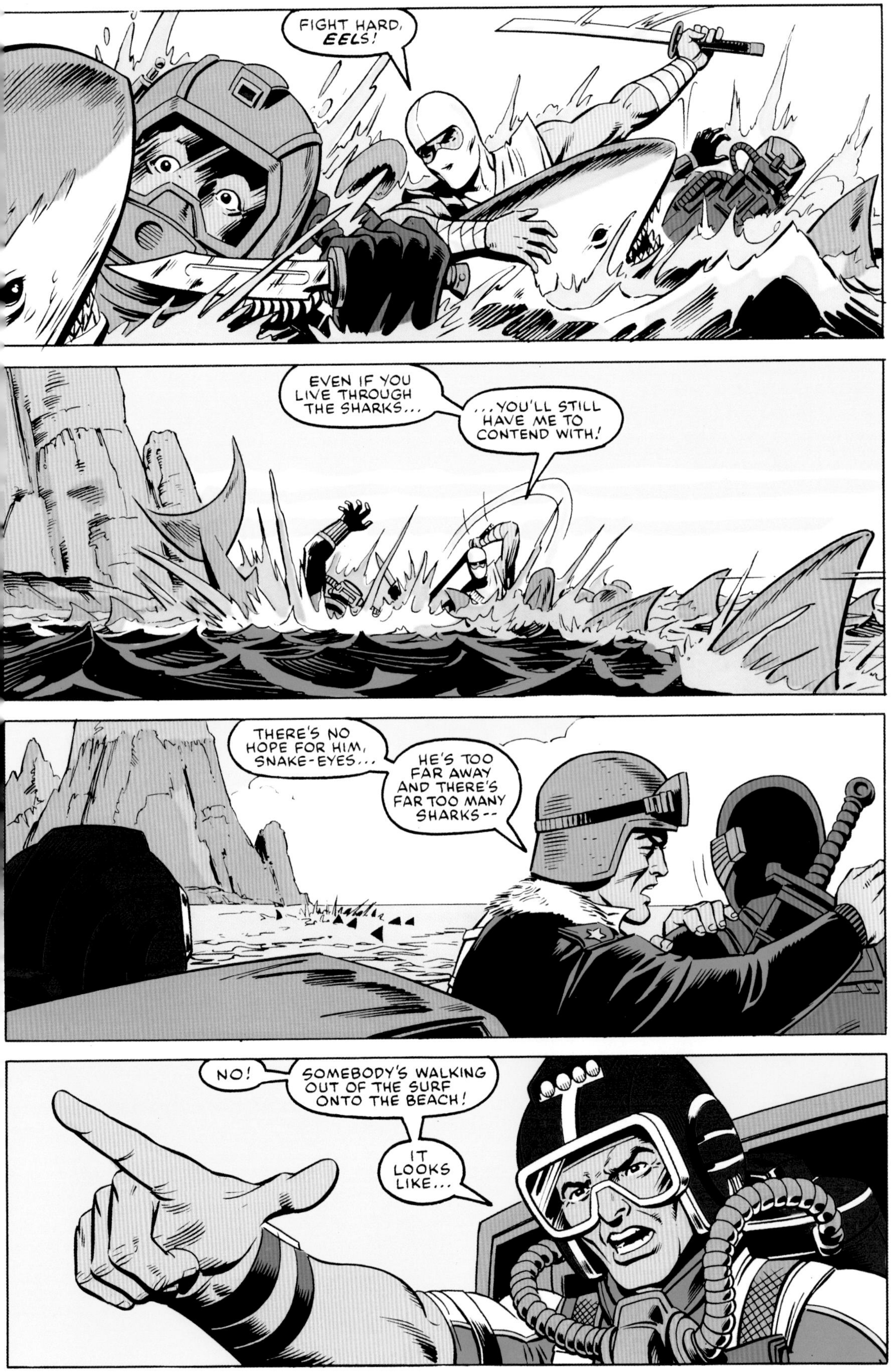

FIGHT HARD, EELS!
EVEN IF YOU LIVE THROUGH THE SHARKS...
...YOU'LL STILL HAVE ME TO CONTEND WITH!
THERE'S NO HOPE FOR HIM, SNAKE-EYES...
HE'S TOO FAR AWAY AND THERE'S FAR TOO MANY SHARKS--
NO!
SOMEBODY'S WALKING OUT OF THE SURF ONTO THE BEACH!
IT LOOKS LIKE...

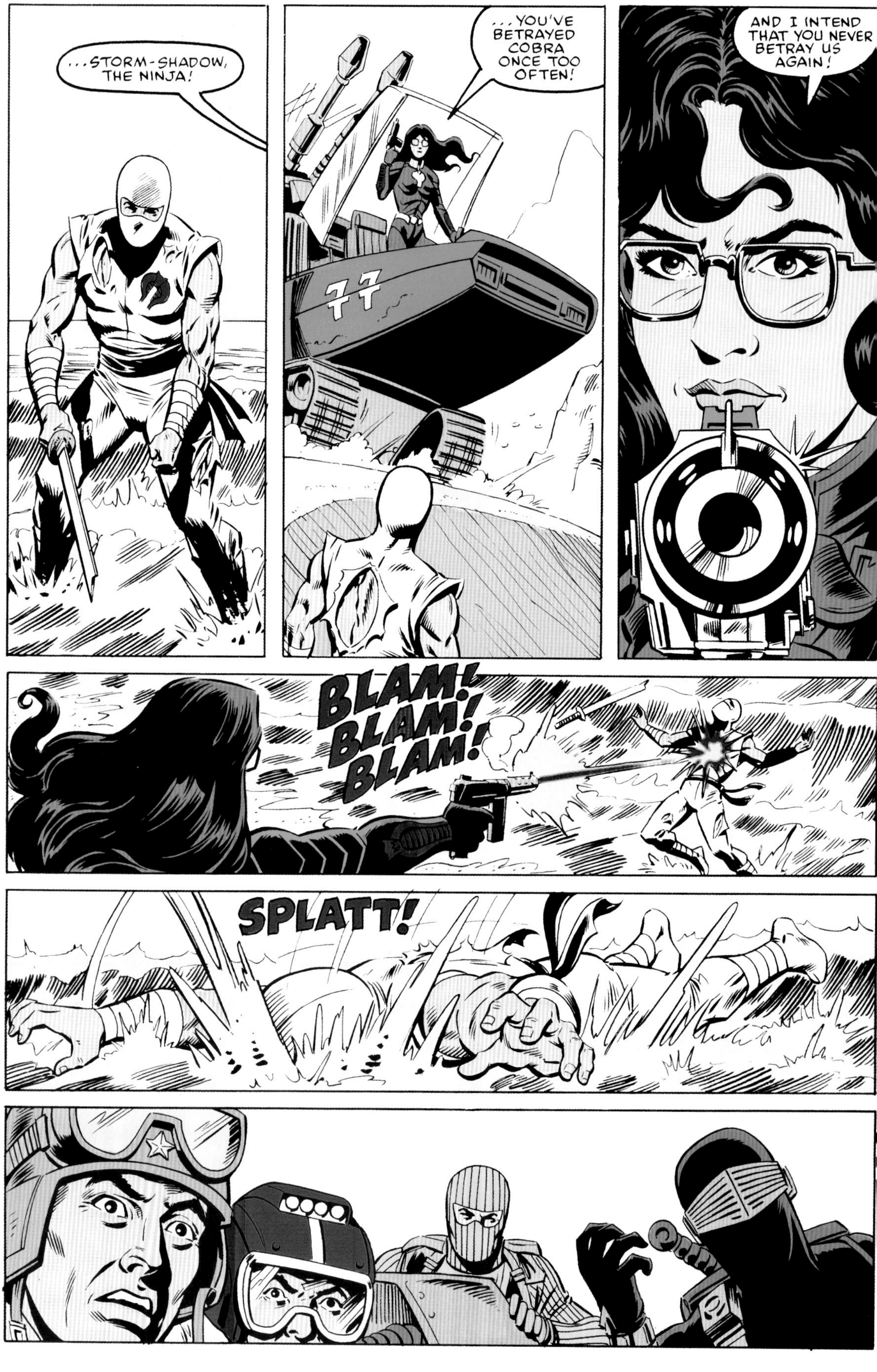
...STORM-SHADOW, THE NINJA!
...YOU'VE BETRAYED COBRA ONCE TOO OFTEN!
AND I INTEND THAT YOU NEVER BETRAY US AGAIN!
BLAM! BLAM! BLAM!
SPLATT!

AT SPRINGFIELD MUNICIPAL AIRPORT...

FIREBAT APPROACHING FOR LANDING! THIS IS AN UNAUTHORIZED LANDING!

SECURITY! HAVE FIREFLY AND THOSE DREDNOKS INVESTIGATE...

...NO SENSE IN WASTING REAL COBRA TROOPERS IN CASE IT'S SOMETHING BAD...

SPRINGFIELD

GOR! IT LOOKS LIKE--

--IT IS! IT'S ZARTAN! WHAT'S HE DOING BACK HERE?

WHAT'S HE DOING ASLEEP AT THE CONTROLS?

THAT PLANE FLEW BACK ON A PRE-SET PROGRAM! ZARTAN MUST HAVE BEEN UNCONSCIOUS FOR THE WHOLE TRIP!

WHAT SHOULD WE DO, RIPPER?

HE'S HURT! BETTER TAKE HIM TO HOSPITAL!

UHHH....C-CANDY....

WHUZZAT? SOUNDED LIKE HE SAID SOMETHIN'...

I DUNNO... SOUNDED LIKE HE WAS ASKIN' FER CANDY...

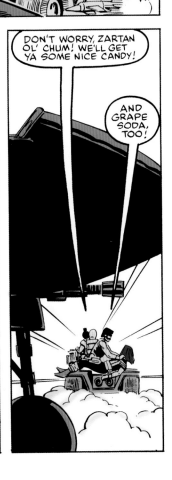

DON'T WORRY, ZARTAN OL' CHUM! WE'LL GET YA SOME NICE CANDY!

AND GRAPE SODA, TOO!

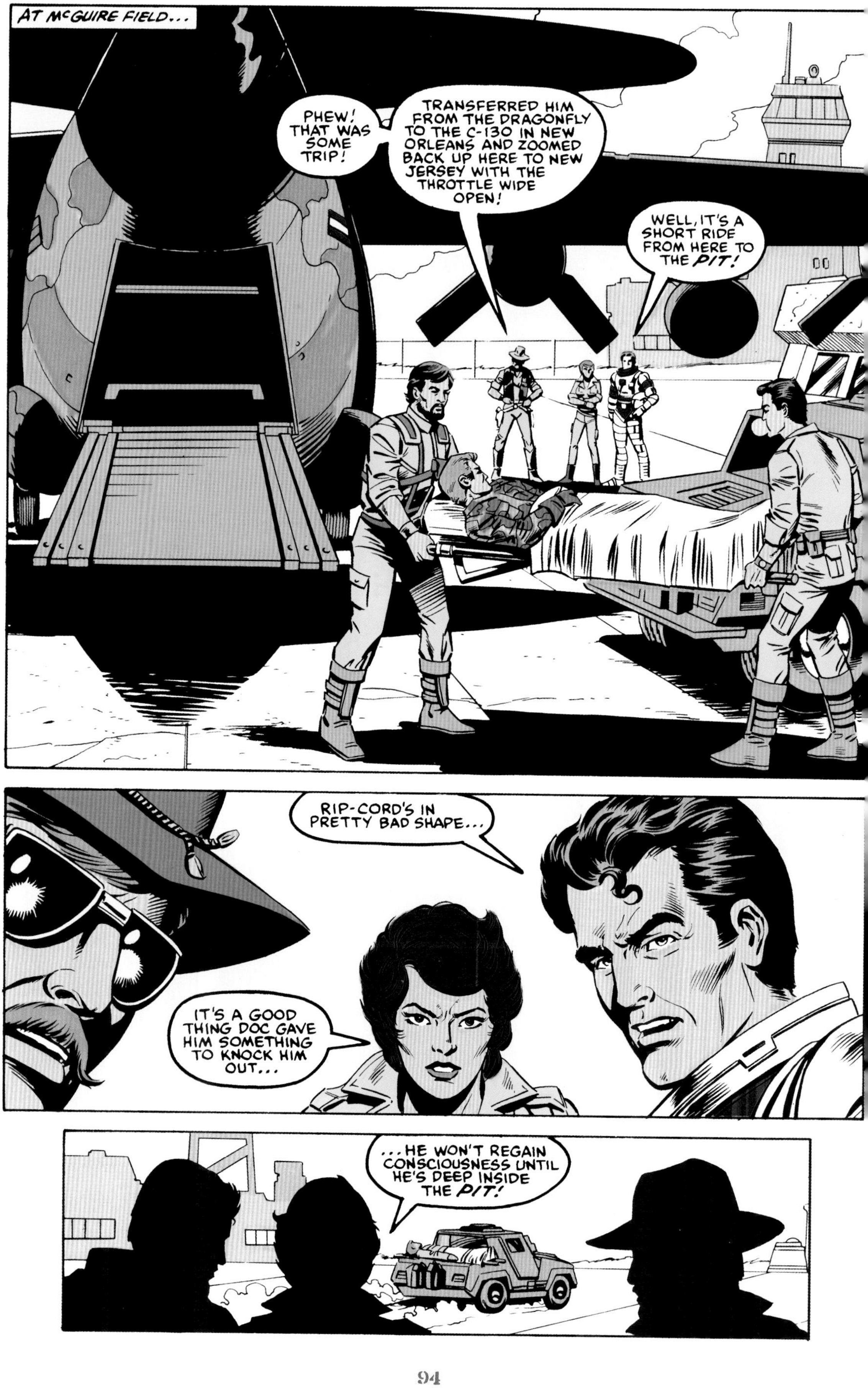
AT McGUIRE FIELD...
PHEW! THAT WAS SOME TRIP!
TRANSFERRED HIM FROM THE DRAGONFLY TO THE C-130 IN NEW ORLEANS AND ZOOMED BACK UP HERE TO NEW JERSEY WITH THE THROTTLE WIDE OPEN!
WELL, IT'S A SHORT RIDE FROM HERE TO THE PIT!
RIP-CORD'S IN PRETTY BAD SHAPE...
IT'S A GOOD THING DOC GAVE HIM SOMETHING TO KNOCK HIM OUT...
...HE WON'T REGAIN CONSCIOUSNESS UNTIL HE'S DEEP INSIDE THE PIT!

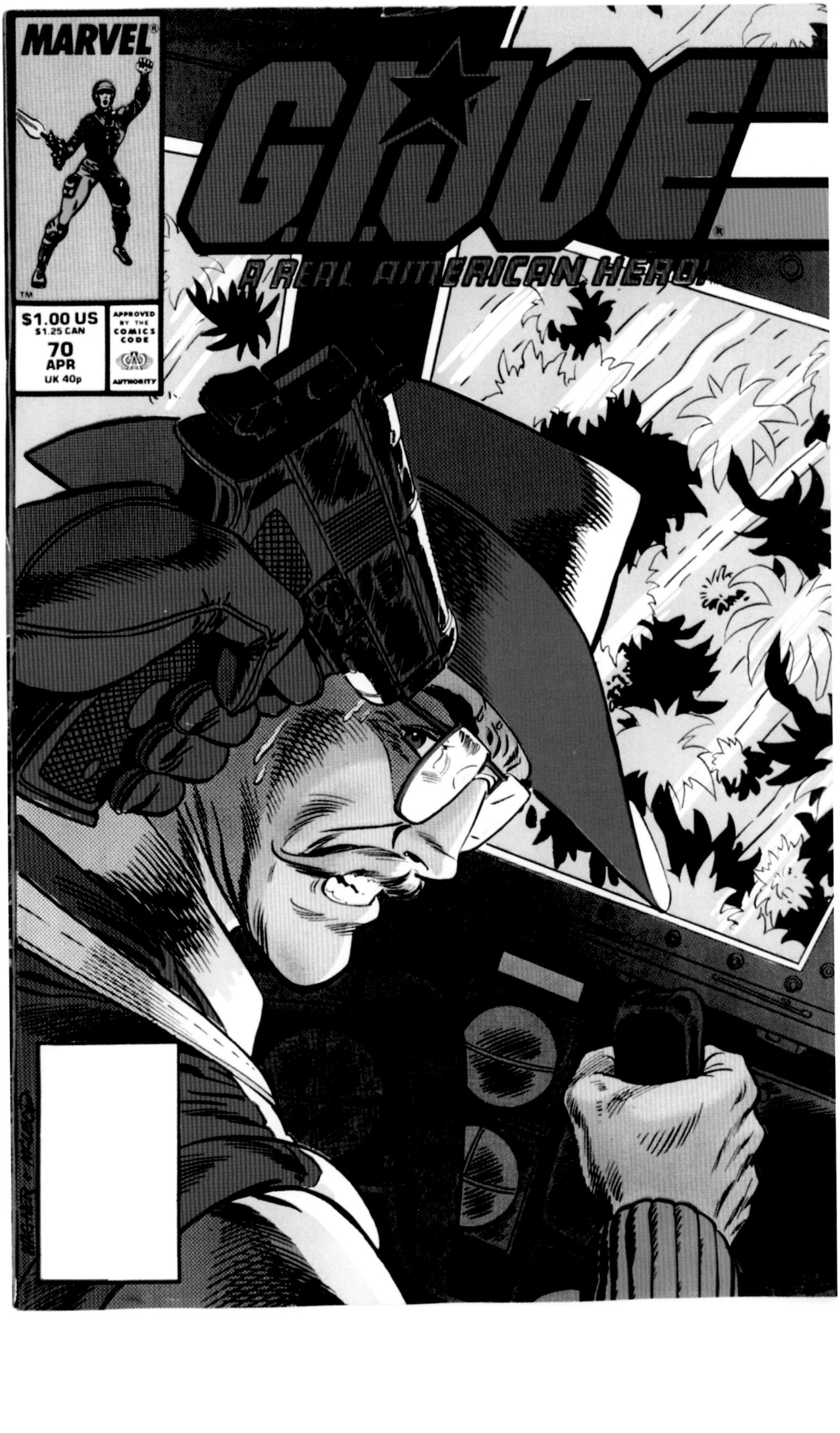
MARVEL
G.I. JOE
A REAL AMERICAN HERO
$1.00 US
$1.25 CAN
70
APR
UK 40p
APPROVED BY THE COMICS CODE AUTHORITY

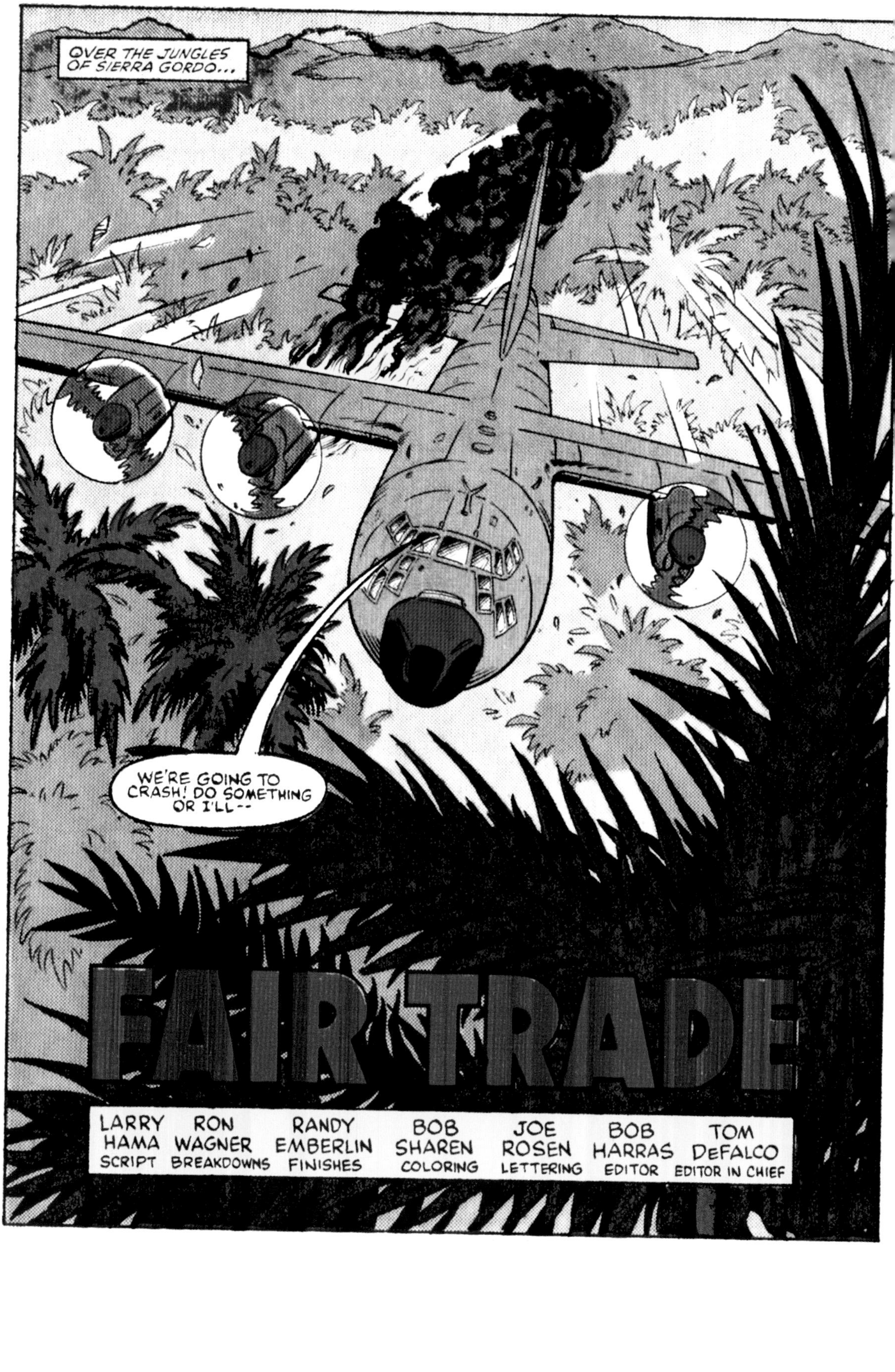
OVER THE JUNGLES OF SIERRA GORDO...
WE'RE GOING TO CRASH! DO SOMETHING OR I'LL--
FAIR TRADE
LARRY HAMA SCRIPT
RON WAGNER BREAKDOWNS
RANDY EMBERLIN FINISHES
BOB SHAREN COLORING
JOE ROSEN LETTERING
BOB HARRAS EDITOR
TOM DeFALCO EDITOR IN CHIEF

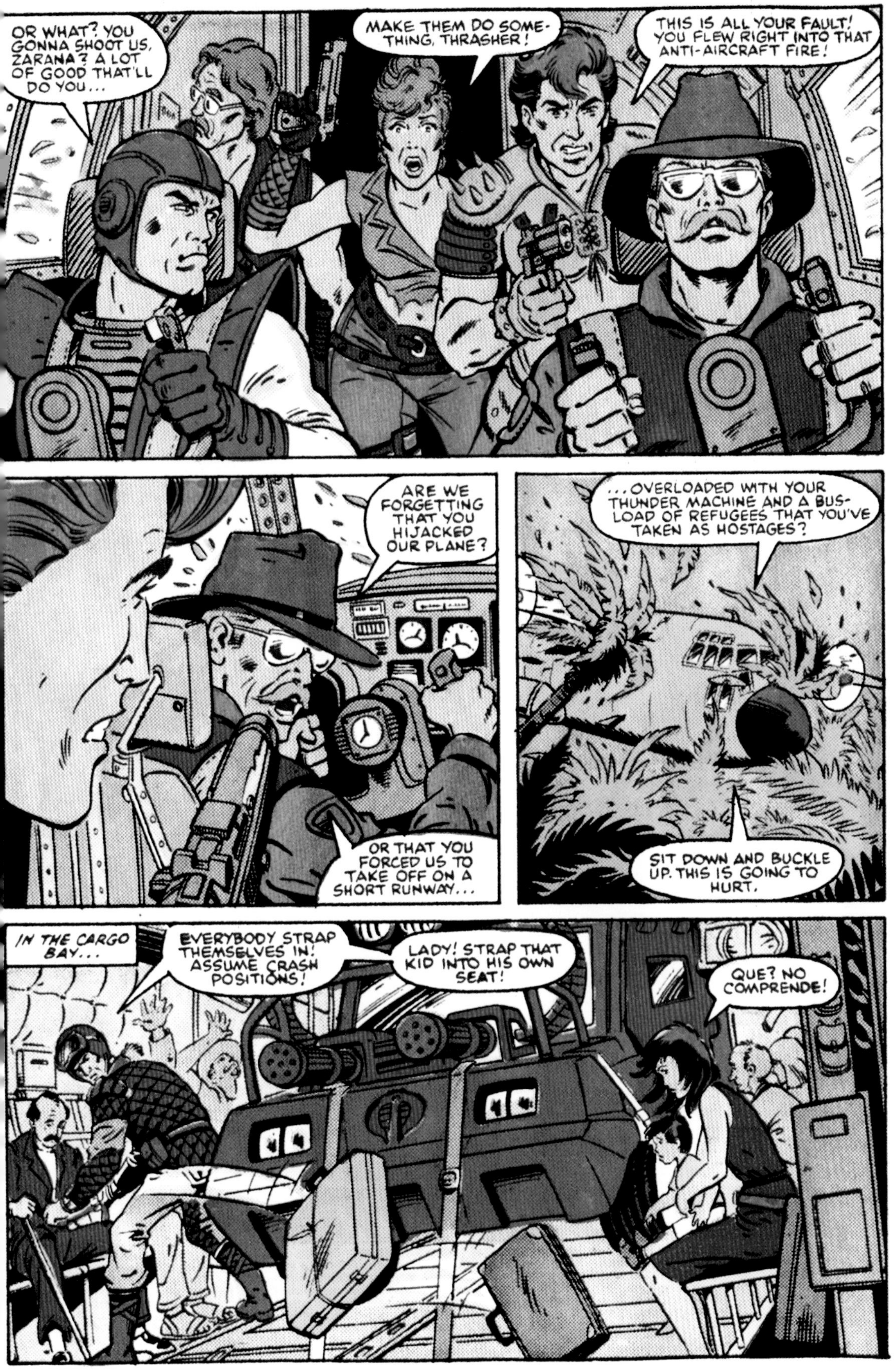
OR WHAT? YOU GONNA SHOOT US, ZARANA? A LOT OF GOOD THAT'LL DO YOU...
MAKE THEM DO SOMETHING, THRASHER!
THIS IS ALL YOUR FAULT! YOU FLEW RIGHT INTO THAT ANTI-AIRCRAFT FIRE!
ARE WE FORGETTING THAT YOU HIJACKED OUR PLANE?
OR THAT YOU FORCED US TO TAKE OFF ON A SHORT RUNWAY...
...OVERLOADED WITH YOUR THUNDER MACHINE AND A BUS-LOAD OF REFUGEES THAT YOU'VE TAKEN AS HOSTAGES?
SIT DOWN AND BUCKLE UP. THIS IS GOING TO HURT.
IN THE CARGO BAY...
EVERYBODY STRAP THEMSELVES IN! ASSUME CRASH POSITIONS!
LADY! STRAP THAT KID INTO HIS OWN SEAT!
QUE? NO COMPRENDE!

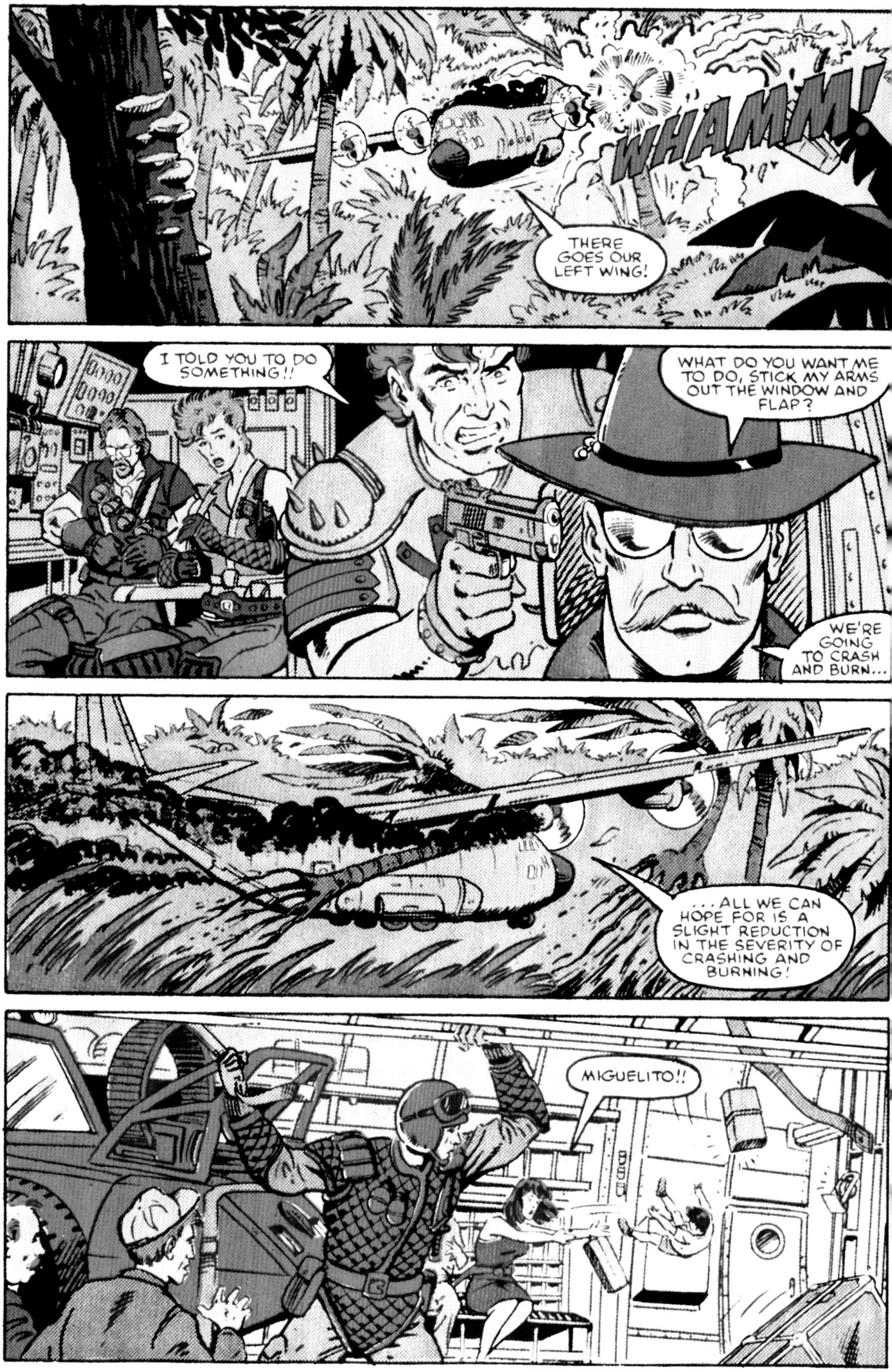
WHAMM!
THERE GOES OUR LEFT WING!
I TOLD YOU TO DO SOMETHING!!
WHAT DO YOU WANT ME TO DO, STICK MY ARMS OUT THE WINDOW AND FLAP?
WE'RE GOING TO CRASH AND BURN...
...ALL WE CAN HOPE FOR IS A SLIGHT REDUCTION IN THE SEVERITY OF CRASHING AND BURNING!
MIGUELITO!!

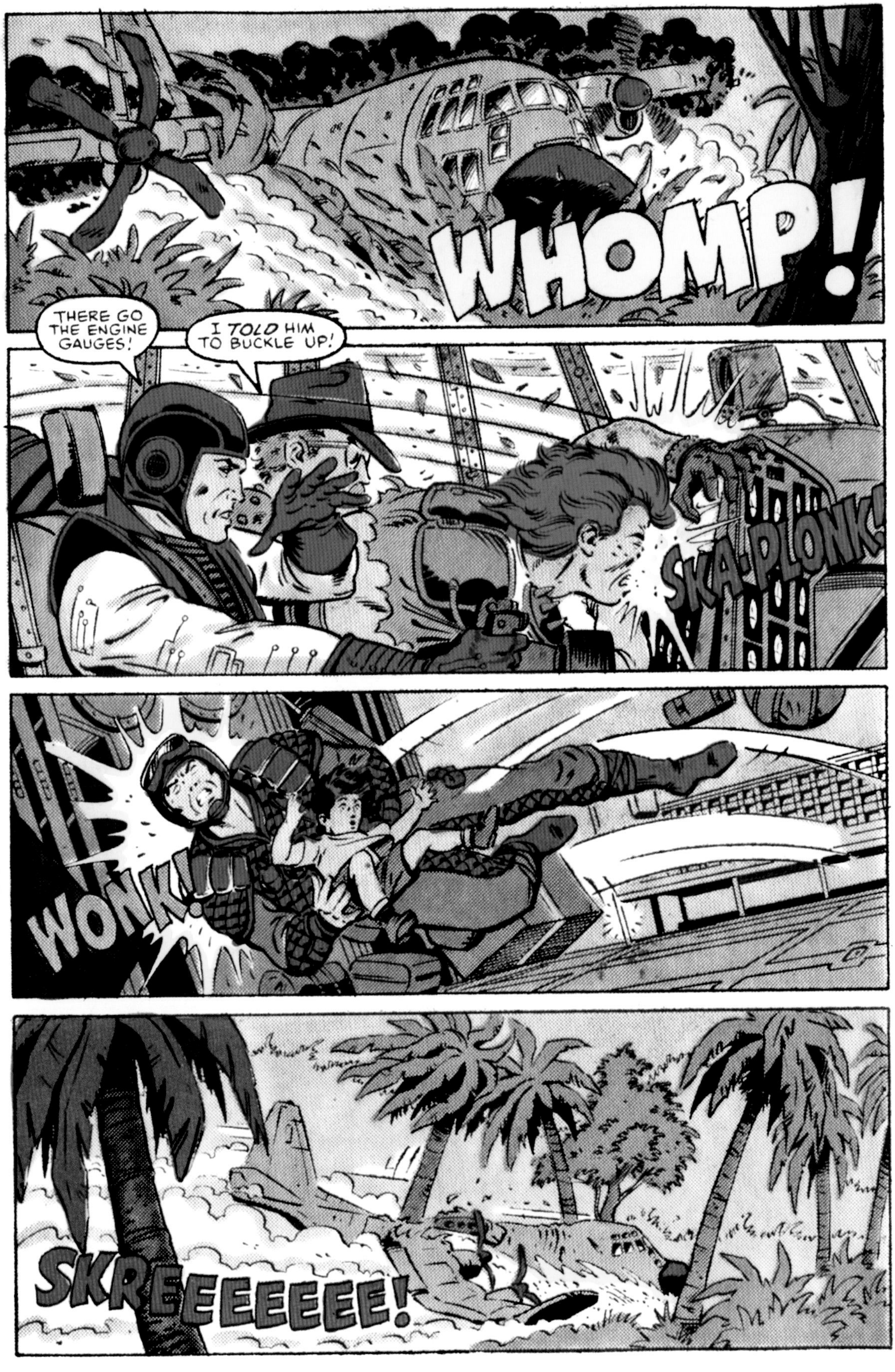
WHOMP!
THERE GO THE ENGINE GAUGES!
I *TOLD* HIM TO BUCKLE UP!
SKA-PLONK!
WONK!
SKREEEEEEEE!

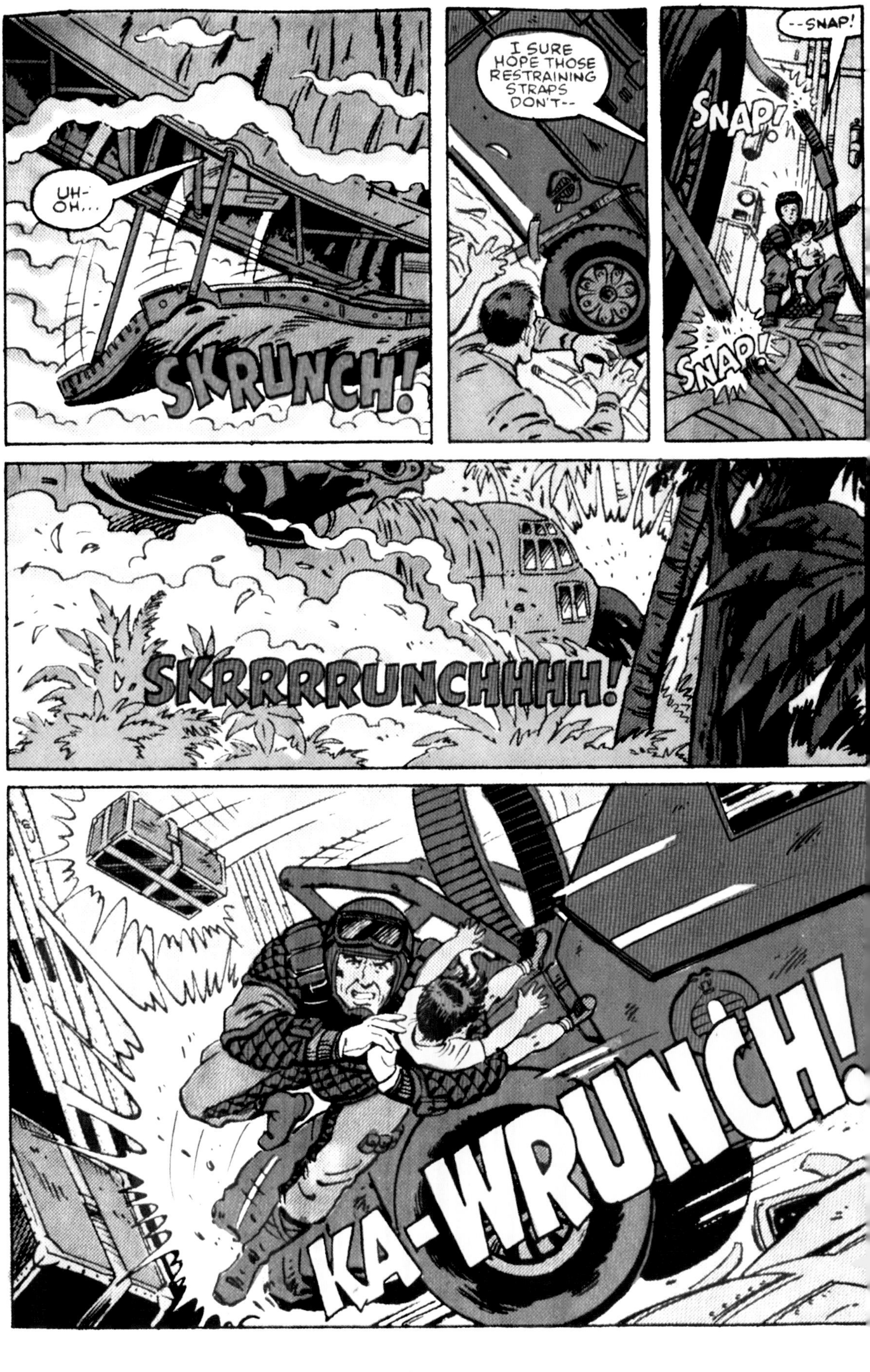
UH-
OH...
SKRUNCH!
I SURE
HOPE THOSE
RESTRAINING
STRAPS
DON'T--
--SNAP!
SNAP!
SNAP!
SKRRRRRUNCHHHH!
KA-WRUNCH!

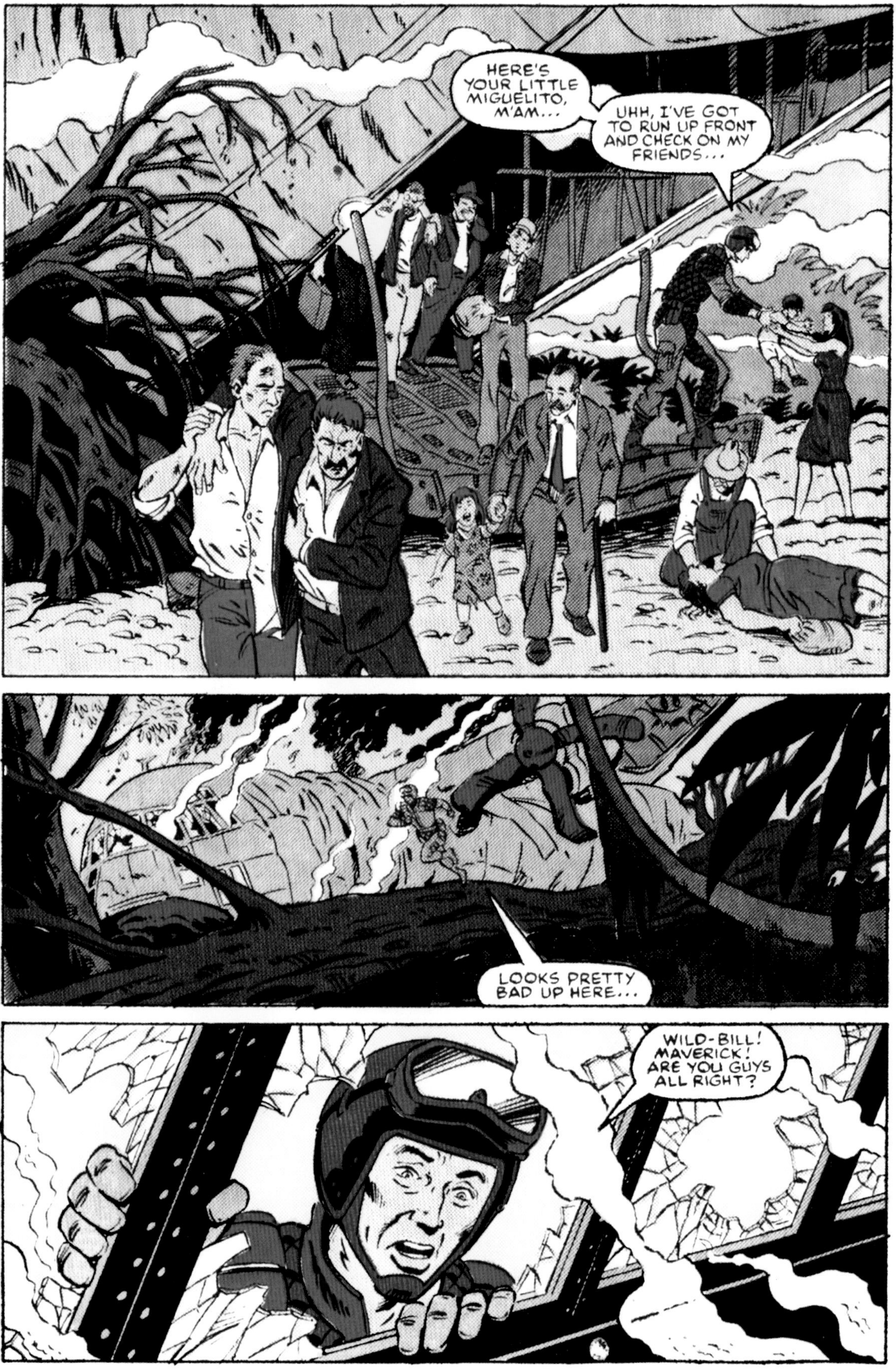
HERE'S YOUR LITTLE MIGUELITO, M'AM...
UHH, I'VE GOT TO RUN UP FRONT AND CHECK ON MY FRIENDS...
LOOKS PRETTY BAD UP HERE...
WILD-BILL! MAVERICK! ARE YOU GUYS ALL RIGHT?

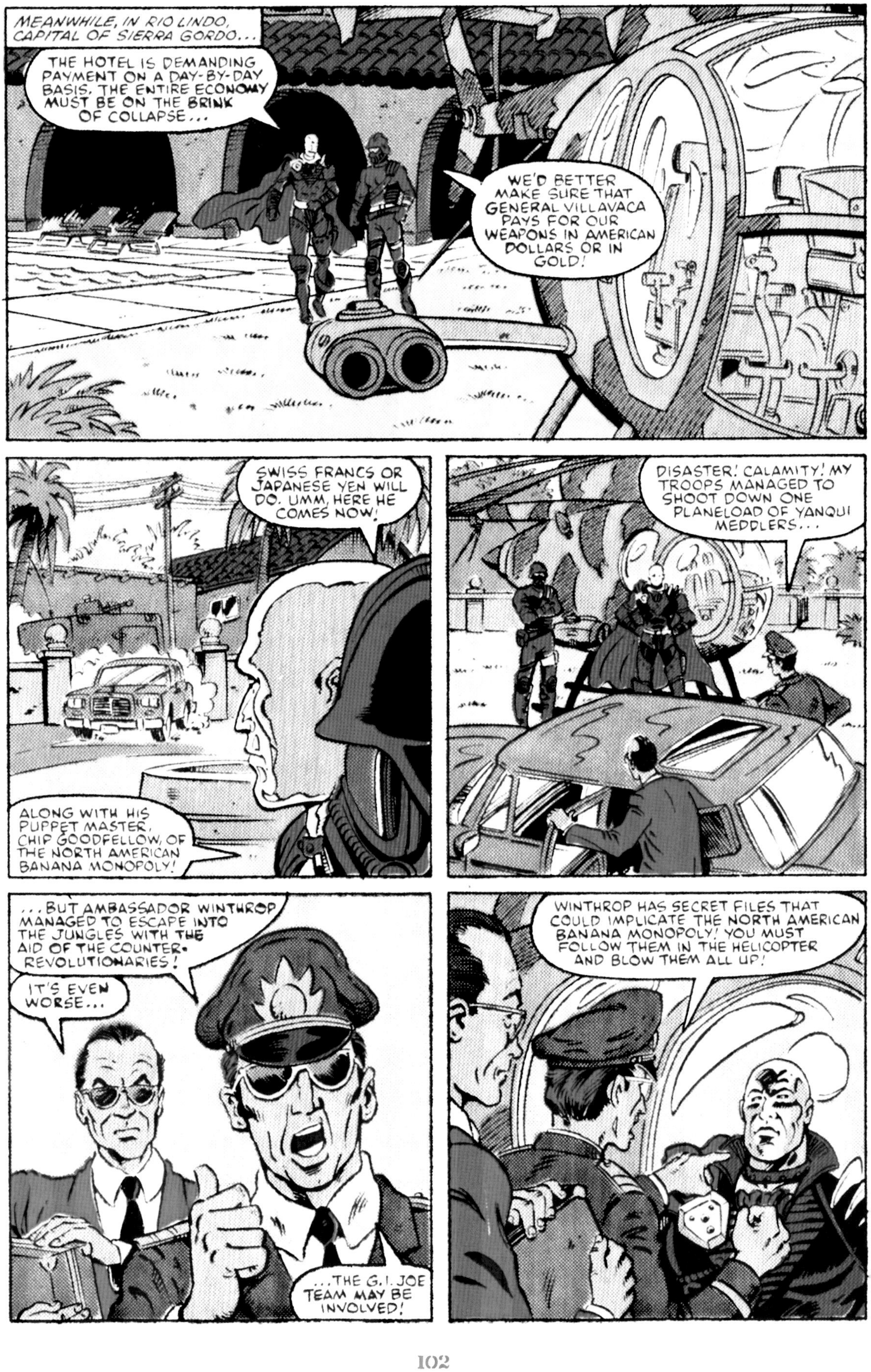
MEANWHILE, IN RIO LINDO, CAPITAL OF SIERRA GORDO...
THE HOTEL IS DEMANDING PAYMENT ON A DAY-BY-DAY BASIS. THE ENTIRE ECONOMY MUST BE ON THE BRINK OF COLLAPSE...
WE'D BETTER MAKE SURE THAT GENERAL VILLAVACA PAYS FOR OUR WEAPONS IN AMERICAN DOLLARS OR IN GOLD!
SWISS FRANCS OR JAPANESE YEN WILL DO. UMM, HERE HE COMES NOW!
ALONG WITH HIS PUPPET MASTER, CHIP GOODFELLOW, OF THE NORTH AMERICAN BANANA MONOPOLY!
DISASTER! CALAMITY! MY TROOPS MANAGED TO SHOOT DOWN ONE PLANELOAD OF YANQUI MEDDLERS...
...BUT AMBASSADOR WINTHROP MANAGED TO ESCAPE INTO THE JUNGLES WITH THE AID OF THE COUNTER-REVOLUTIONARIES!
IT'S EVEN WORSE...
...THE G.I. JOE TEAM MAY BE INVOLVED!
WINTHROP HAS SECRET FILES THAT COULD IMPLICATE THE NORTH AMERICAN BANANA MONOPOLY! YOU MUST FOLLOW THEM IN THE HELICOPTER AND BLOW THEM ALL UP!

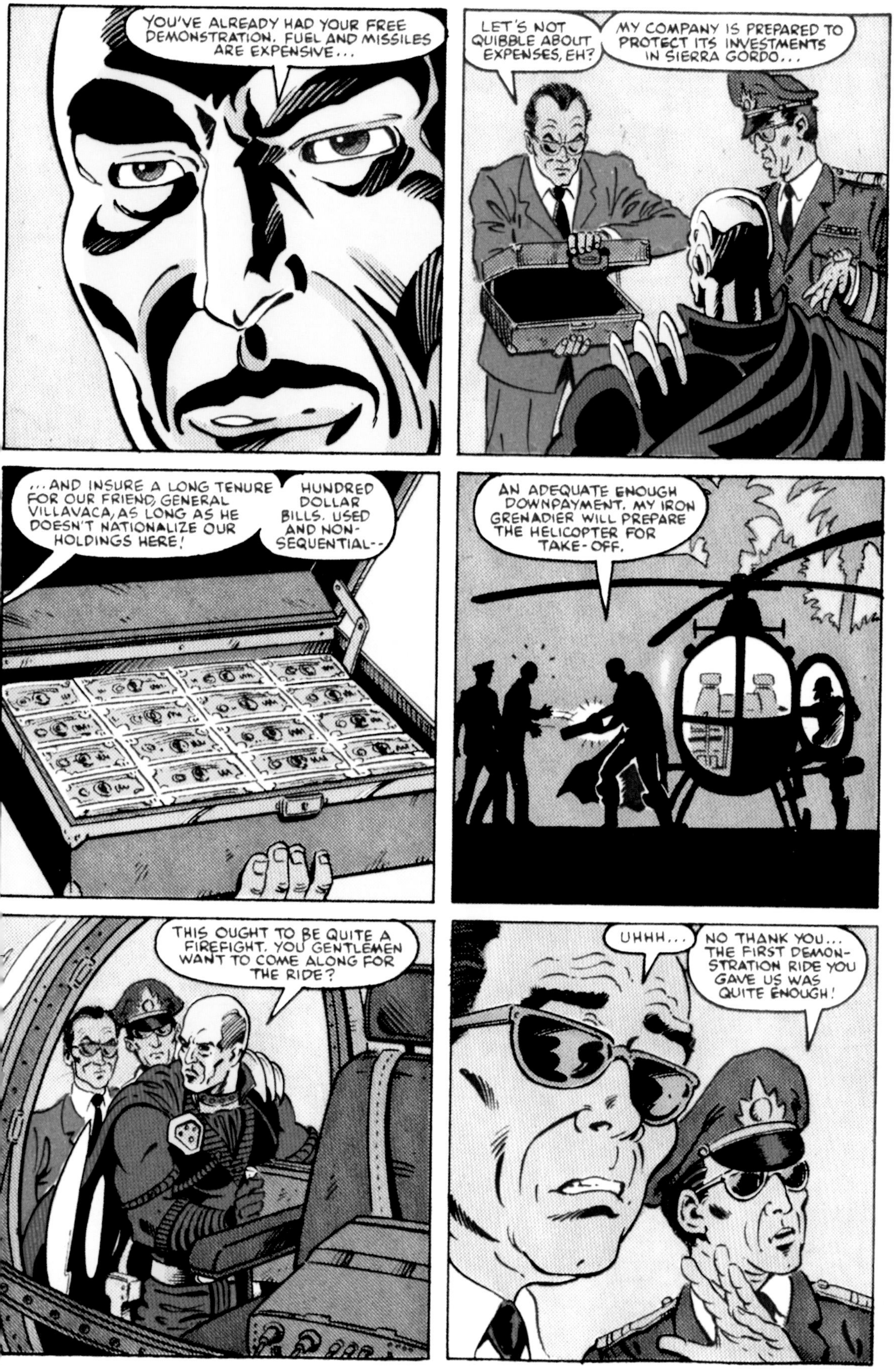
YOU'VE ALREADY HAD YOUR FREE DEMONSTRATION. FUEL AND MISSILES ARE EXPENSIVE...
LET'S NOT QUIBBLE ABOUT EXPENSES, EH?
MY COMPANY IS PREPARED TO PROTECT ITS INVESTMENTS IN SIERRA GORDO...
...AND INSURE A LONG TENURE FOR OUR FRIEND, GENERAL VILLAVACA, AS LONG AS HE DOESN'T NATIONALIZE OUR HOLDINGS HERE!
HUNDRED DOLLAR BILLS. USED AND NON-SEQUENTIAL--
AN ADEQUATE ENOUGH DOWNPAYMENT. MY IRON GRENADIER WILL PREPARE THE HELICOPTER FOR TAKE-OFF.
THIS OUGHT TO BE QUITE A FIREFIGHT. YOU GENTLEMEN WANT TO COME ALONG FOR THE RIDE?
UHHH...
NO THANK YOU... THE FIRST DEMONSTRATION RIDE YOU GAVE US WAS QUITE ENOUGH!

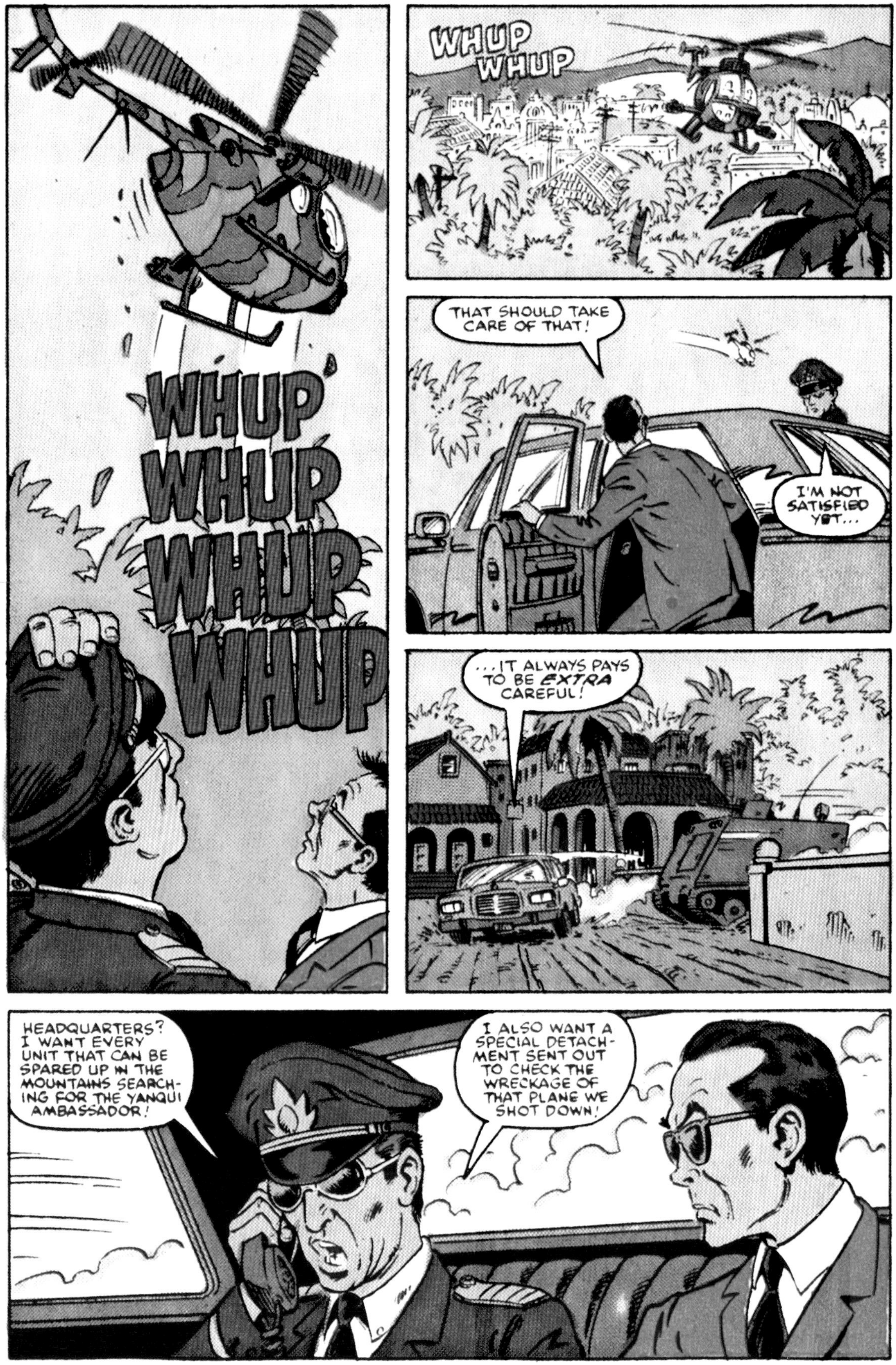
WHUP
WHUP
WHUP
WHUP
WHUP
WHUP
THAT SHOULD TAKE CARE OF THAT!
I'M NOT SATISFIED YET...
...IT ALWAYS PAYS TO BE EXTRA CAREFUL!
HEADQUARTERS? I WANT EVERY UNIT THAT CAN BE SPARED UP IN THE MOUNTAINS SEARCHING FOR THE YANQUI AMBASSADOR!
I ALSO WANT A SPECIAL DETACHMENT SENT OUT TO CHECK THE WRECKAGE OF THAT PLANE WE SHOT DOWN!

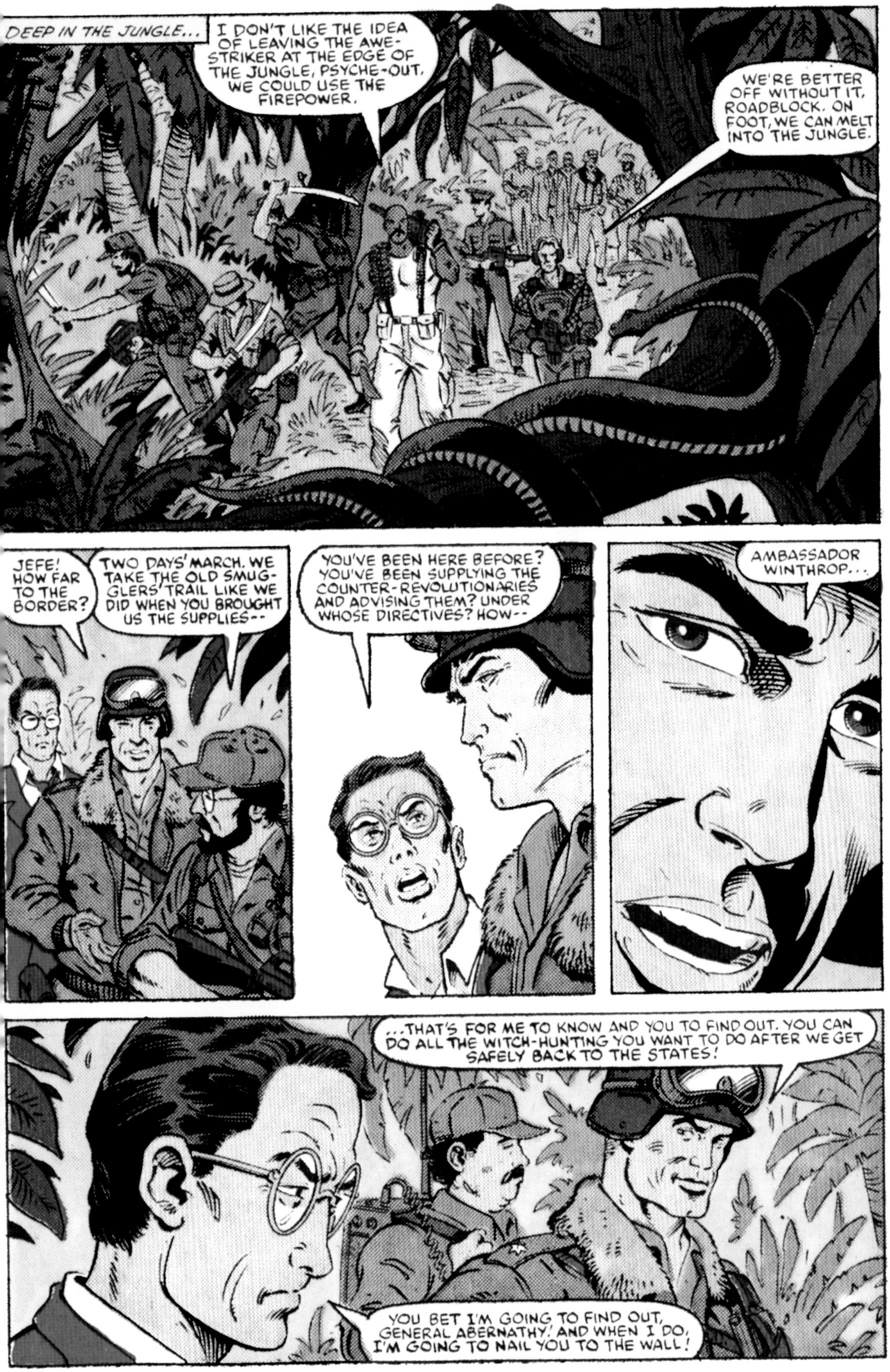
DEEP IN THE JUNGLE...
I DON'T LIKE THE IDEA OF LEAVING THE AWE-STRIKER AT THE EDGE OF THE JUNGLE, PSYCHE-OUT. WE COULD USE THE FIREPOWER.
WE'RE BETTER OFF WITHOUT IT, ROADBLOCK. ON FOOT, WE CAN MELT INTO THE JUNGLE.
JEFE! HOW FAR TO THE BORDER?
TWO DAYS' MARCH. WE TAKE THE OLD SMUGGLERS' TRAIL LIKE WE DID WHEN YOU BROUGHT US THE SUPPLIES--
YOU'VE BEEN HERE BEFORE? YOU'VE BEEN SUPPLYING THE COUNTER-REVOLUTIONARIES AND ADVISING THEM? UNDER WHOSE DIRECTIVES? HOW--
AMBASSADOR WINTHROP...
...THAT'S FOR ME TO KNOW AND YOU TO FIND OUT. YOU CAN DO ALL THE WITCH-HUNTING YOU WANT TO DO AFTER WE GET SAFELY BACK TO THE STATES!
YOU BET I'M GOING TO FIND OUT, GENERAL ABERNATHY! AND WHEN I DO, I'M GOING TO NAIL YOU TO THE WALL!

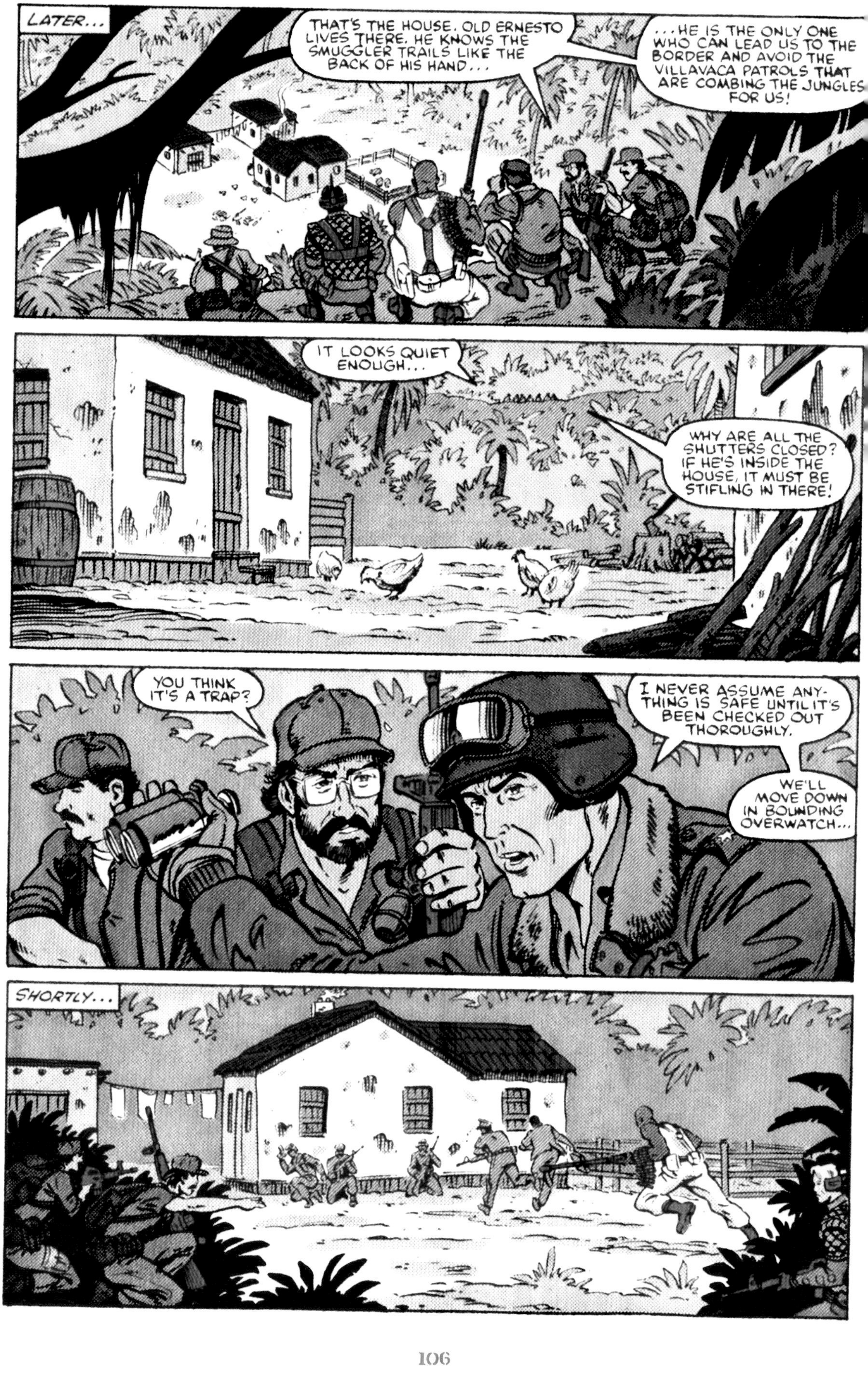

LATER...
THAT'S THE HOUSE. OLD ERNESTO LIVES THERE. HE KNOWS THE SMUGGLER TRAILS LIKE THE BACK OF HIS HAND...
...HE IS THE ONLY ONE WHO CAN LEAD US TO THE BORDER AND AVOID THE VILLAVACA PATROLS THAT ARE COMBING THE JUNGLES FOR US!
IT LOOKS QUIET ENOUGH...
WHY ARE ALL THE SHUTTERS CLOSED? IF HE'S INSIDE THE HOUSE, IT MUST BE STIFLING IN THERE!
YOU THINK IT'S A TRAP?
I NEVER ASSUME ANYTHING IS SAFE UNTIL IT'S BEEN CHECKED OUT THOROUGHLY.
WE'LL MOVE DOWN IN BOUNDING OVERWATCH...
SHORTLY...

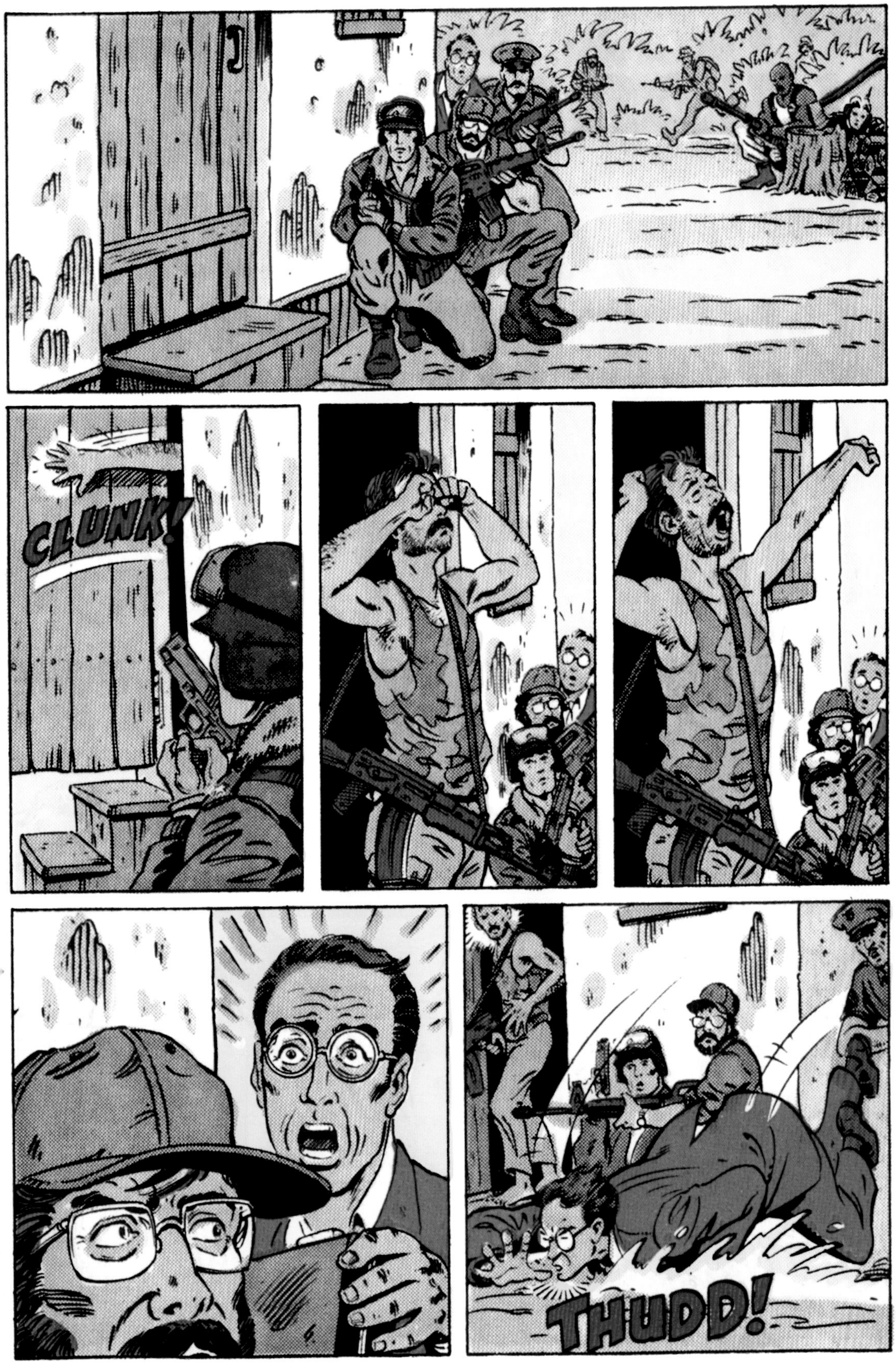
CLUNK!
THUDD!

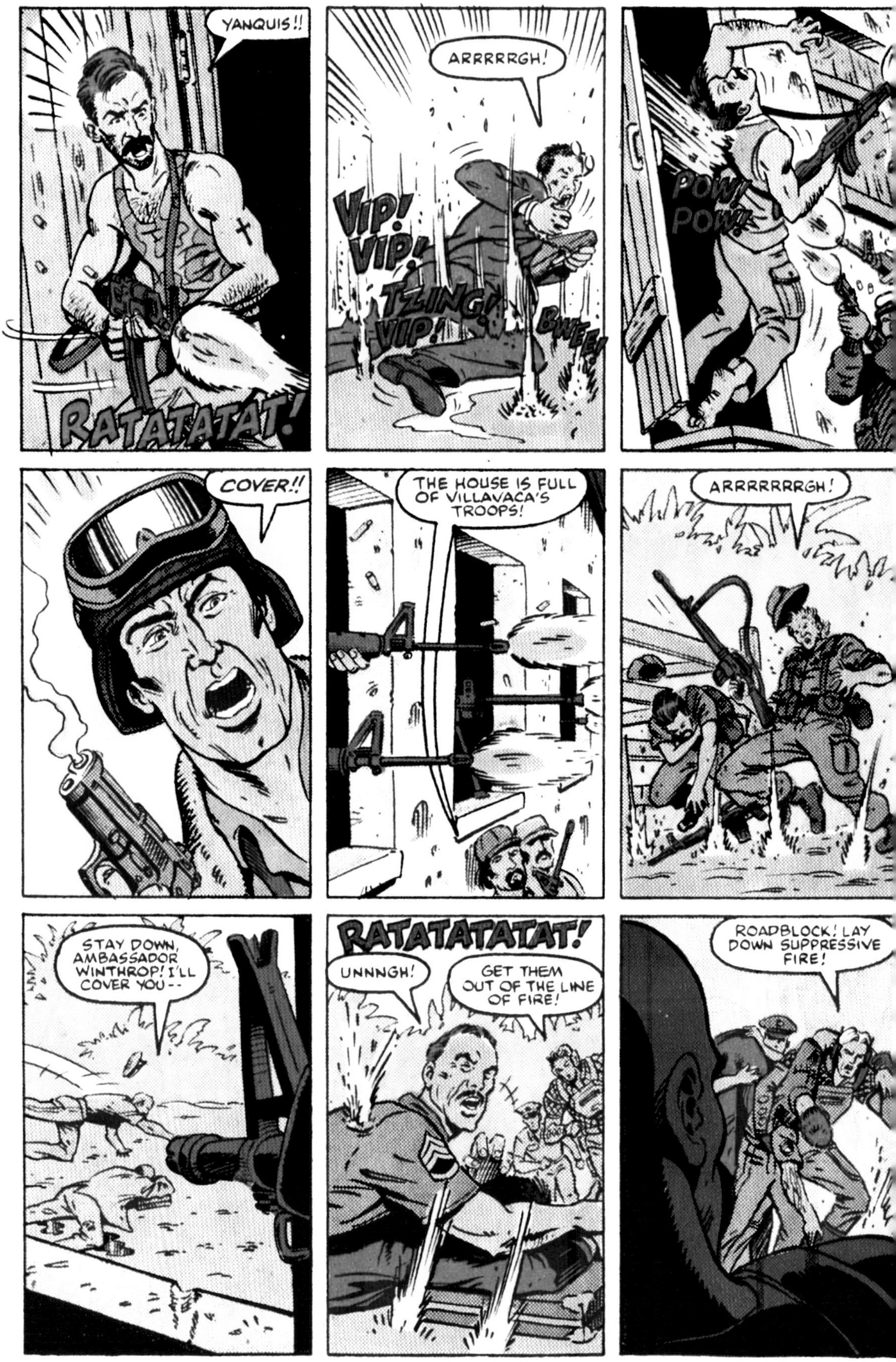
YANQUIS!!
RATATATAT!
ARRRRRGH!
VIP! VIP!
TZING!
VIP!
BWEE!
POW! POW!
COVER!!
THE HOUSE IS FULL OF VILLAVACA'S TROOPS!
ARRRRRRRGH!
STAY DOWN, AMBASSADOR WINTHROP! I'LL COVER YOU--
RATATATATAT!
UNNNGH!
GET THEM OUT OF THE LINE OF FIRE!
ROADBLOCK! LAY DOWN SUPPRESSIVE FIRE!

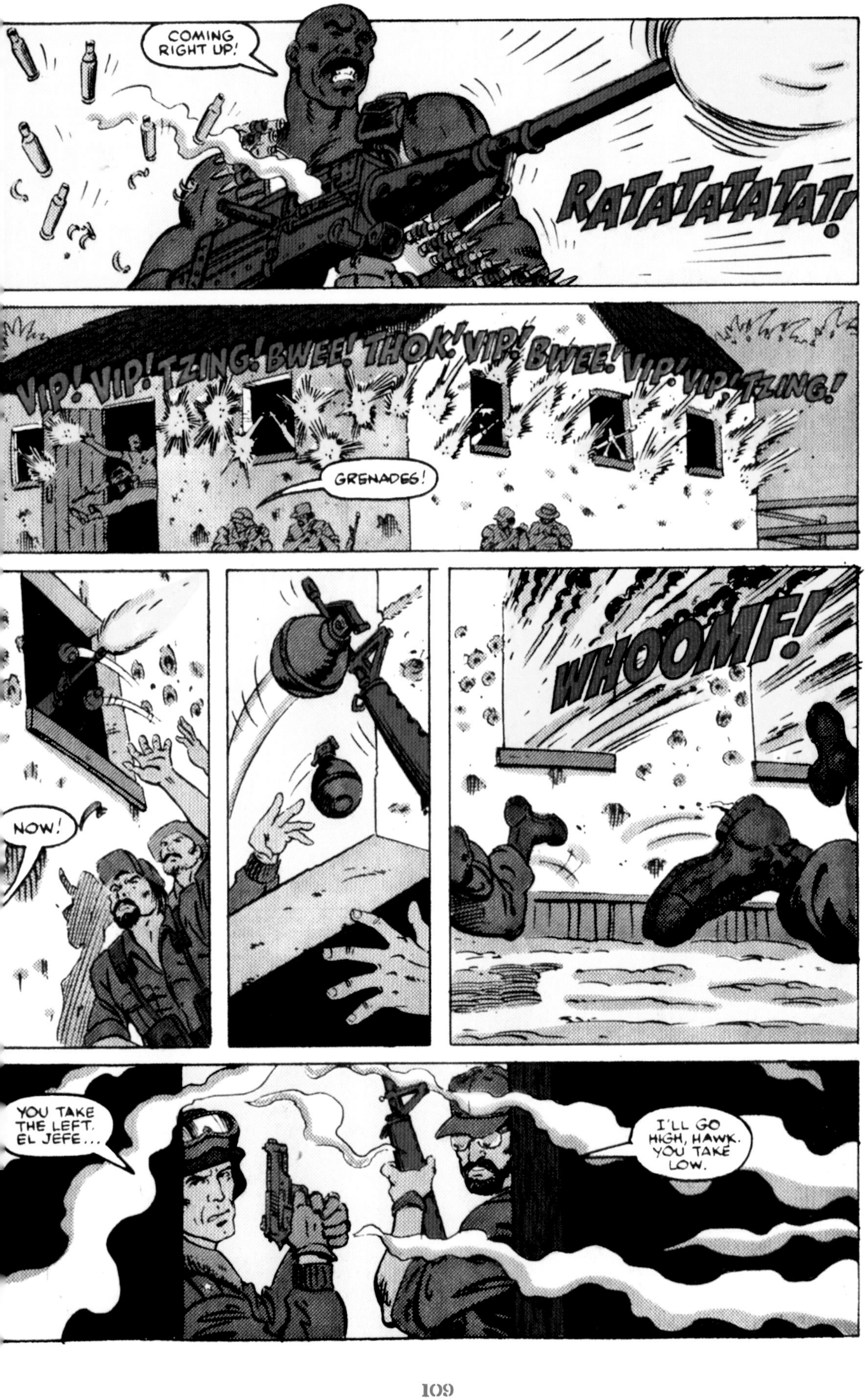
COMING RIGHT UP!
RATATATATAT!
VIP! VIP! TZING! BWEE! THOK! VIP! BWEE! VIP! VIP! TZING!
GRENADES!
NOW!
WHOOMF!
YOU TAKE THE LEFT. EL JEFE...
I'LL GO HIGH, HAWK. YOU TAKE LOW.

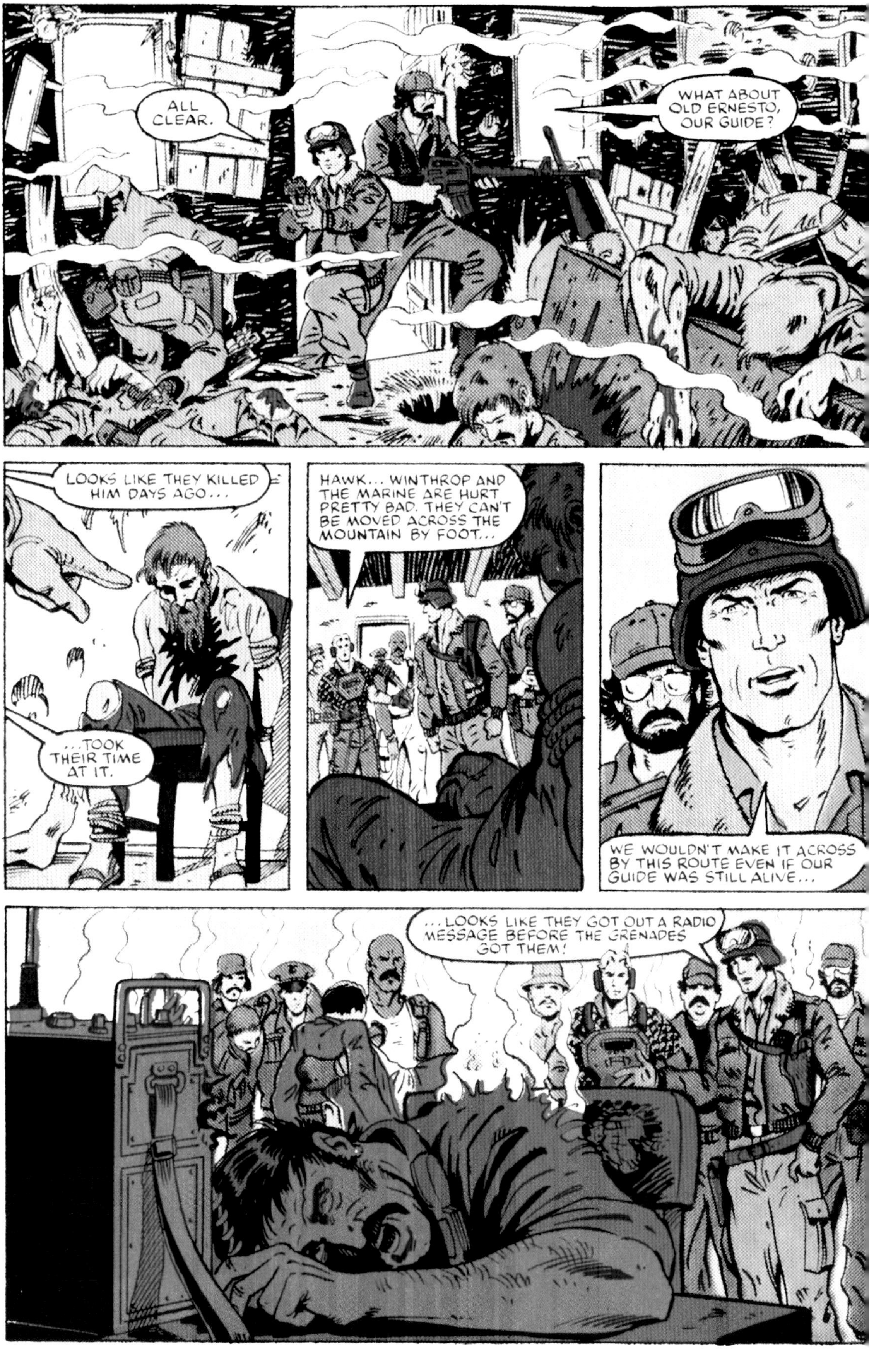
ALL CLEAR.
WHAT ABOUT OLD ERNESTO, OUR GUIDE?
LOOKS LIKE THEY KILLED HIM DAYS AGO...
...TOOK THEIR TIME AT IT.
HAWK... WINTHROP AND THE MARINE ARE HURT PRETTY BAD. THEY CAN'T BE MOVED ACROSS THE MOUNTAIN BY FOOT...
WE WOULDN'T MAKE IT ACROSS BY THIS ROUTE EVEN IF OUR GUIDE WAS STILL ALIVE...
...LOOKS LIKE THEY GOT OUT A RADIO MESSAGE BEFORE THE GRENADES GOT THEM!

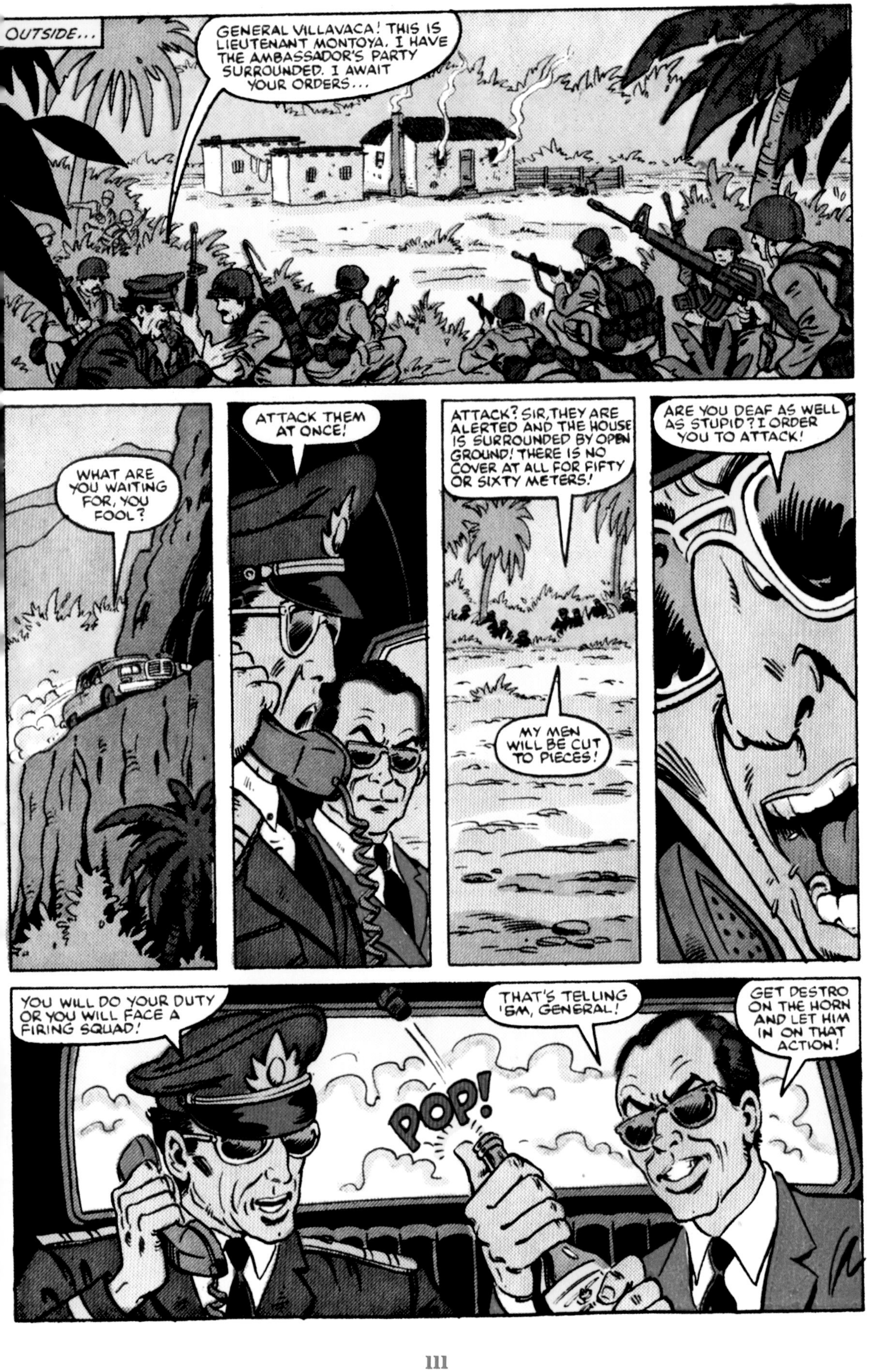
OUTSIDE...
GENERAL VILLAVACA! THIS IS LIEUTENANT MONTOYA. I HAVE THE AMBASSADOR'S PARTY SURROUNDED. I AWAIT YOUR ORDERS...
WHAT ARE YOU WAITING FOR, YOU FOOL?
ATTACK THEM AT ONCE!
ATTACK? SIR, THEY ARE ALERTED AND THE HOUSE IS SURROUNDED BY OPEN GROUND! THERE IS NO COVER AT ALL FOR FIFTY OR SIXTY METERS!
MY MEN WILL BE CUT TO PIECES!
ARE YOU DEAF AS WELL AS STUPID? I ORDER YOU TO ATTACK!
YOU WILL DO YOUR DUTY OR YOU WILL FACE A FIRING SQUAD!
THAT'S TELLING 'EM, GENERAL!
GET DESTRO ON THE HORN AND LET HIM IN ON THAT ACTION!
POP!

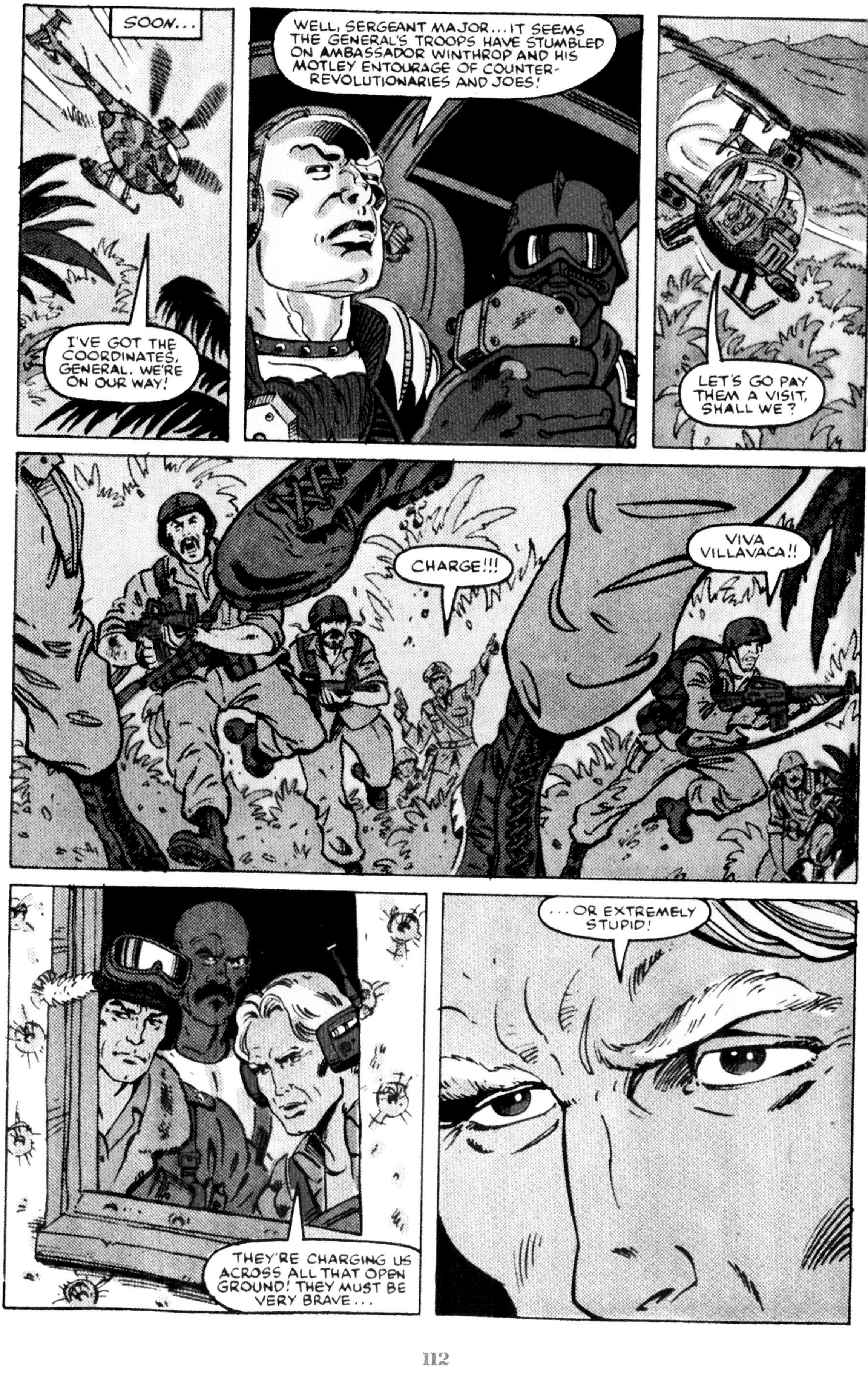
SOON...
I'VE GOT THE COORDINATES, GENERAL. WE'RE ON OUR WAY!
WELL, SERGEANT MAJOR... IT SEEMS THE GENERAL'S TROOPS HAVE STUMBLED ON AMBASSADOR WINTHROP AND HIS MOTLEY ENTOURAGE OF COUNTER-REVOLUTIONARIES AND JOES!
LET'S GO PAY THEM A VISIT, SHALL WE?
CHARGE!!!
VIVA VILLAVACA!!
THEY'RE CHARGING US ACROSS ALL THAT OPEN GROUND! THEY MUST BE VERY BRAVE...
...OR EXTREMELY STUPID!

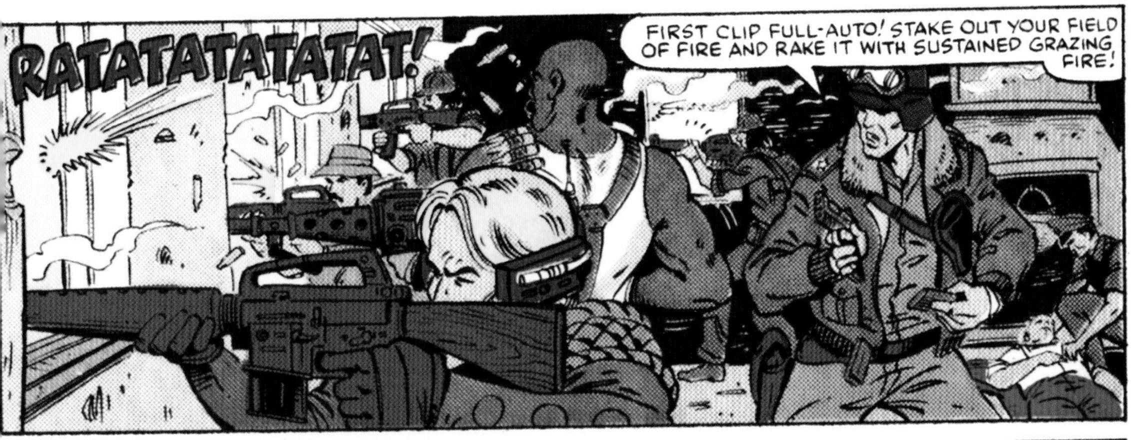
RATATATATATAT!
FIRST CLIP FULL-AUTO! STAKE OUT YOUR FIELD OF FIRE AND RAKE IT WITH SUSTAINED GRAZING FIRE!

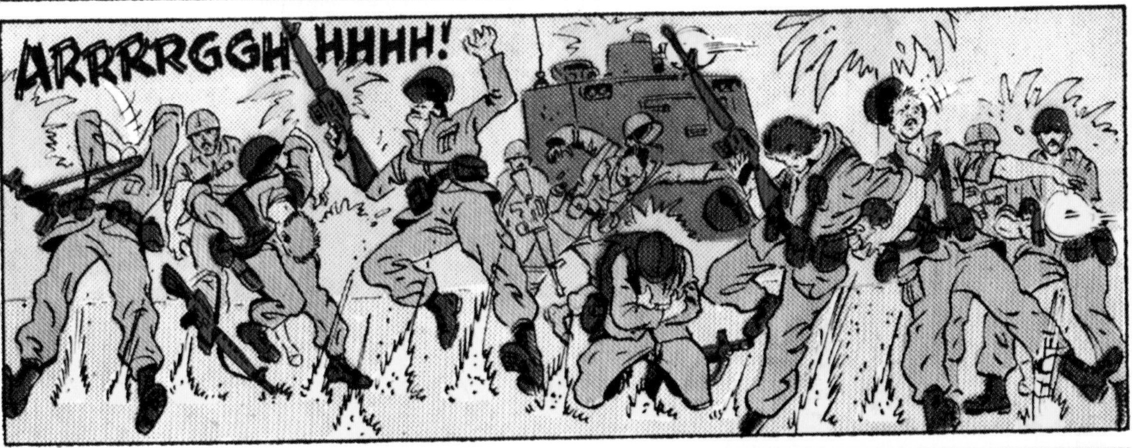
ARRRRGGH HHHH!

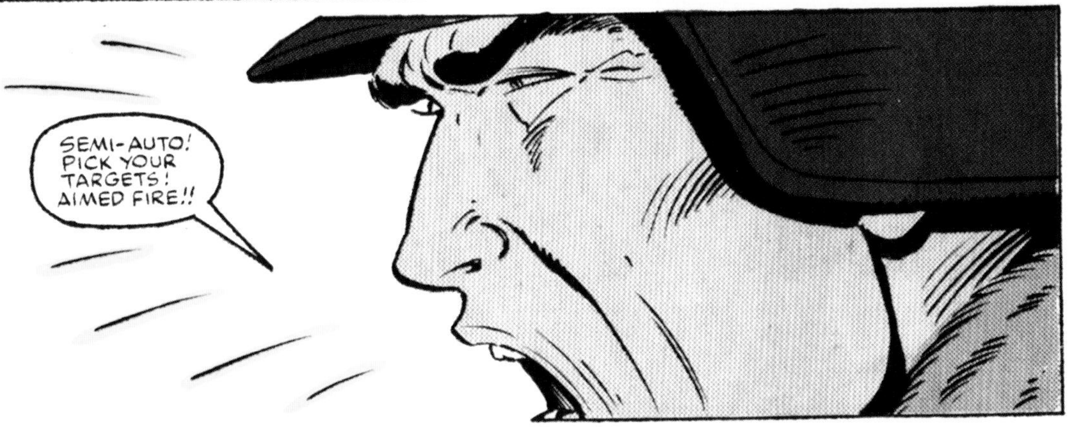
SEMI-AUTO! PICK YOUR TARGETS! AIMED FIRE!!

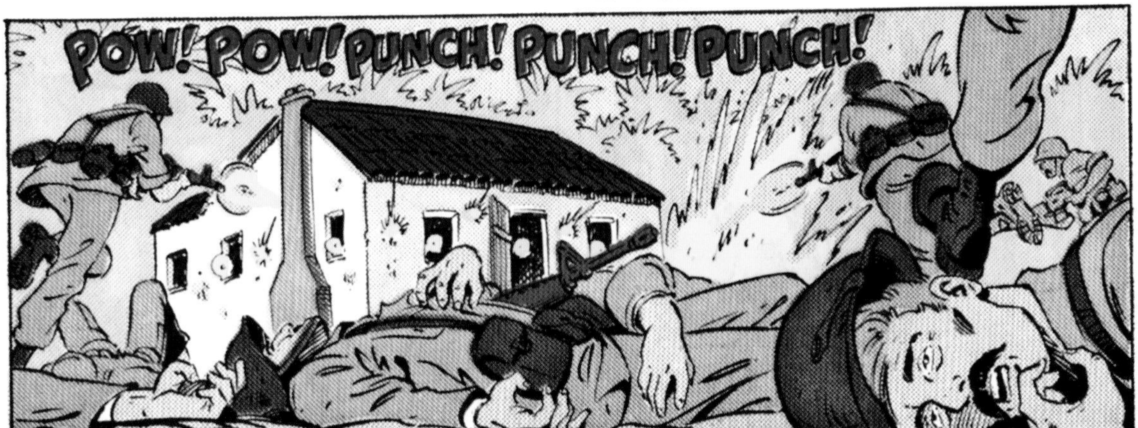
POW! POW! PUNCH! PUNCH! PUNCH!

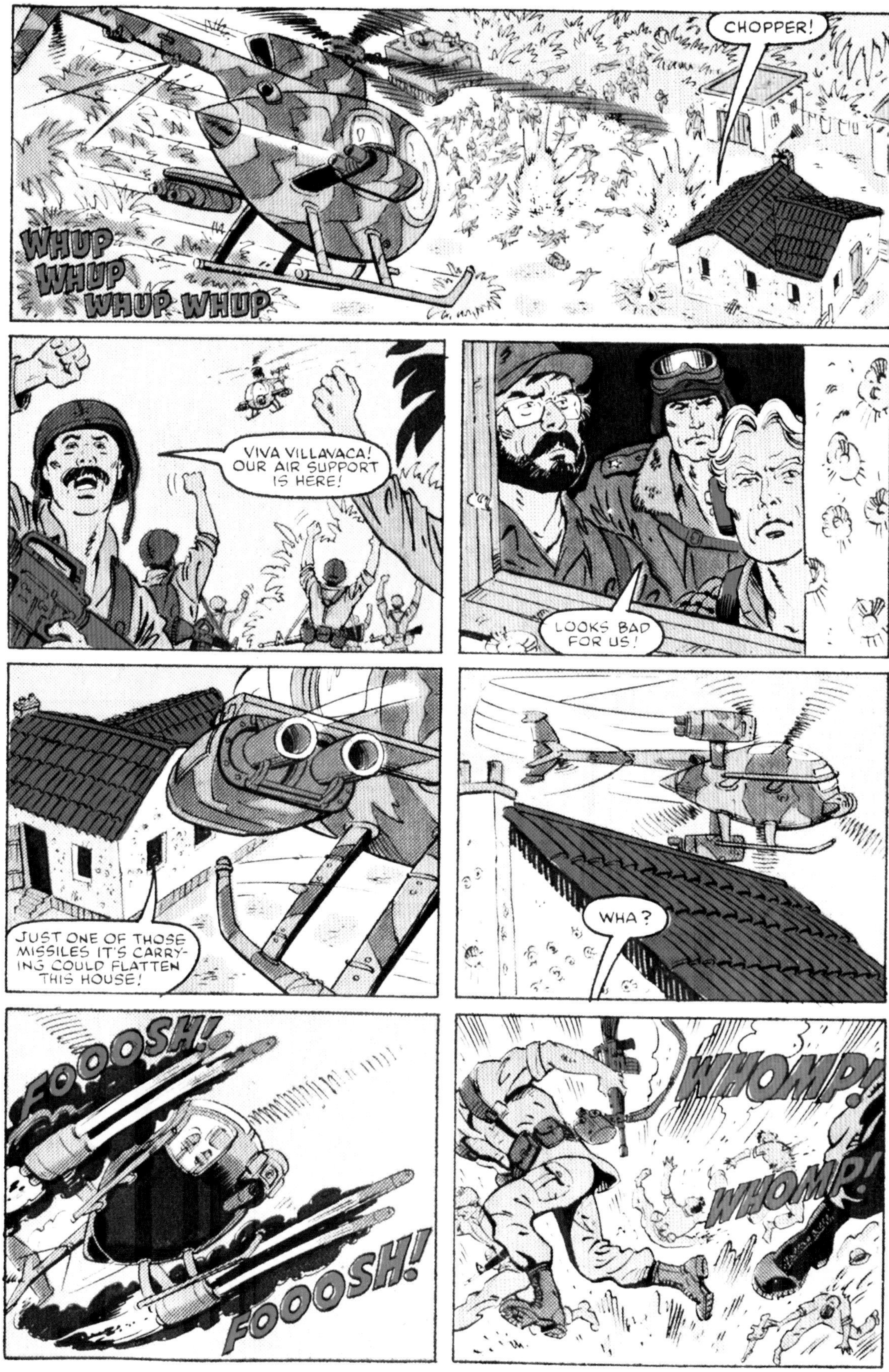
WHUP WHUP WHUP WHUP
CHOPPER!
VIVA VILLAVACA! OUR AIR SUPPORT IS HERE!
LOOKS BAD FOR US!
JUST ONE OF THOSE MISSILES IT'S CARRYING COULD FLATTEN THIS HOUSE!
WHA?
FOOOSH!
FOOOSH!
WHOMP!
WHOMP!

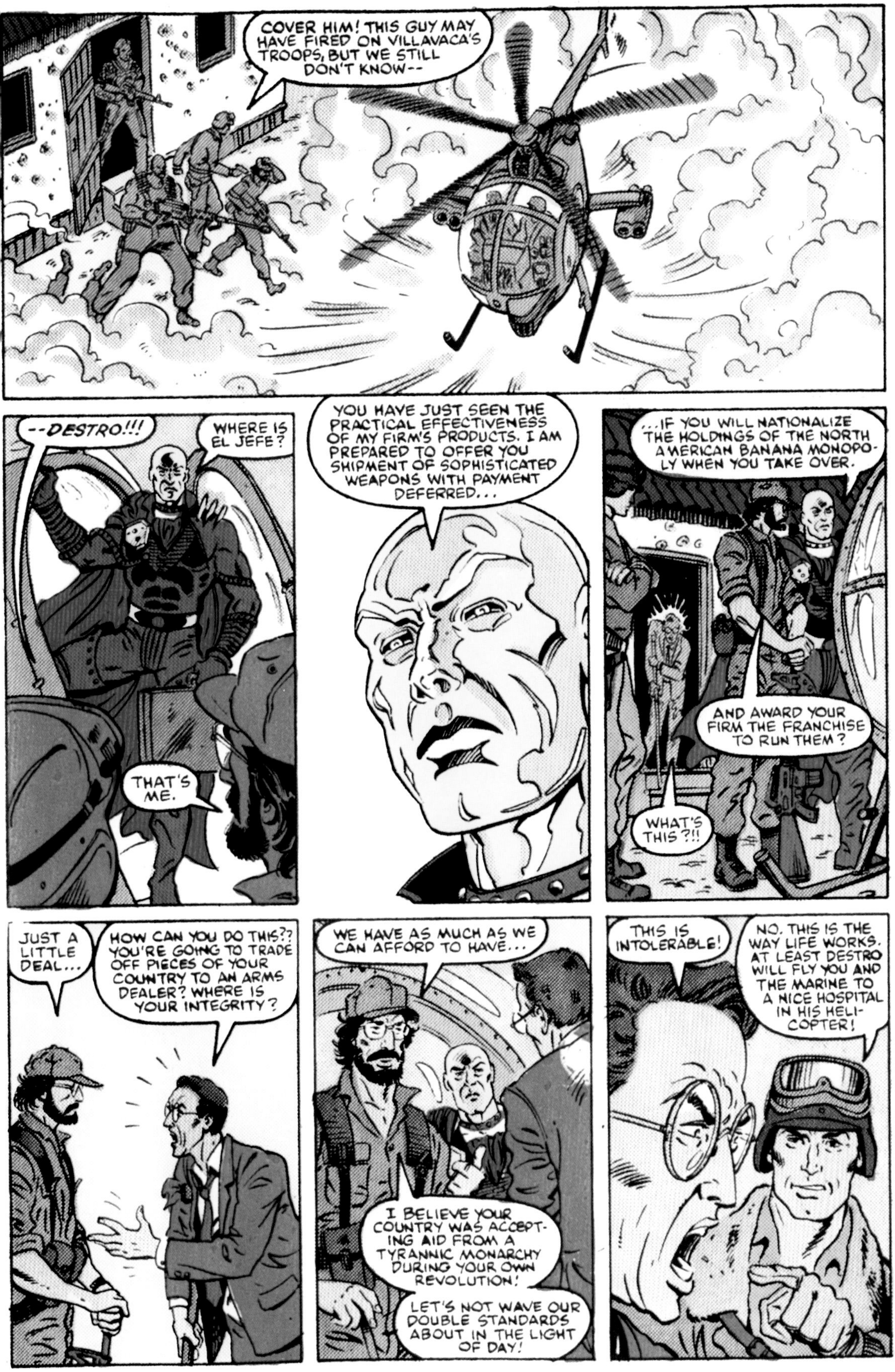

COVER HIM! THIS GUY MAY HAVE FIRED ON VILLAVACA'S TROOPS, BUT WE STILL DON'T KNOW--
--DESTRO!!!
WHERE IS EL JEFE?
THAT'S ME.
YOU HAVE JUST SEEN THE PRACTICAL EFFECTIVENESS OF MY FIRM'S PRODUCTS. I AM PREPARED TO OFFER YOU SHIPMENT OF SOPHISTICATED WEAPONS WITH PAYMENT DEFERRED...
...IF YOU WILL NATIONALIZE THE HOLDINGS OF THE NORTH AMERICAN BANANA MONOPOLY WHEN YOU TAKE OVER.
AND AWARD YOUR FIRM THE FRANCHISE TO RUN THEM?
WHAT'S THIS?!!
JUST A LITTLE DEAL...
HOW CAN YOU DO THIS?? YOU'RE GOING TO TRADE OFF PIECES OF YOUR COUNTRY TO AN ARMS DEALER? WHERE IS YOUR INTEGRITY?
WE HAVE AS MUCH AS WE CAN AFFORD TO HAVE...
I BELIEVE YOUR COUNTRY WAS ACCEPTING AID FROM A TYRANNIC MONARCHY DURING YOUR OWN REVOLUTION!
LET'S NOT WAVE OUR DOUBLE STANDARDS ABOUT IN THE LIGHT OF DAY!
THIS IS INTOLERABLE!
NO. THIS IS THE WAY LIFE WORKS. AT LEAST DESTRO WILL FLY YOU AND THE MARINE TO A NICE HOSPITAL IN HIS HELICOPTER!

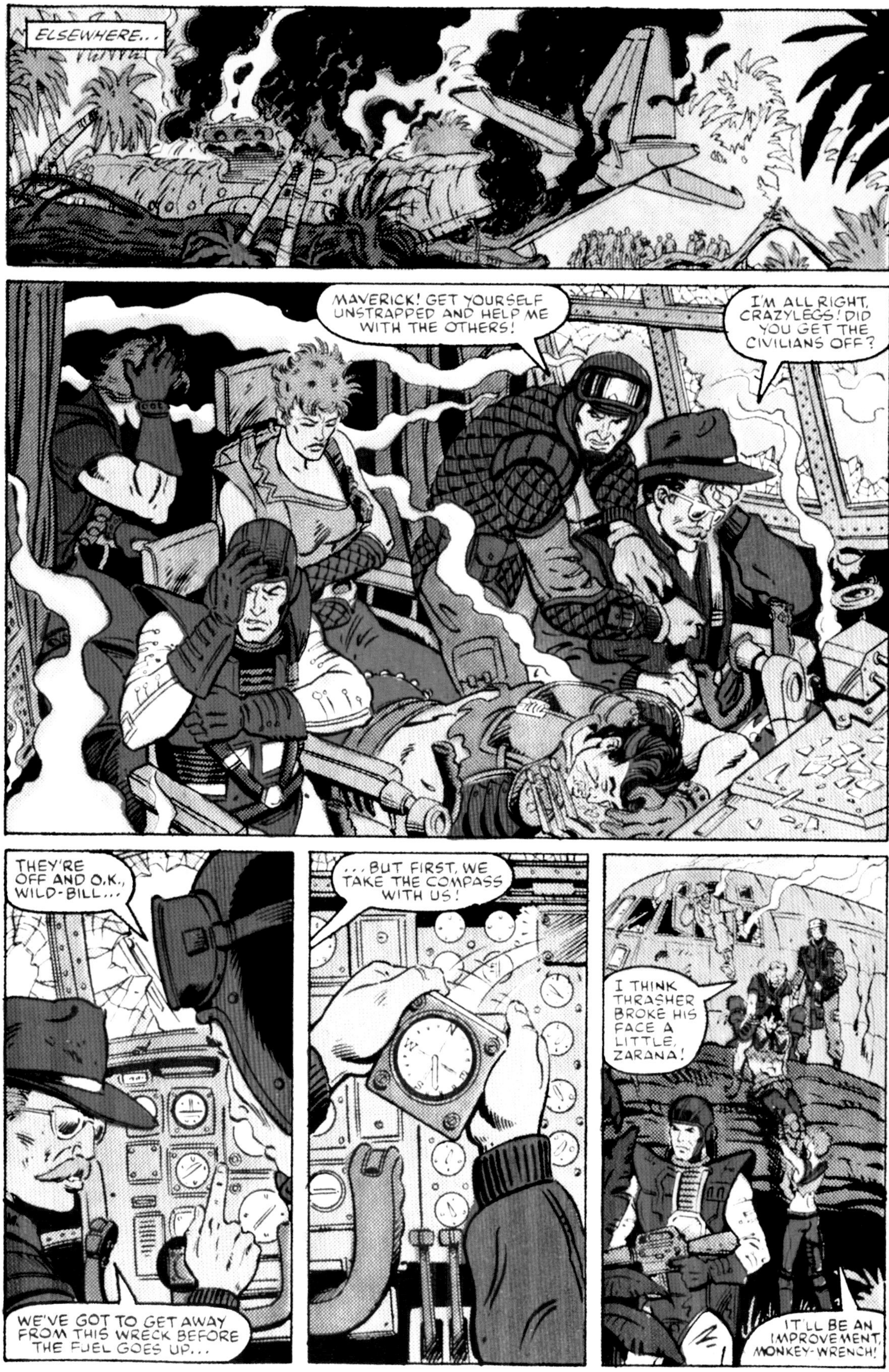
ELSEWHERE...
MAVERICK! GET YOURSELF UNSTRAPPED AND HELP ME WITH THE OTHERS!
I'M ALL RIGHT, CRAZYLEGS! DID YOU GET THE CIVILIANS OFF?
THEY'RE OFF AND O.K., WILD-BILL...
WE'VE GOT TO GET AWAY FROM THIS WRECK BEFORE THE FUEL GOES UP...
...BUT FIRST, WE TAKE THE COMPASS WITH US!
I THINK THRASHER BROKE HIS FACE A LITTLE, ZARANA!
IT'LL BE AN IMPROVEMENT, MONKEY-WRENCH!

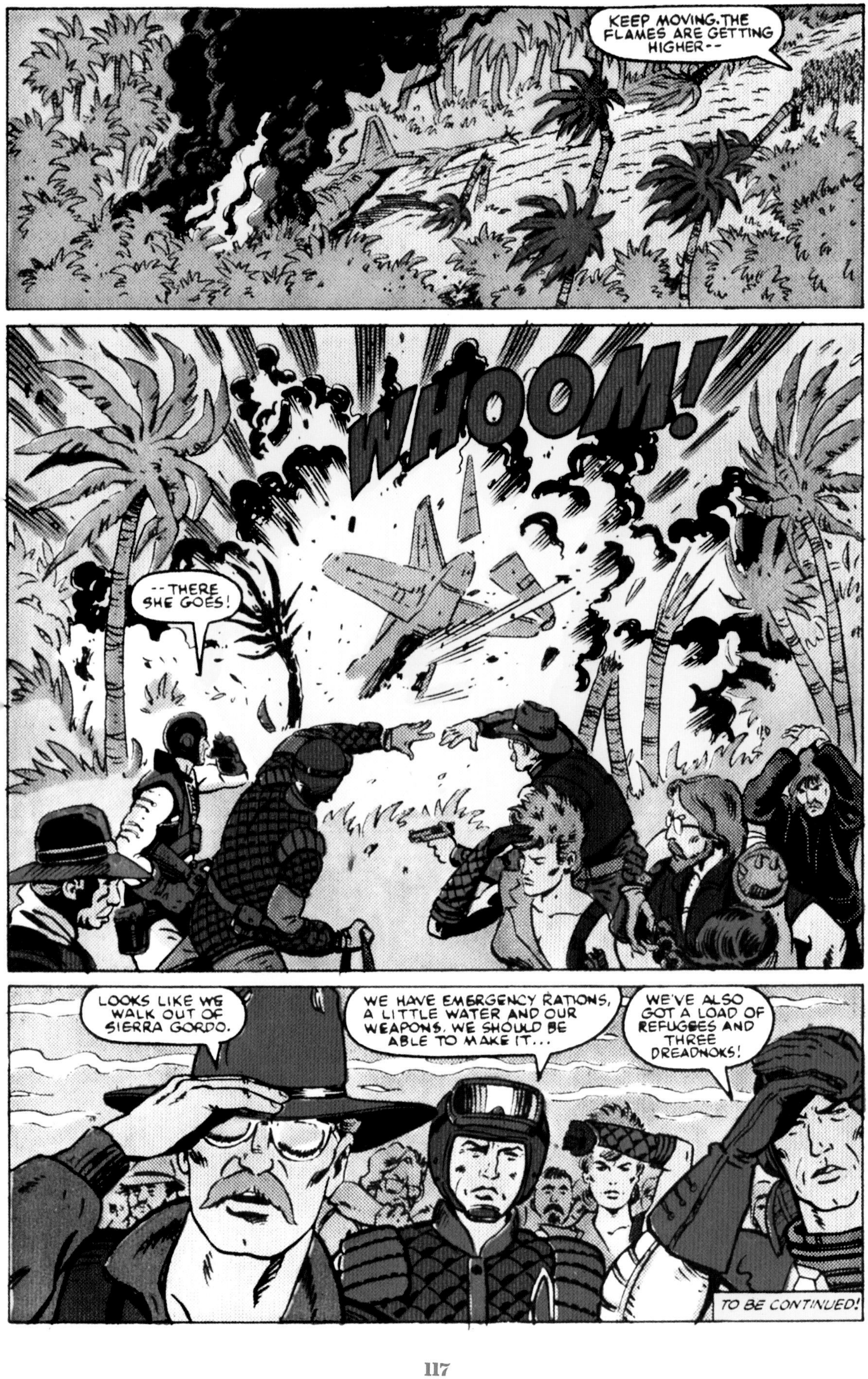
KEEP MOVING. THE FLAMES ARE GETTING HIGHER--
WHOOM!
--THERE SHE GOES!
LOOKS LIKE WE WALK OUT OF SIERRA GORDO.
WE HAVE EMERGENCY RATIONS, A LITTLE WATER AND OUR WEAPONS. WE SHOULD BE ABLE TO MAKE IT...
WE'VE ALSO GOT A LOAD OF REFUGEES AND THREE DREADNOKS!
TO BE CONTINUED!

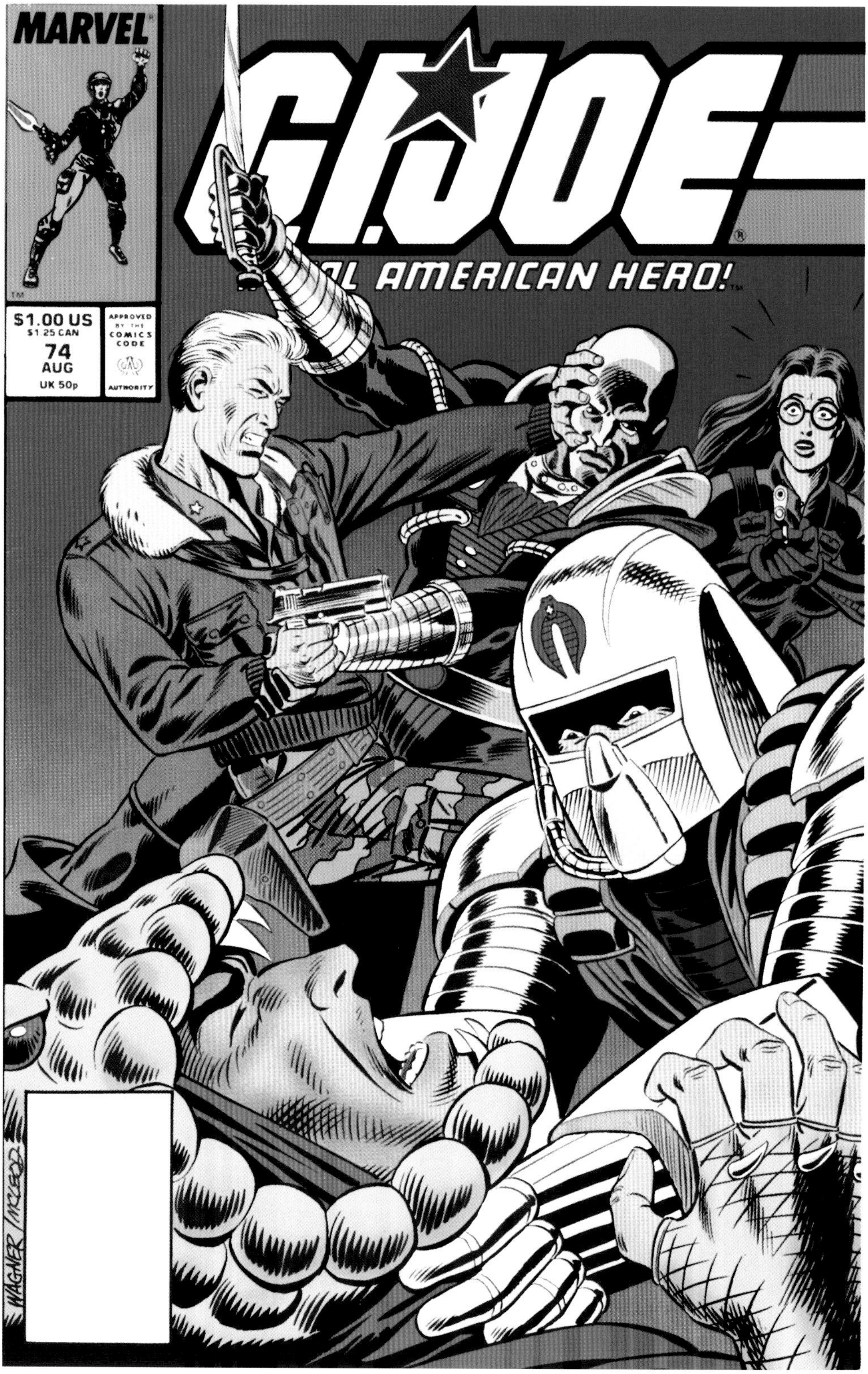
MARVEL
G.I. JOE
AL AMERICAN HERO!
$1.00 US
$1.25 CAN
74
AUG
UK 50p
APPROVED BY THE COMICS CODE AUTHORITY

ALLIANCE OF CONVENIENCE

ON COBRA ISLAND...

I DON'T SEE HOW THE BARONESS CAN KEEP THIS ASSAULT UP FOR MUCH LONGER, SNEAK-PEEK...

SHE'S NOT EVEN MAKING A DENT IN SERPENTOR'S DEFENSIVE LINE, LT. FALCON. WHY DOESN'T COBRA COMMANDER HAVE HER PULL BACK AND POUND THE FREIGHTER WITH ARTILLERY?

TOO MUCH EXPENSIVE HARDWARE ON THE FREIGHTER, INCLUDING THE COBRA SHUTTLE. THEY WANT TO TAKE IT AS INTACT AS POSSIBLE.

WHOEVER MADE THAT DECISION SURE WASN'T OUT THERE GETTING SHOT AT, SPIRIT!

| LARRY HAMA SCRIPT | RON WAGNER PENCILS | RANDY EMBERLIN INKS | BOB SHAREN COLOR | RICK PARKER LETTERS | BOBBIE CHASE EDITOR | TOM DeFALCO ED. IN CHIEF |

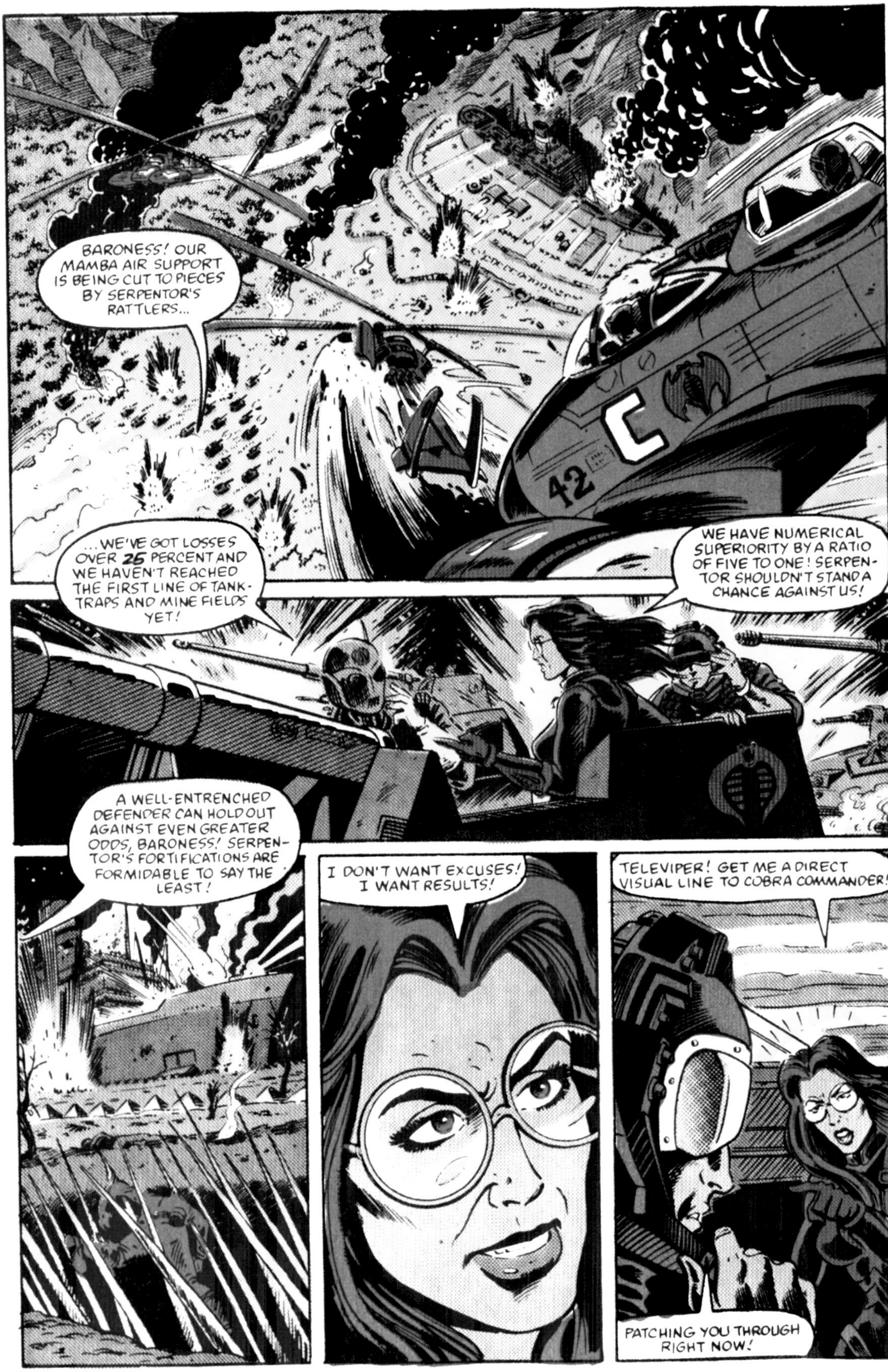
BARONESS! OUR MAMBA AIR SUPPORT IS BEING CUT TO PIECES BY SERPENTOR'S RATTLERS...
...WE'VE GOT LOSSES OVER 25 PERCENT AND WE HAVEN'T REACHED THE FIRST LINE OF TANK-TRAPS AND MINE FIELDS YET!
42
WE HAVE NUMERICAL SUPERIORITY BY A RATIO OF FIVE TO ONE! SERPENTOR SHOULDN'T STAND A CHANCE AGAINST US!
A WELL-ENTRENCHED DEFENDER CAN HOLD OUT AGAINST EVEN GREATER ODDS, BARONESS! SERPENTOR'S FORTIFICATIONS ARE FORMIDABLE TO SAY THE LEAST!
I DON'T WANT EXCUSES! I WANT RESULTS!
TELEVIPER! GET ME A DIRECT VISUAL LINE TO COBRA COMMANDER!
PATCHING YOU THROUGH RIGHT NOW!

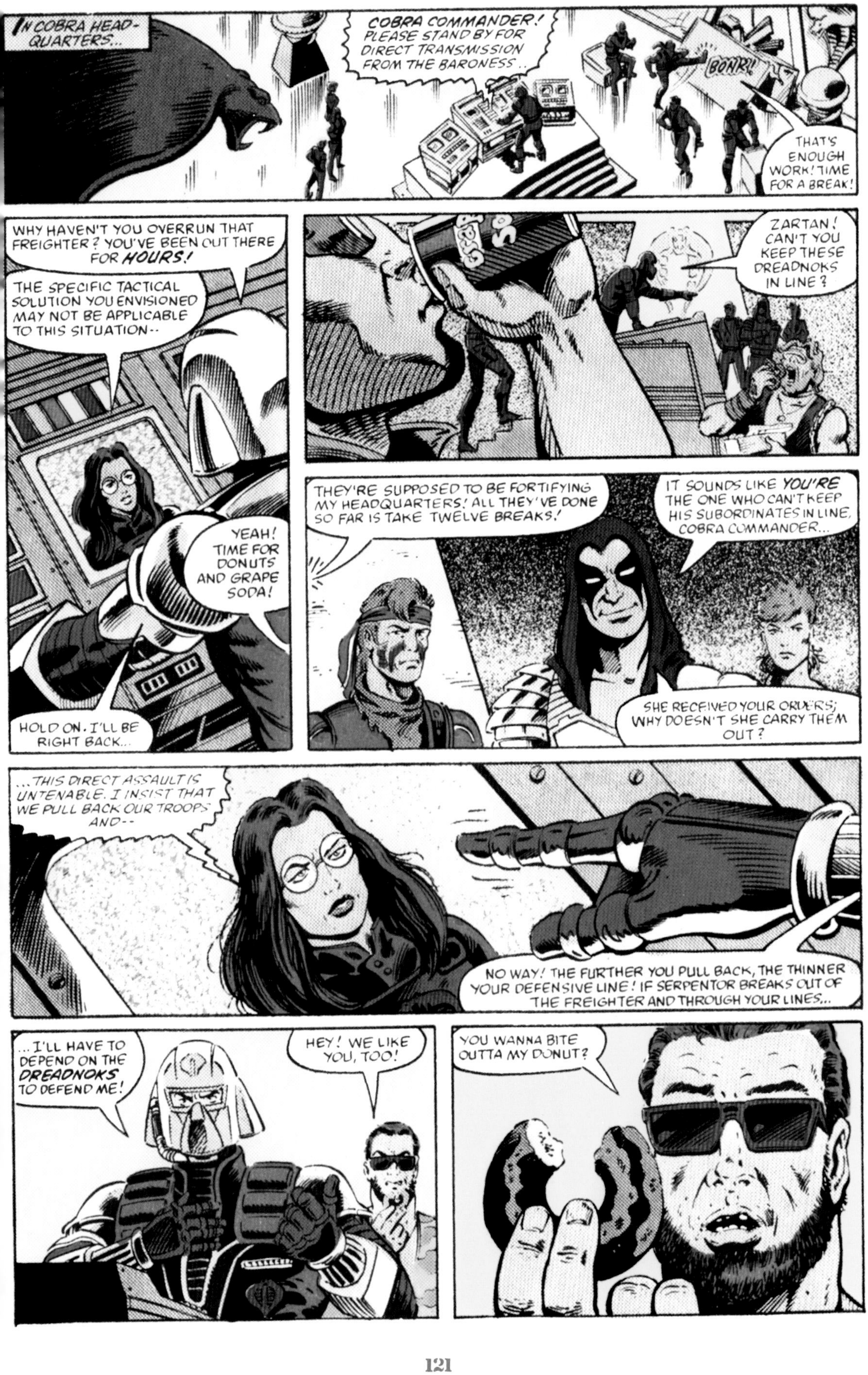
IN COBRA HEAD-QUARTERS...
COBRA COMMANDER! PLEASE STAND BY FOR DIRECT TRANSMISSION FROM THE BARONESS...
BONK!
THAT'S ENOUGH WORK! TIME FOR A BREAK!
WHY HAVEN'T YOU OVERRUN THAT FREIGHTER? YOU'VE BEEN OUT THERE FOR HOURS!
THE SPECIFIC TACTICAL SOLUTION YOU ENVISIONED MAY NOT BE APPLICABLE TO THIS SITUATION--
YEAH! TIME FOR DONUTS AND GRAPE SODA!
HOLD ON. I'LL BE RIGHT BACK...
ZARTAN! CAN'T YOU KEEP THESE DREADNOKS IN LINE?
THEY'RE SUPPOSED TO BE FORTIFYING MY HEADQUARTERS! ALL THEY'VE DONE SO FAR IS TAKE TWELVE BREAKS!
IT SOUNDS LIKE YOU'RE THE ONE WHO CAN'T KEEP HIS SUBORDINATES IN LINE, COBRA COMMANDER...
SHE RECEIVED YOUR ORDERS; WHY DOESN'T SHE CARRY THEM OUT?
...THIS DIRECT ASSAULT IS UNTENABLE. I INSIST THAT WE PULL BACK OUR TROOPS AND--
NO WAY! THE FURTHER YOU PULL BACK, THE THINNER YOUR DEFENSIVE LINE! IF SERPENTOR BREAKS OUT OF THE FREIGHTER AND THROUGH YOUR LINES...
...I'LL HAVE TO DEPEND ON THE DREADNOKS TO DEFEND ME!
HEY! WE LIKE YOU, TOO!
YOU WANNA BITE OUTTA MY DONUT?

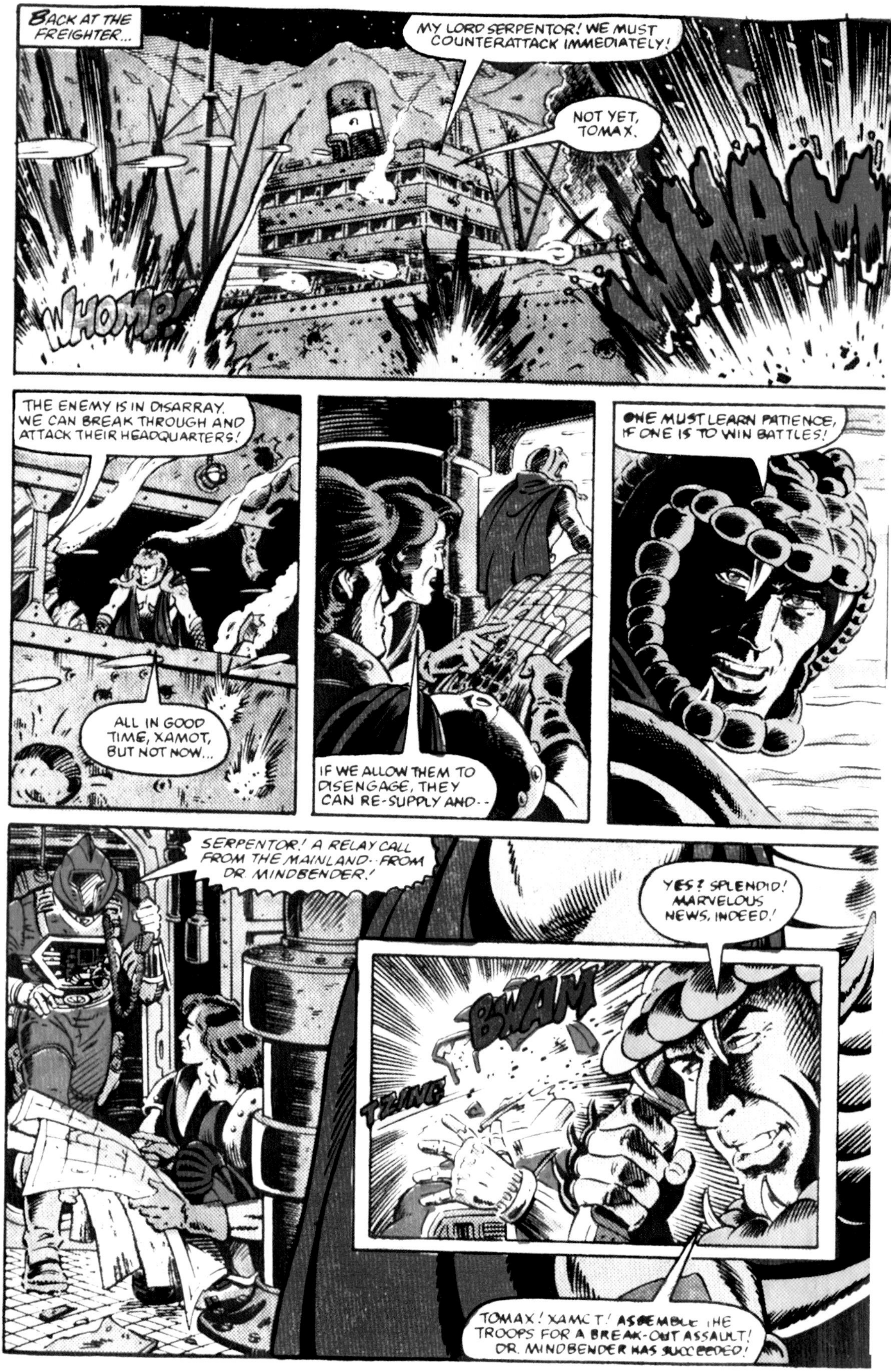
BACK AT THE FREIGHTER...
MY LORD SERPENTOR! WE MUST COUNTERATTACK IMMEDIATELY!
NOT YET, TOMAX.
WHOMP!
WHAM
THE ENEMY IS IN DISARRAY. WE CAN BREAK THROUGH AND ATTACK THEIR HEADQUARTERS!
ALL IN GOOD TIME, XAMOT, BUT NOT NOW...
IF WE ALLOW THEM TO DISENGAGE, THEY CAN RE-SUPPLY AND--
ONE MUST LEARN PATIENCE, IF ONE IS TO WIN BATTLES!
SERPENTOR! A RELAY CALL FROM THE MAINLAND--FROM DR. MINDBENDER!
YES? SPLENDID! MARVELOUS NEWS, INDEED!
BWAM
TZING!
TOMAX! XAMOT! ASSEMBLE THE TROOPS FOR A BREAK-OUT ASSAULT! DR. MINDBENDER HAS SUCCEEDED!

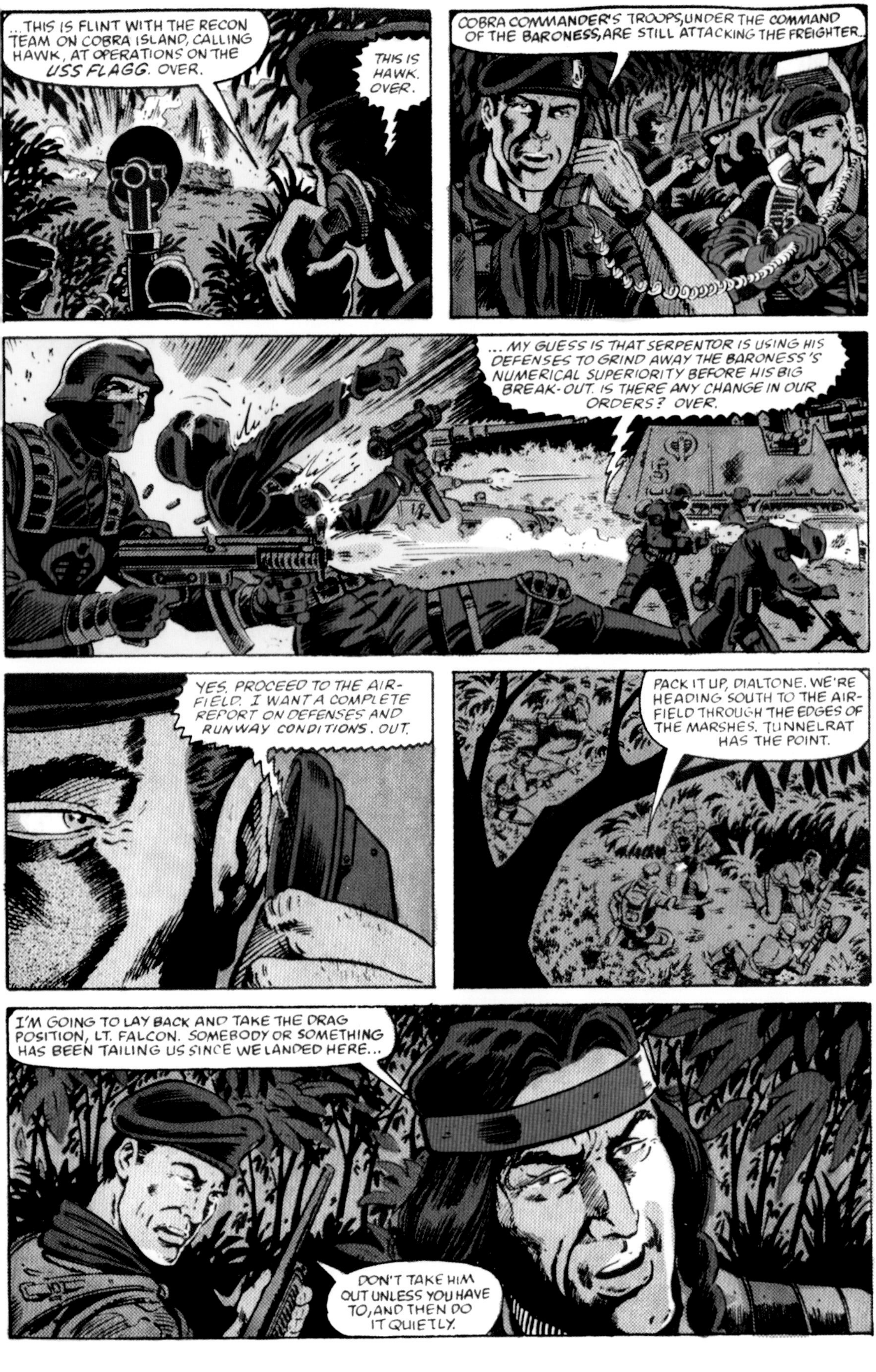
...THIS IS FLINT WITH THE RECON TEAM ON COBRA ISLAND, CALLING HAWK, AT OPERATIONS ON THE USS FLAGG. OVER.
THIS IS HAWK. OVER.
COBRA COMMANDER'S TROOPS, UNDER THE COMMAND OF THE BARONESS, ARE STILL ATTACKING THE FREIGHTER...
... MY GUESS IS THAT SERPENTOR IS USING HIS DEFENSES TO GRIND AWAY THE BARONESS'S NUMERICAL SUPERIORITY BEFORE HIS BIG BREAK-OUT. IS THERE ANY CHANGE IN OUR ORDERS? OVER.
YES. PROCEED TO THE AIR-FIELD. I WANT A COMPLETE REPORT ON DEFENSES AND RUNWAY CONDITIONS. OUT.
PACK IT UP, DIALTONE. WE'RE HEADING SOUTH TO THE AIR-FIELD THROUGH THE EDGES OF THE MARSHES. TUNNELRAT HAS THE POINT.
I'M GOING TO LAY BACK AND TAKE THE DRAG POSITION, LT. FALCON. SOMEBODY OR SOMETHING HAS BEEN TAILING US SINCE WE LANDED HERE...
DON'T TAKE HIM OUT UNLESS YOU HAVE TO, AND THEN DO IT QUIETLY.

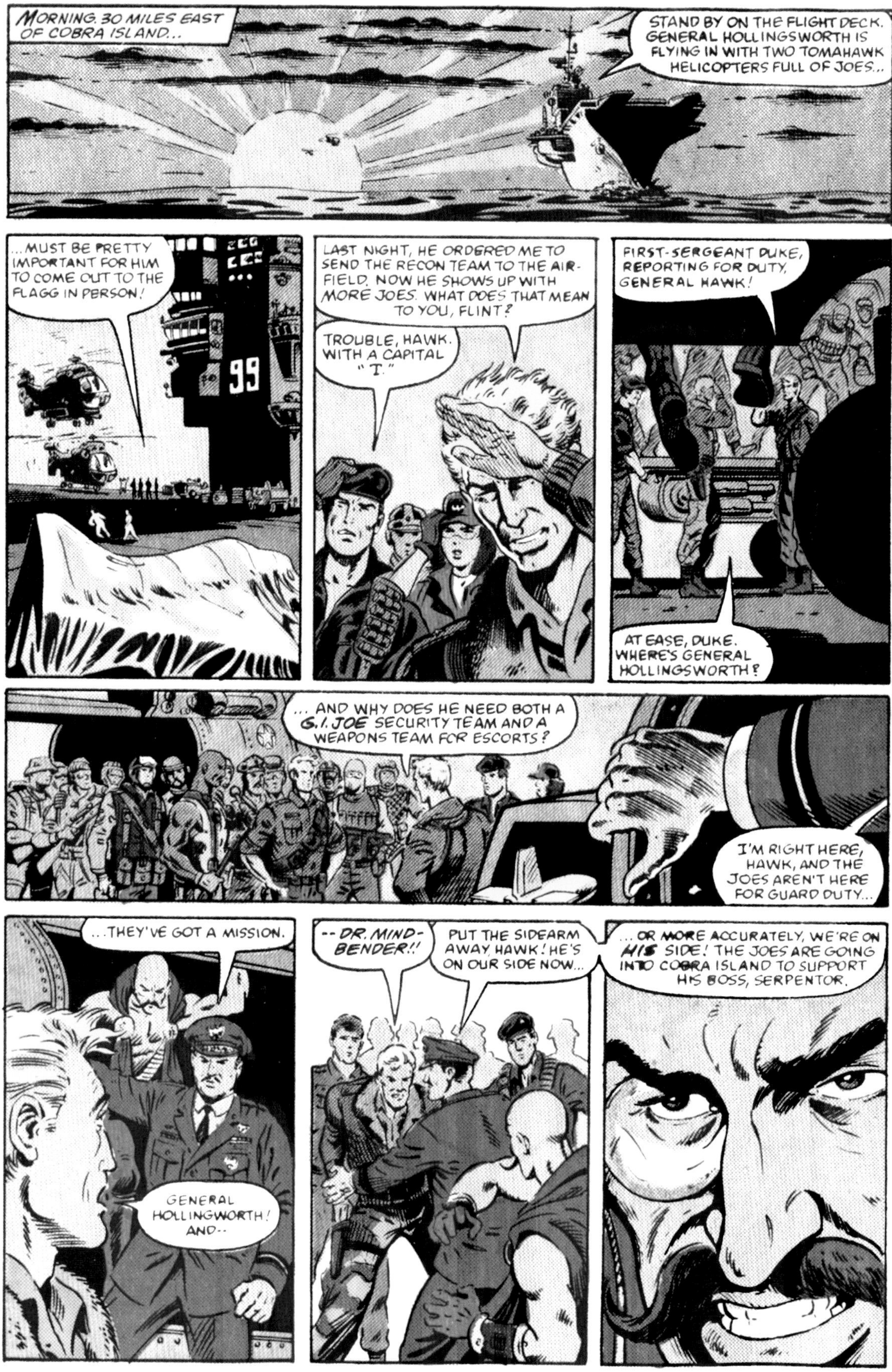
MORNING. 30 MILES EAST OF COBRA ISLAND...
STAND BY ON THE FLIGHT DECK. GENERAL HOLLINGSWORTH IS FLYING IN WITH TWO TOMAHAWK HELICOPTERS FULL OF JOES...
...MUST BE PRETTY IMPORTANT FOR HIM TO COME OUT TO THE FLAGG IN PERSON!
99
LAST NIGHT, HE ORDERED ME TO SEND THE RECON TEAM TO THE AIR-FIELD. NOW HE SHOWS UP WITH MORE JOES. WHAT DOES THAT MEAN TO YOU, FLINT?
TROUBLE, HAWK. WITH A CAPITAL "T."
FIRST-SERGEANT DUKE, REPORTING FOR DUTY, GENERAL HAWK!
AT EASE, DUKE. WHERE'S GENERAL HOLLINGSWORTH?
... AND WHY DOES HE NEED BOTH A G.I. JOE SECURITY TEAM AND A WEAPONS TEAM FOR ESCORTS?
I'M RIGHT HERE, HAWK, AND THE JOES AREN'T HERE FOR GUARD DUTY...
...THEY'VE GOT A MISSION.
GENERAL HOLLINGWORTH! AND--
--DR. MIND-BENDER!!
PUT THE SIDEARM AWAY, HAWK! HE'S ON OUR SIDE NOW...
...OR MORE ACCURATELY, WE'RE ON HIS SIDE! THE JOES ARE GOING INTO COBRA ISLAND TO SUPPORT HIS BOSS, SERPENTOR.

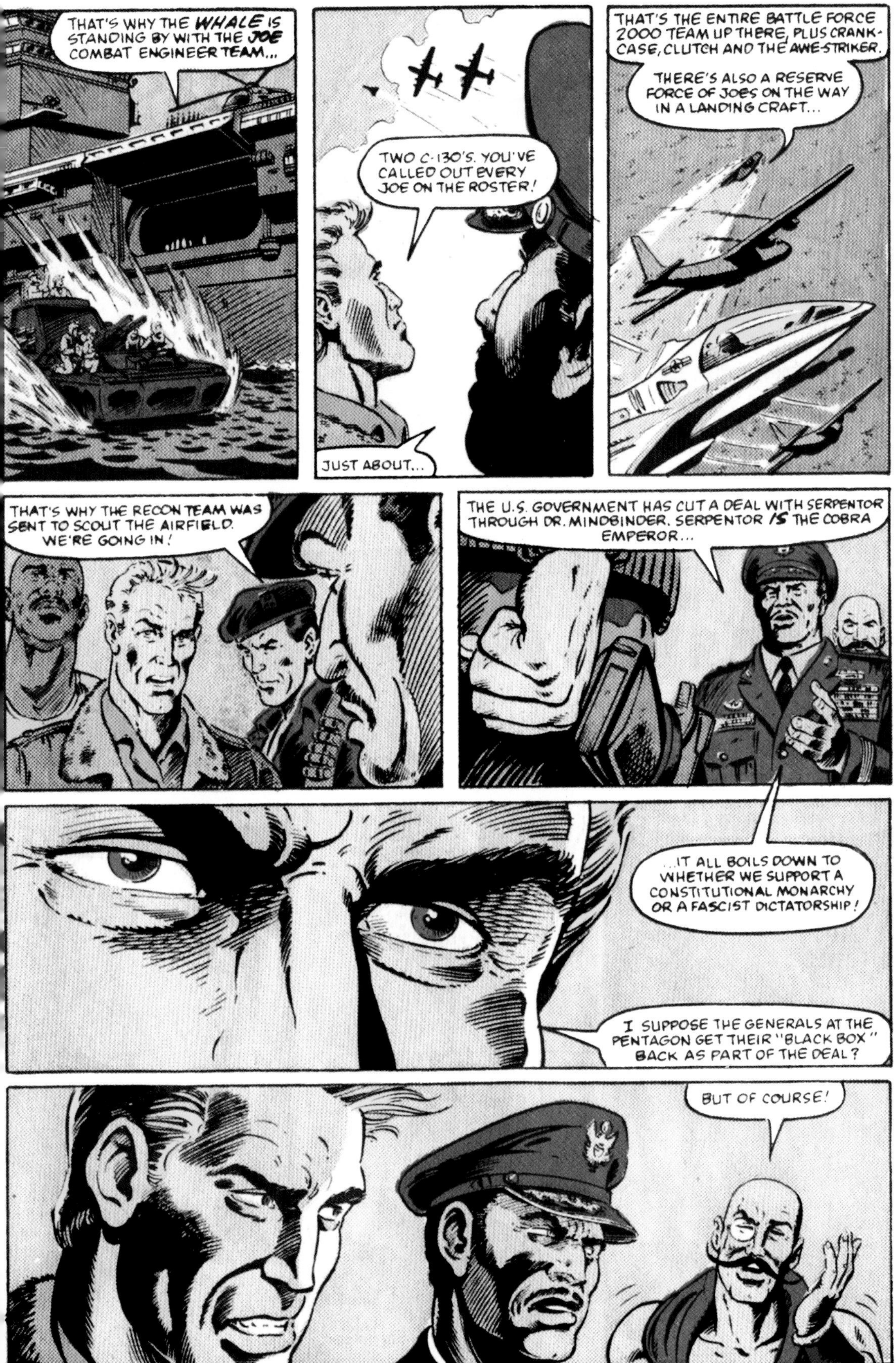

THAT'S WHY THE WHALE IS STANDING BY WITH THE JOE COMBAT ENGINEER TEAM...
TWO C-130'S. YOU'VE CALLED OUT EVERY JOE ON THE ROSTER!
JUST ABOUT...
THAT'S THE ENTIRE BATTLE FORCE 2000 TEAM UP THERE, PLUS CRANK-CASE, CLUTCH AND THE AWE-STRIKER.
THERE'S ALSO A RESERVE FORCE OF JOES ON THE WAY IN A LANDING CRAFT...
THAT'S WHY THE RECON TEAM WAS SENT TO SCOUT THE AIRFIELD. WE'RE GOING IN!
THE U.S. GOVERNMENT HAS CUT A DEAL WITH SERPENTOR THROUGH DR. MINDBINDER. SERPENTOR IS THE COBRA EMPEROR...
...IT ALL BOILS DOWN TO WHETHER WE SUPPORT A CONSTITUTIONAL MONARCHY OR A FASCIST DICTATORSHIP!
I SUPPOSE THE GENERALS AT THE PENTAGON GET THEIR "BLACK BOX" BACK AS PART OF THE DEAL?
BUT OF COURSE!

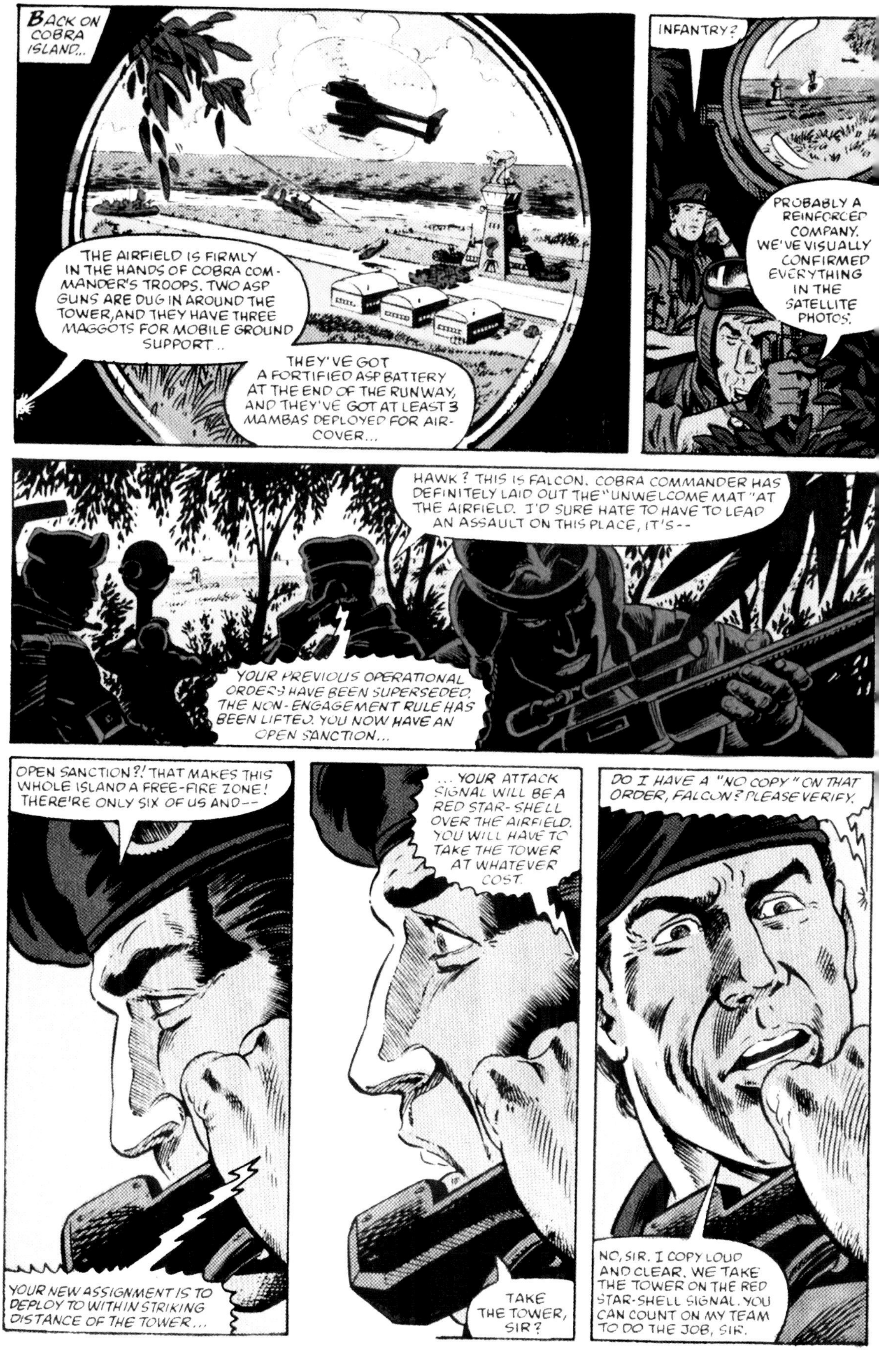
BACK ON COBRA ISLAND...
THE AIRFIELD IS FIRMLY IN THE HANDS OF COBRA COMMANDER'S TROOPS. TWO ASP GUNS ARE DUG IN AROUND THE TOWER, AND THEY HAVE THREE MAGGOTS FOR MOBILE GROUND SUPPORT...
THEY'VE GOT A FORTIFIED ASP BATTERY AT THE END OF THE RUNWAY, AND THEY'VE GOT AT LEAST 3 MAMBAS DEPLOYED FOR AIR-COVER...
INFANTRY?
PROBABLY A REINFORCED COMPANY. WE'VE VISUALLY CONFIRMED EVERYTHING IN THE SATELLITE PHOTOS.
HAWK? THIS IS FALCON. COBRA COMMANDER HAS DEFINITELY LAID OUT THE "UNWELCOME MAT" AT THE AIRFIELD. I'D SURE HATE TO HAVE TO LEAD AN ASSAULT ON THIS PLACE, IT'S--
YOUR PREVIOUS OPERATIONAL ORDERS HAVE BEEN SUPERSEDED. THE NON-ENGAGEMENT RULE HAS BEEN LIFTED. YOU NOW HAVE AN OPEN SANCTION...
OPEN SANCTION?! THAT MAKES THIS WHOLE ISLAND A FREE-FIRE ZONE! THERE'RE ONLY SIX OF US AND--
YOUR NEW ASSIGNMENT IS TO DEPLOY TO WITHIN STRIKING DISTANCE OF THE TOWER...
...YOUR ATTACK SIGNAL WILL BE A RED STAR-SHELL OVER THE AIRFIELD. YOU WILL HAVE TO TAKE THE TOWER AT WHATEVER COST.
TAKE THE TOWER, SIR?
DO I HAVE A "NO COPY" ON THAT ORDER, FALCON? PLEASE VERIFY.
NO, SIR. I COPY LOUD AND CLEAR. WE TAKE THE TOWER ON THE RED STAR-SHELL SIGNAL. YOU CAN COUNT ON MY TEAM TO DO THE JOB, SIR.

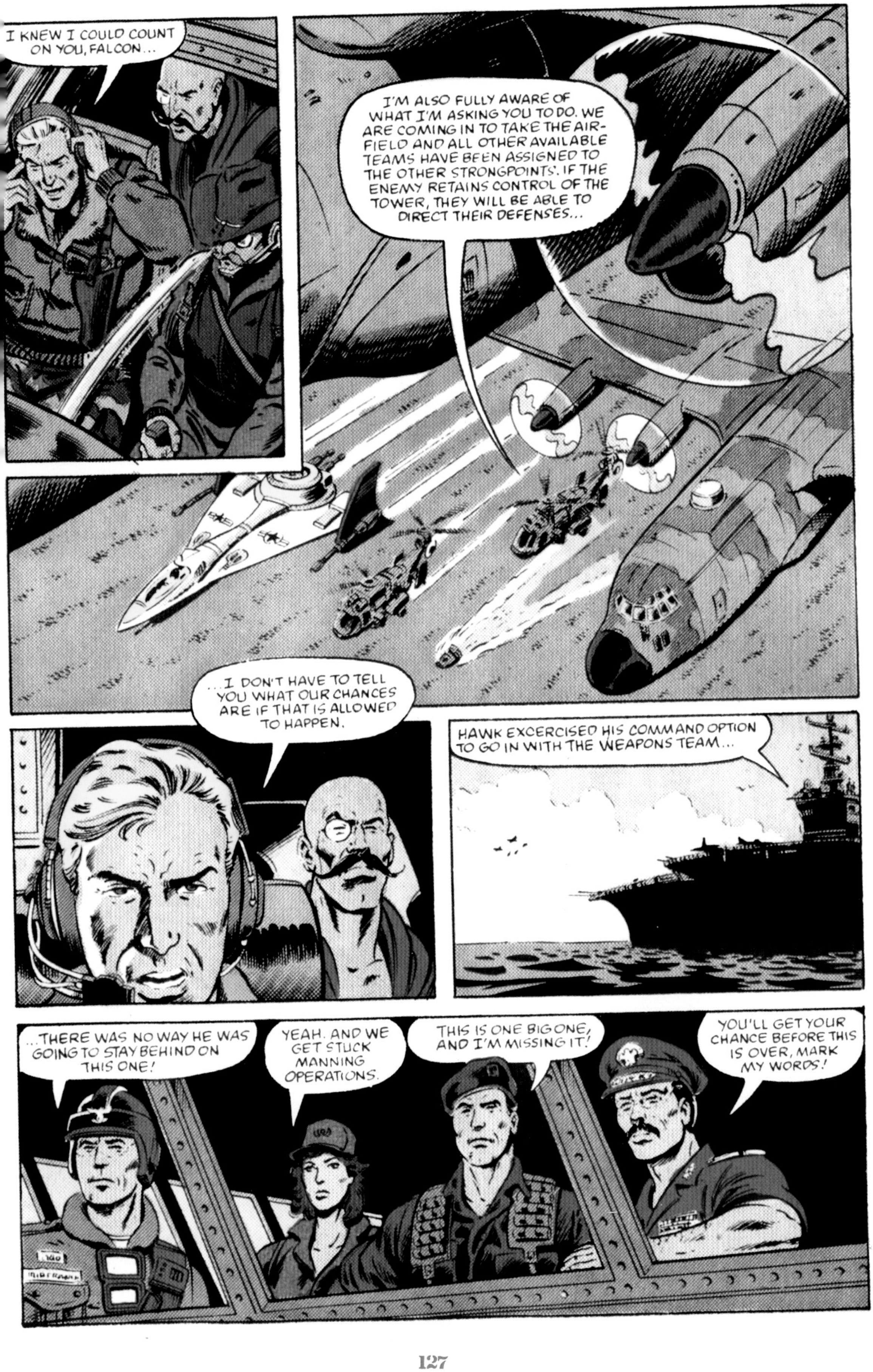
I KNEW I COULD COUNT ON YOU, FALCON...
I'M ALSO FULLY AWARE OF WHAT I'M ASKING YOU TO DO. WE ARE COMING IN TO TAKE THE AIR-FIELD AND ALL OTHER AVAILABLE TEAMS HAVE BEEN ASSIGNED TO THE OTHER STRONGPOINTS. IF THE ENEMY RETAINS CONTROL OF THE TOWER, THEY WILL BE ABLE TO DIRECT THEIR DEFENSES...
...I DON'T HAVE TO TELL YOU WHAT OUR CHANCES ARE IF THAT IS ALLOWED TO HAPPEN.
HAWK EXCERCISED HIS COMMAND OPTION TO GO IN WITH THE WEAPONS TEAM...
...THERE WAS NO WAY HE WAS GOING TO STAY BEHIND ON THIS ONE!
YEAH. AND WE GET STUCK MANNING OPERATIONS.
THIS IS ONE BIG ONE, AND I'M MISSING IT!
YOU'LL GET YOUR CHANCE BEFORE THIS IS OVER, MARK MY WORDS!

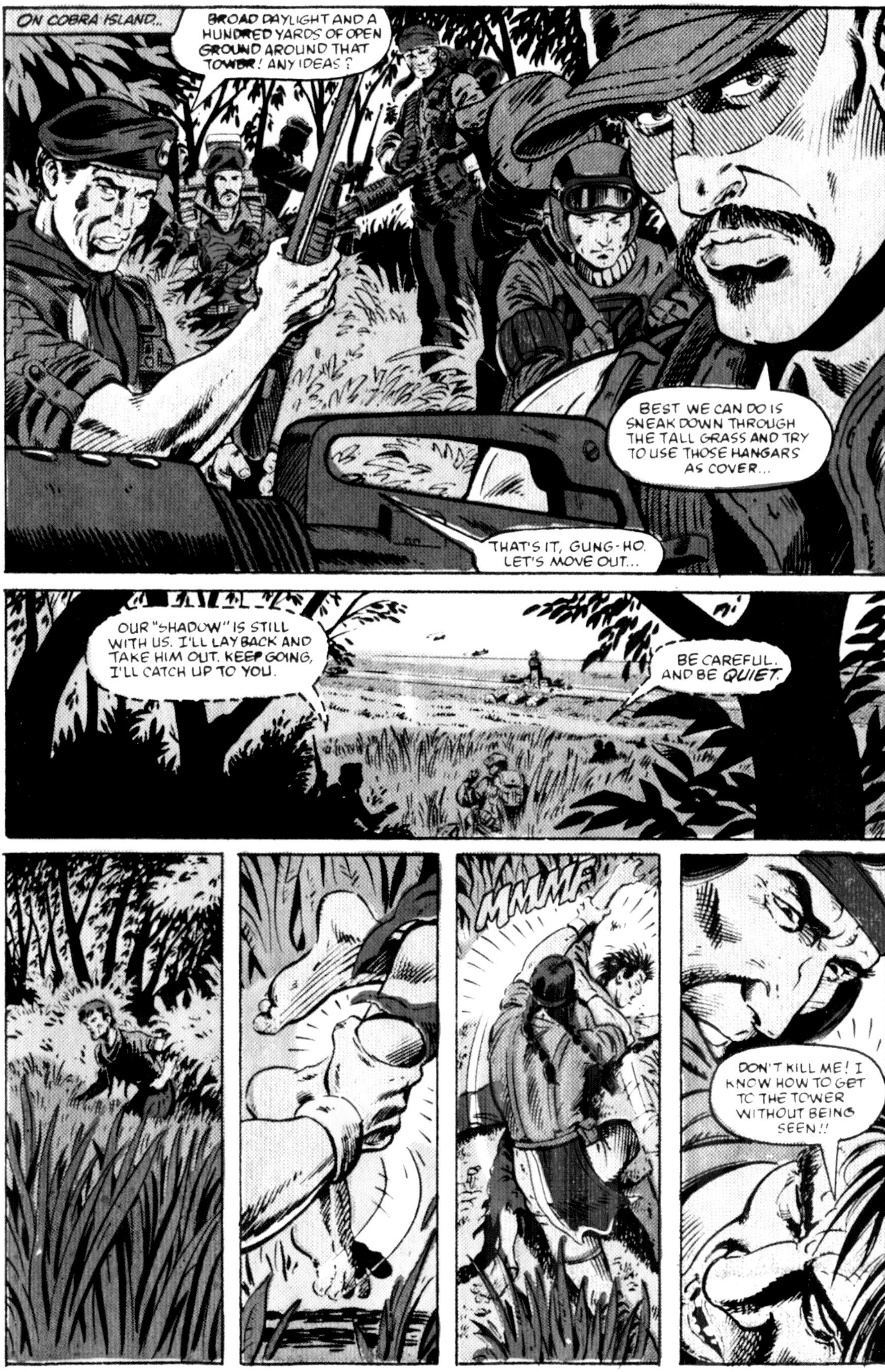
ON COBRA ISLAND...
BROAD DAYLIGHT AND A HUNDRED YARDS OF OPEN GROUND AROUND THAT TOWER! ANY IDEAS?
BEST WE CAN DO IS SNEAK DOWN THROUGH THE TALL GRASS AND TRY TO USE THOSE HANGARS AS COVER...
THAT'S IT, GUNG-HO. LET'S MOVE OUT...
OUR "SHADOW" IS STILL WITH US. I'LL LAY BACK AND TAKE HIM OUT. KEEP GOING, I'LL CATCH UP TO YOU.
BE CAREFUL. AND BE QUIET.
MMMF
DON'T KILL ME! I KNOW HOW TO GET TO THE TOWER WITHOUT BEING SEEN!!

NOTHING'S COMING OUT TO MEET US! IS THIS A TRAP?

THEY'RE EXPECTING TROUBLE FROM THE OPPOSITE DIRECTION: INLAND, FROM SERPENTOR'S FORCES!

I GO IN FIRST WITH THE WEAPONS TEAM, DUKE FOLLOWS WITH THE SECURITY TEAM. WE KNOCK OUT THE MAIN AIRFIELD DEFENSES.

I HEAR YOU, HAWK THE SECURITY TEAM BACKS UP YOUR ASSAULT.

CUTTER AND THE ENGINEER TEAM DEPLOY FROM THE **WHALE** AND TAKE OUT THE **ASP** EMPLACEMENTS AT THE END OF THE RUNWAY...

LOCK AND LOAD! GUNNERS, TEST YOUR WEAPONS!

FOOOMP!

GIVE 'EM THE RED STAR-SHELL, SHIPWRECK!

TRIPWIRE AND SHORT-FUSE, STAND-BY WITH THE SATCHEL CHARGES!

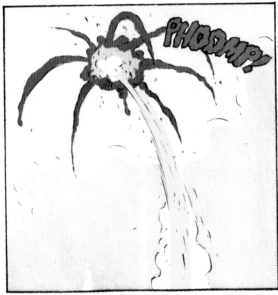

PHOOMP!

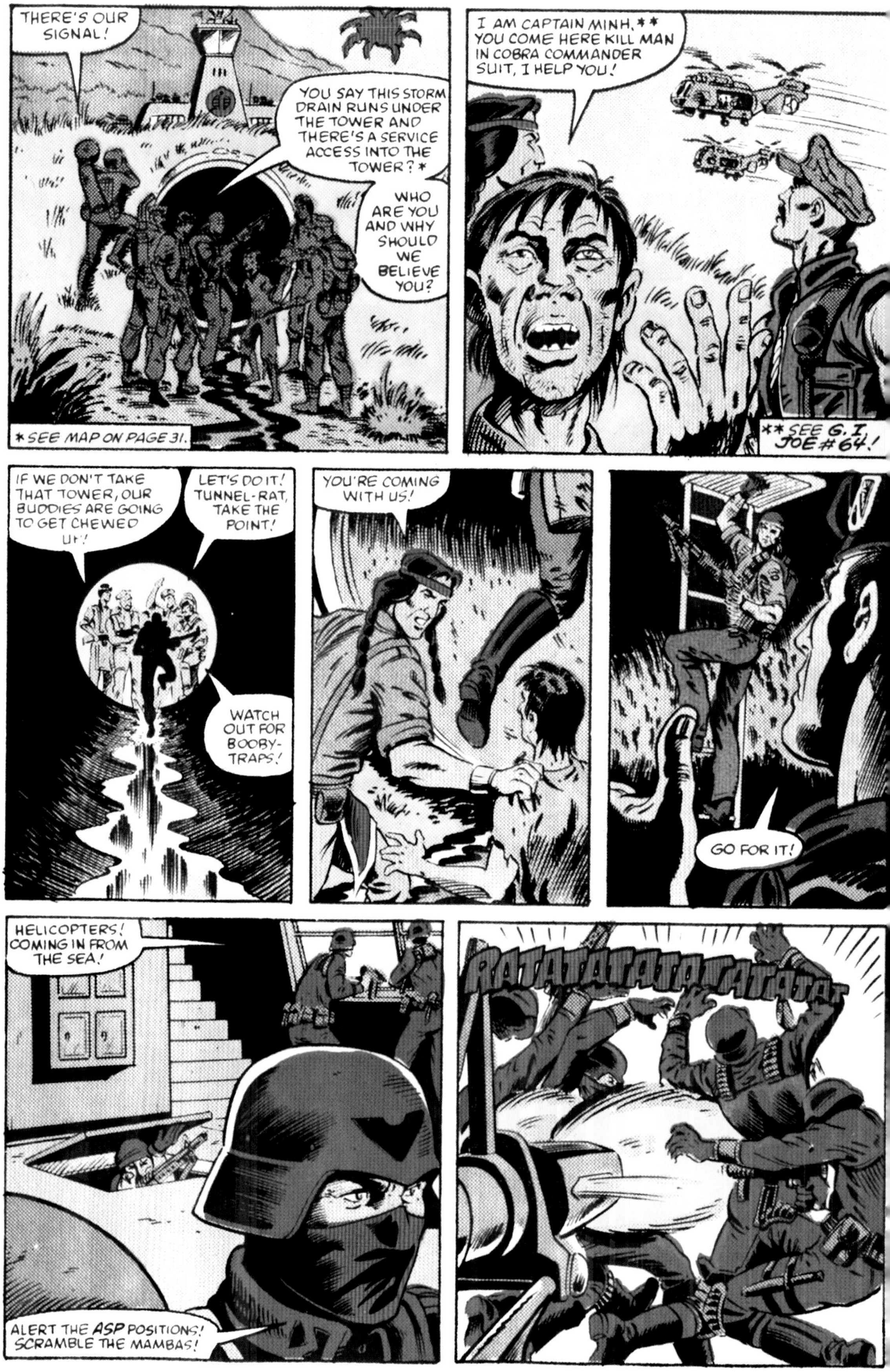
THERE'S OUR SIGNAL!
YOU SAY THIS STORM DRAIN RUNS UNDER THE TOWER AND THERE'S A SERVICE ACCESS INTO THE TOWER? *
WHO ARE YOU AND WHY SHOULD WE BELIEVE YOU?
* SEE MAP ON PAGE 31.
I AM CAPTAIN MINH, ** YOU COME HERE KILL MAN IN COBRA COMMANDER SUIT, I HELP YOU!
** SEE G.I. JOE #64!
IF WE DON'T TAKE THAT TOWER, OUR BUDDIES ARE GOING TO GET CHEWED UP!
LET'S DO IT! TUNNEL-RAT, TAKE THE POINT!
WATCH OUT FOR BOOBY-TRAPS!
YOU'RE COMING WITH US!
GO FOR IT!
HELICOPTERS! COMING IN FROM THE SEA!
ALERT THE ASP POSITIONS! SCRAMBLE THE MAMBAS!
RATATATATATATATATAT

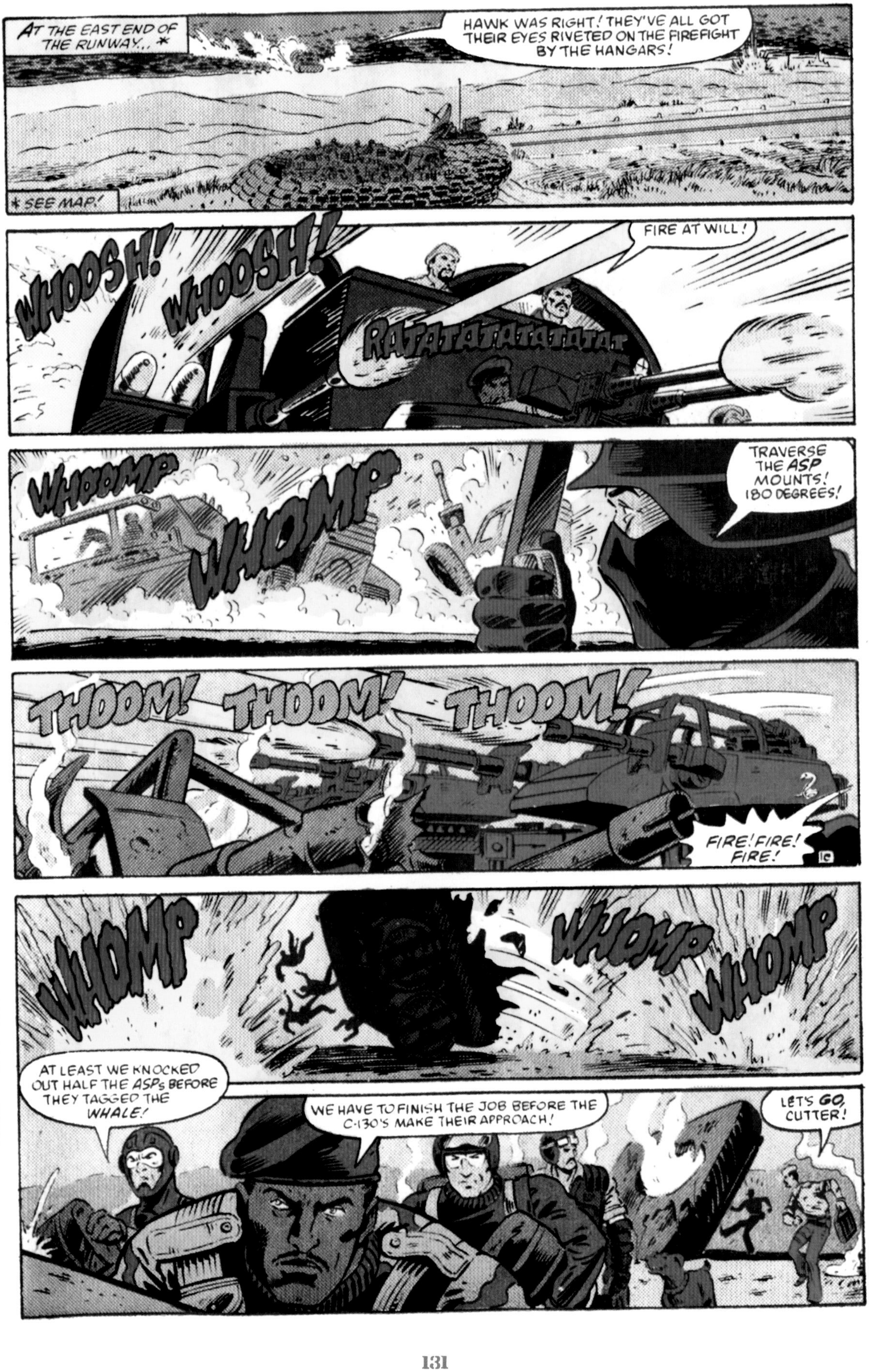
AT THE EAST END OF THE RUNWAY... *
HAWK WAS RIGHT! THEY'VE ALL GOT THEIR EYES RIVETED ON THE FIREFIGHT BY THE HANGARS!
* SEE MAP!
WHOOSH! WHOOSH!
FIRE AT WILL!
RATATATATATATATAT
WHOOMP
WHOMP
TRAVERSE THE ASP MOUNTS! 180 DEGREES!
THOOM! THOOM! THOOM!
FIRE! FIRE! FIRE!
WHOMP
WHOMP WHOMP
AT LEAST WE KNOCKED OUT HALF THE ASPs BEFORE THEY TAGGED THE WHALE!
WE HAVE TO FINISH THE JOB BEFORE THE C-130'S MAKE THEIR APPROACH!
LET'S GO, CUTTER!

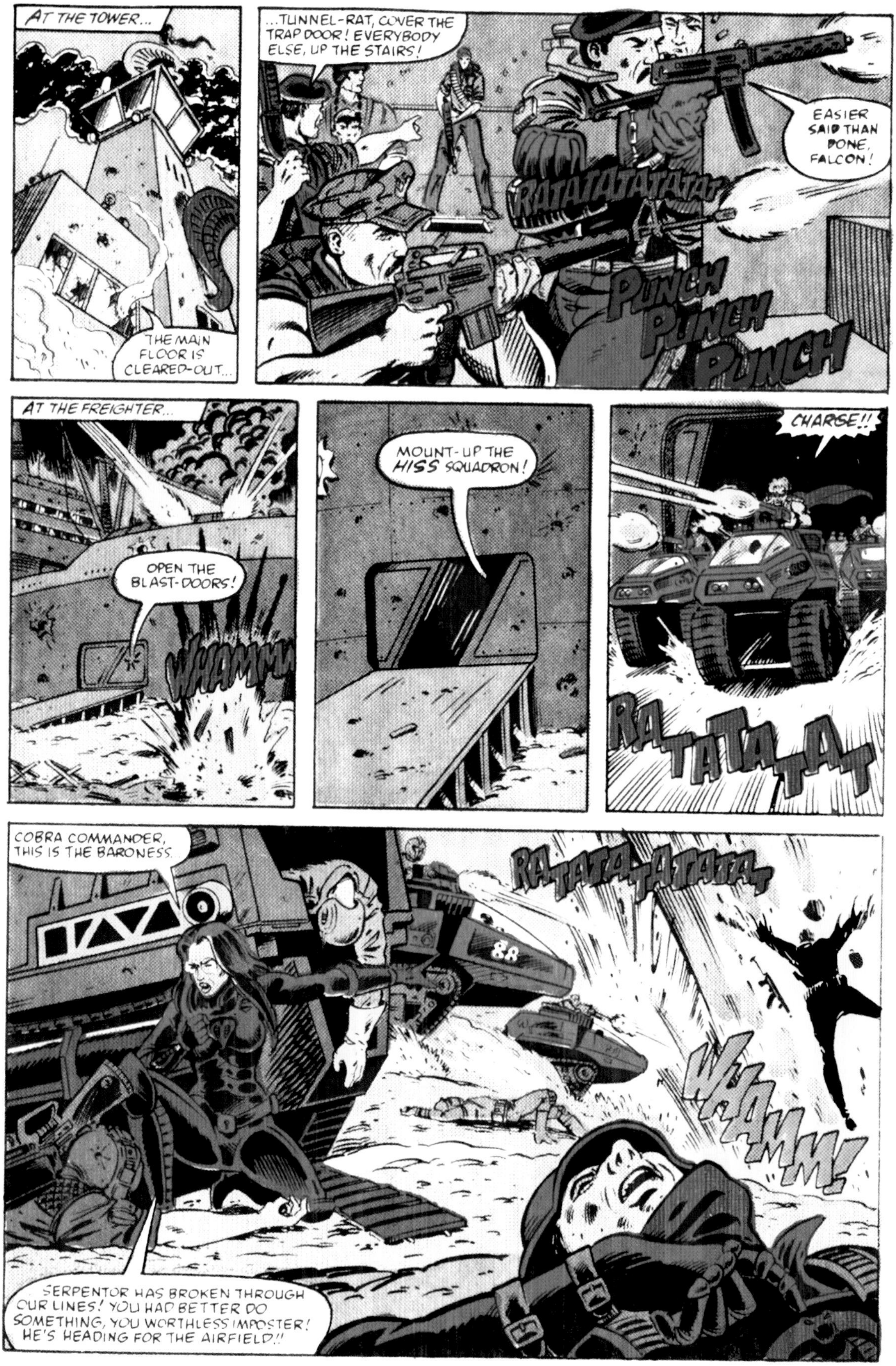
AT THE TOWER...
THE MAIN FLOOR IS CLEARED-OUT...
...TUNNEL-RAT, COVER THE TRAP DOOR! EVERYBODY ELSE, UP THE STAIRS!
EASIER SAID THAN DONE, FALCON!
RATATATATATATAT
PUNCH PUNCH PUNCH
AT THE FREIGHTER...
OPEN THE BLAST-DOORS!
WHAMMM
MOUNT-UP THE HISS SQUADRON!
CHARGE!!
RA TATA TAT
COBRA COMMANDER, THIS IS THE BARONESS...
RATATATATATATA
WHAMM!
SERPENTOR HAS BROKEN THROUGH OUR LINES! YOU HAD BETTER DO SOMETHING, YOU WORTHLESS IMPOSTER! HE'S HEADING FOR THE AIRFIELD!!

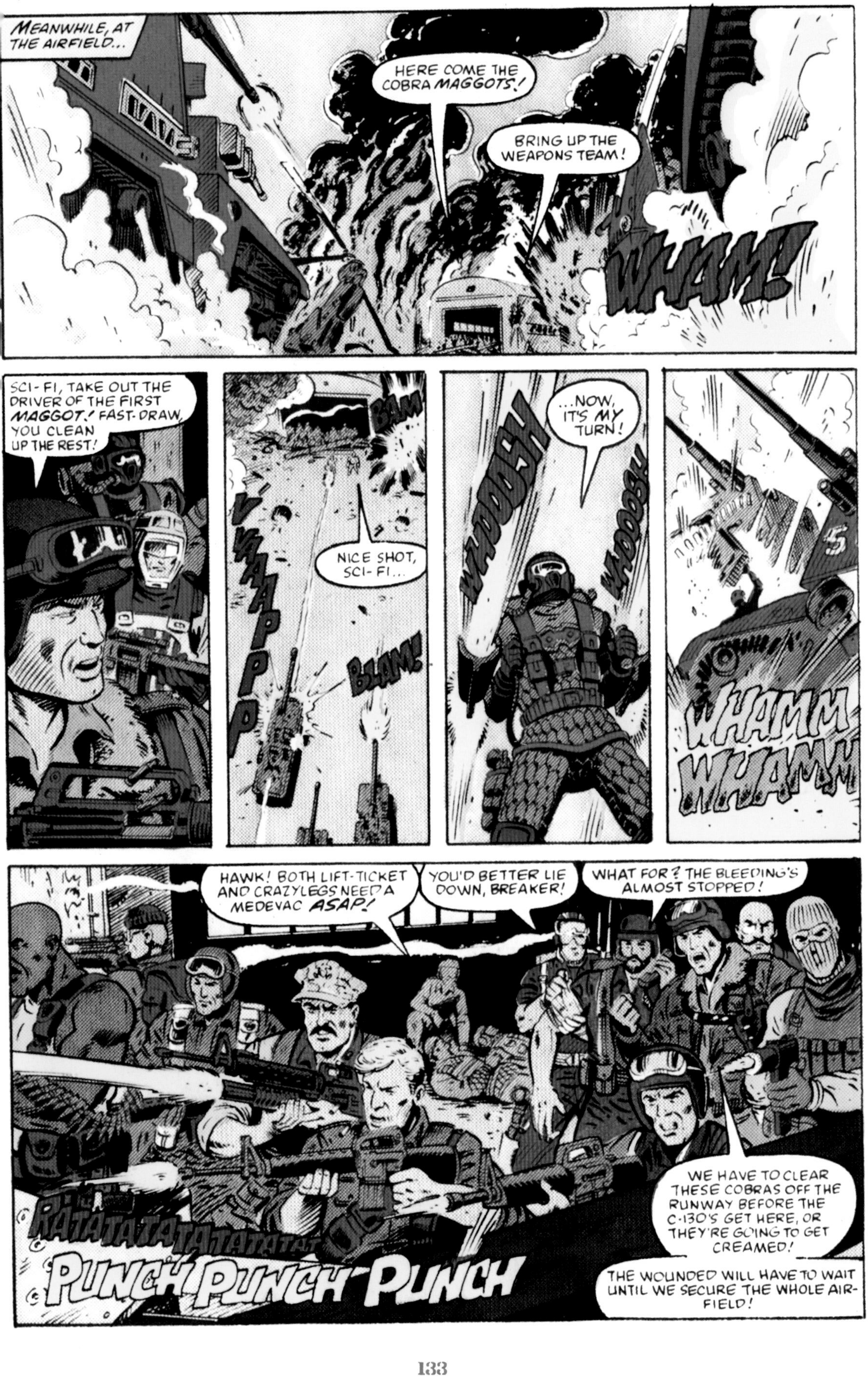
MEANWHILE, AT THE AIRFIELD...
HERE COME THE COBRA MAGGOTS!
BRING UP THE WEAPONS TEAM!
WHAM!
SCI-FI, TAKE OUT THE DRIVER OF THE FIRST MAGGOT! FAST-DRAW, YOU CLEAN UP THE REST!
BAM
VVAAAPPP
NICE SHOT, SCI-FI...
BLAM!
...NOW, IT'S MY TURN!
WHOOSH
WHOOSH
WHAMM
WHAMM
HAWK! BOTH LIFT-TICKET AND CRAZYLEGS NEED A MEDEVAC ASAP!
YOU'D BETTER LIE DOWN, BREAKER!
WHAT FOR? THE BLEEDING'S ALMOST STOPPED!
RATATATATATATATATAT
PUNCH PUNCH PUNCH
WE HAVE TO CLEAR THESE COBRAS OFF THE RUNWAY BEFORE THE C-130'S GET HERE, OR THEY'RE GOING TO GET CREAMED!
THE WOUNDED WILL HAVE TO WAIT UNTIL WE SECURE THE WHOLE AIR-FIELD!

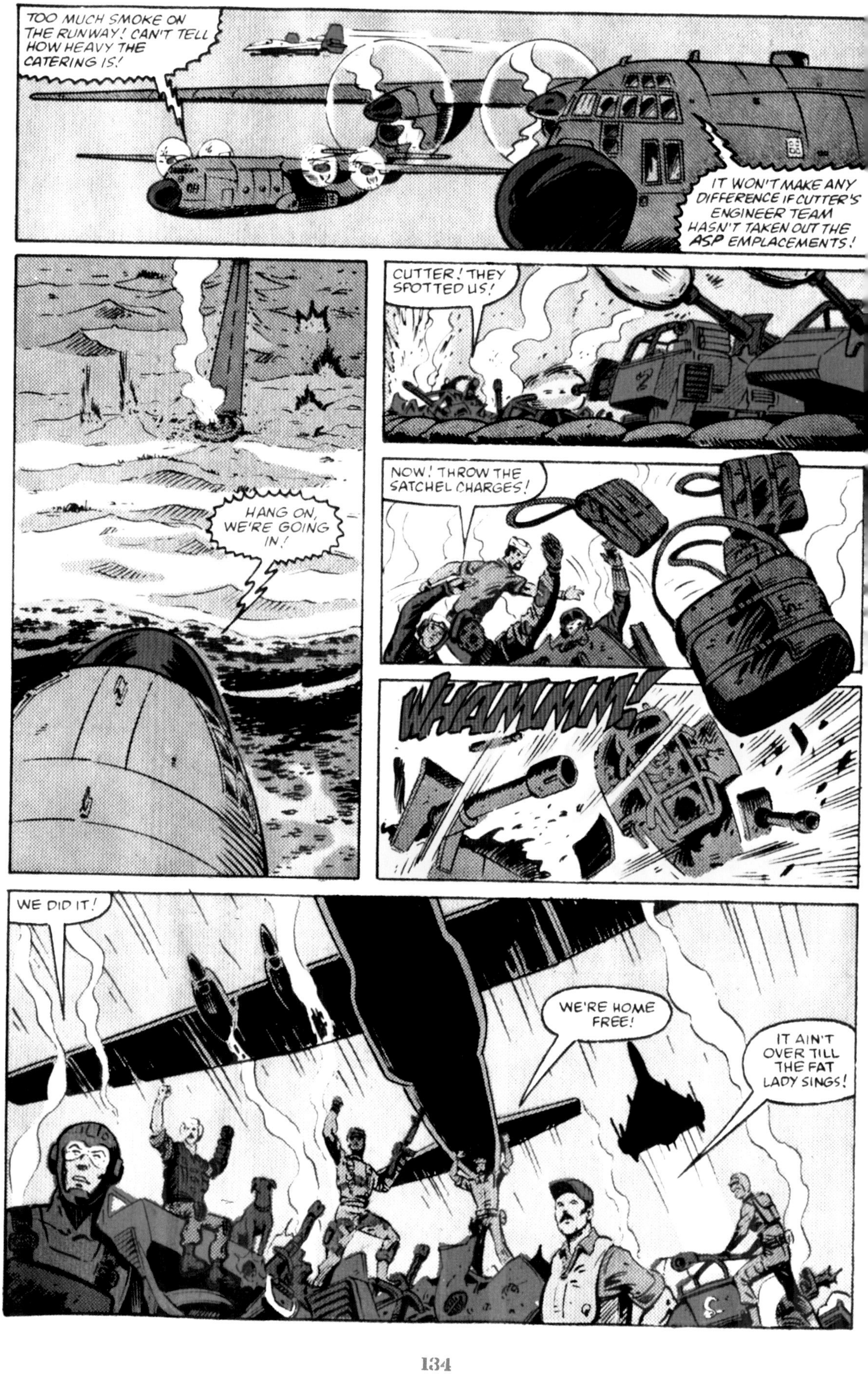
TOO MUCH SMOKE ON THE RUNWAY! CAN'T TELL HOW HEAVY THE CATERING IS!
IT WON'T MAKE ANY DIFFERENCE IF CUTTER'S ENGINEER TEAM HASN'T TAKEN OUT THE ASP EMPLACEMENTS!
HANG ON, WE'RE GOING IN!
CUTTER! THEY SPOTTED US!
NOW! THROW THE SATCHEL CHARGES!
WHAMMM!
WE DID IT!
WE'RE HOME FREE!
IT AIN'T OVER TILL THE FAT LADY SINGS!

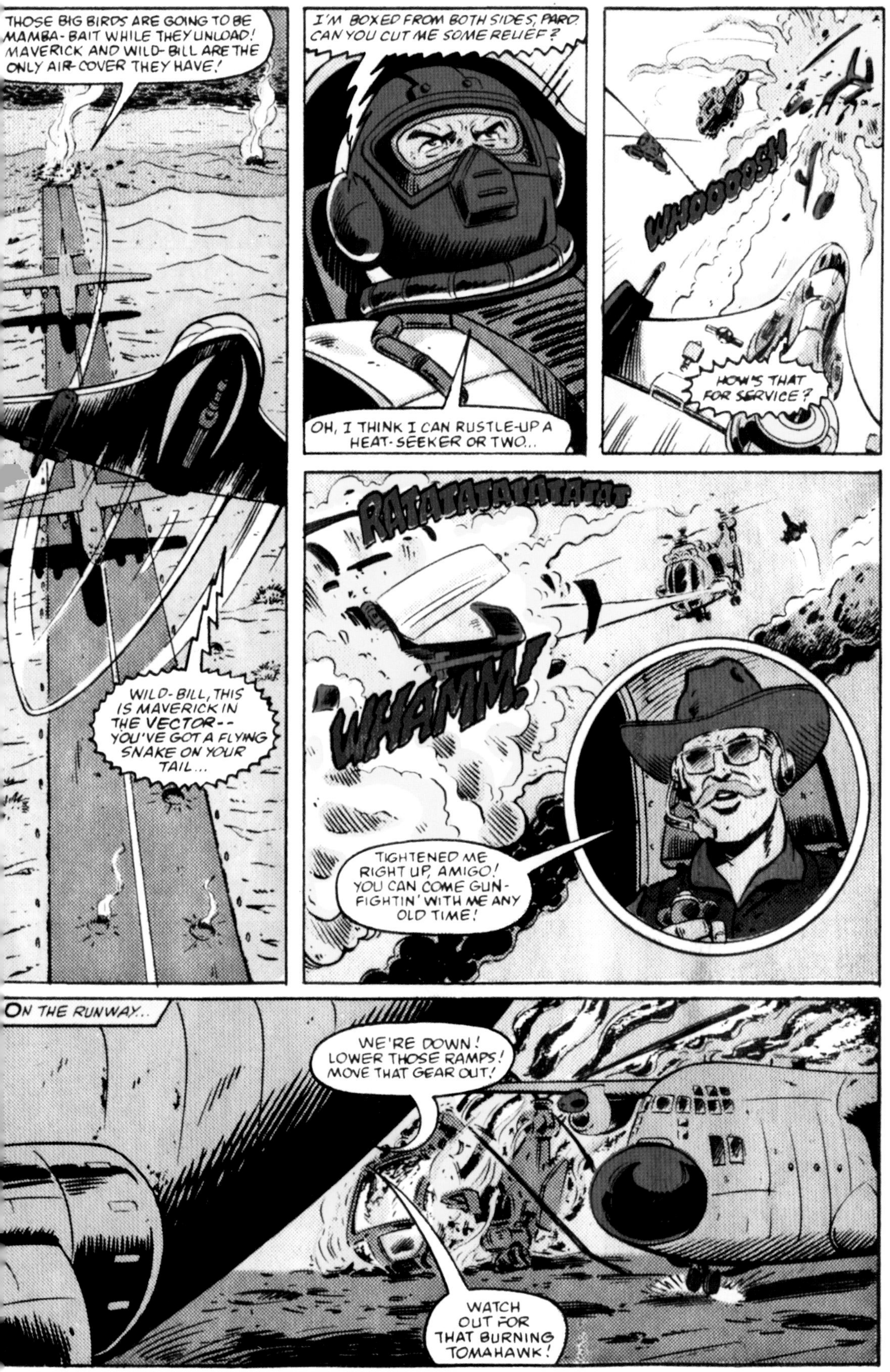
THOSE BIG BIRDS ARE GOING TO BE MAMBA-BAIT WHILE THEY UNLOAD! MAVERICK AND WILD-BILL ARE THE ONLY AIR-COVER THEY HAVE!
WILD-BILL, THIS IS MAVERICK IN THE VECTOR-- YOU'VE GOT A FLYING SNAKE ON YOUR TAIL...
I'M BOXED FROM BOTH SIDES, PARD. CAN YOU CUT ME SOME RELIEF?
OH, I THINK I CAN RUSTLE-UP A HEAT-SEEKER OR TWO...
WHOOOOOSH
HOW'S THAT FOR SERVICE?
RATATATATATATATAT
WHAMM!
TIGHTENED ME RIGHT UP, AMIGO! YOU CAN COME GUN-FIGHTIN' WITH ME ANY OLD TIME!
ON THE RUNWAY...
WE'RE DOWN! LOWER THOSE RAMPS! MOVE THAT GEAR OUT!
WATCH OUT FOR THAT BURNING TOMAHAWK!

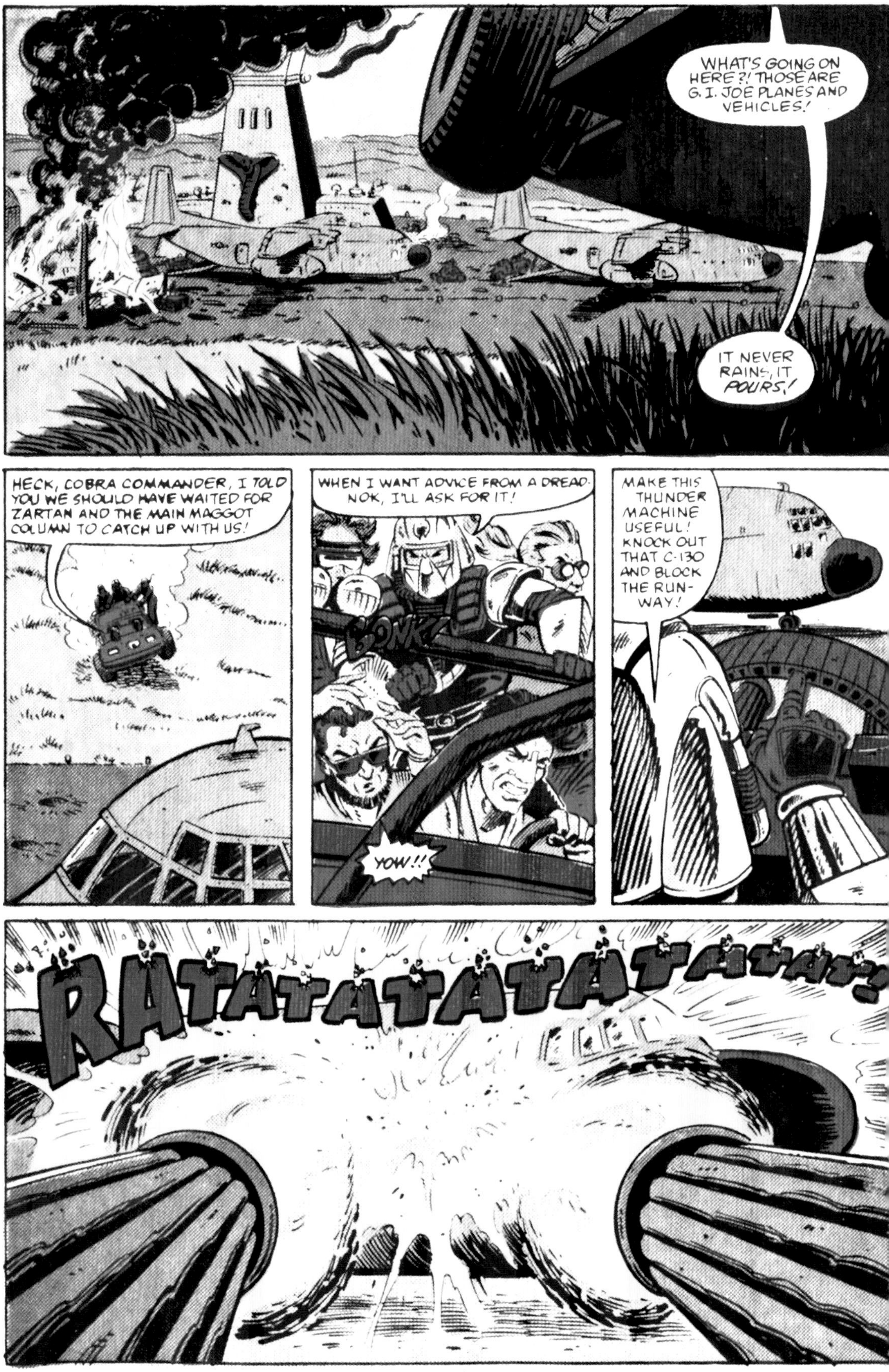
WHAT'S GOING ON HERE?! THOSE ARE G.I. JOE PLANES AND VEHICLES!
IT NEVER RAINS, IT POURS!
HECK, COBRA COMMANDER, I TOLD YOU WE SHOULD HAVE WAITED FOR ZARTAN AND THE MAIN MAGGOT COLUMN TO CATCH UP WITH US!
WHEN I WANT ADVICE FROM A DREAD-NOK, I'LL ASK FOR IT!
BONK!
YOW!!
MAKE THIS THUNDER MACHINE USEFUL! KNOCK OUT THAT C-130 AND BLOCK THE RUN-WAY!
RATATATATATATATAT!

MOVE IT OUT! GET THAT GEAR OFF THAT BURNING PLANE!

HEY! LOOK WHO'S HERE!! THE JOE COMMANDER!

DON'T SLOW DOWN, THRASHER, I'LL SNAG HIM ON THE RUN!

VROOOM

THWOOOP!

GET HIM UNDER CONTROL, OR I'LL--

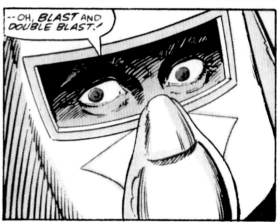

-- OH, BLAST AND DOUBLE BLAST!

IT'S SERPENTOR AND HIS HISS COLUMN!

ALL HAIL, SERPENTOR!

THAT'S COBRA COMMANDER HIMSELF ON THAT THUNDER MACHINE!

TAKE HIM DOWN! BRACKET YOUR SHOTS! YOUR WEIGHT IN COBRA STOCK CERTIFICATES TO THE CREW WHO HITS HIM!

ALL HAIL, SERPENTOR!

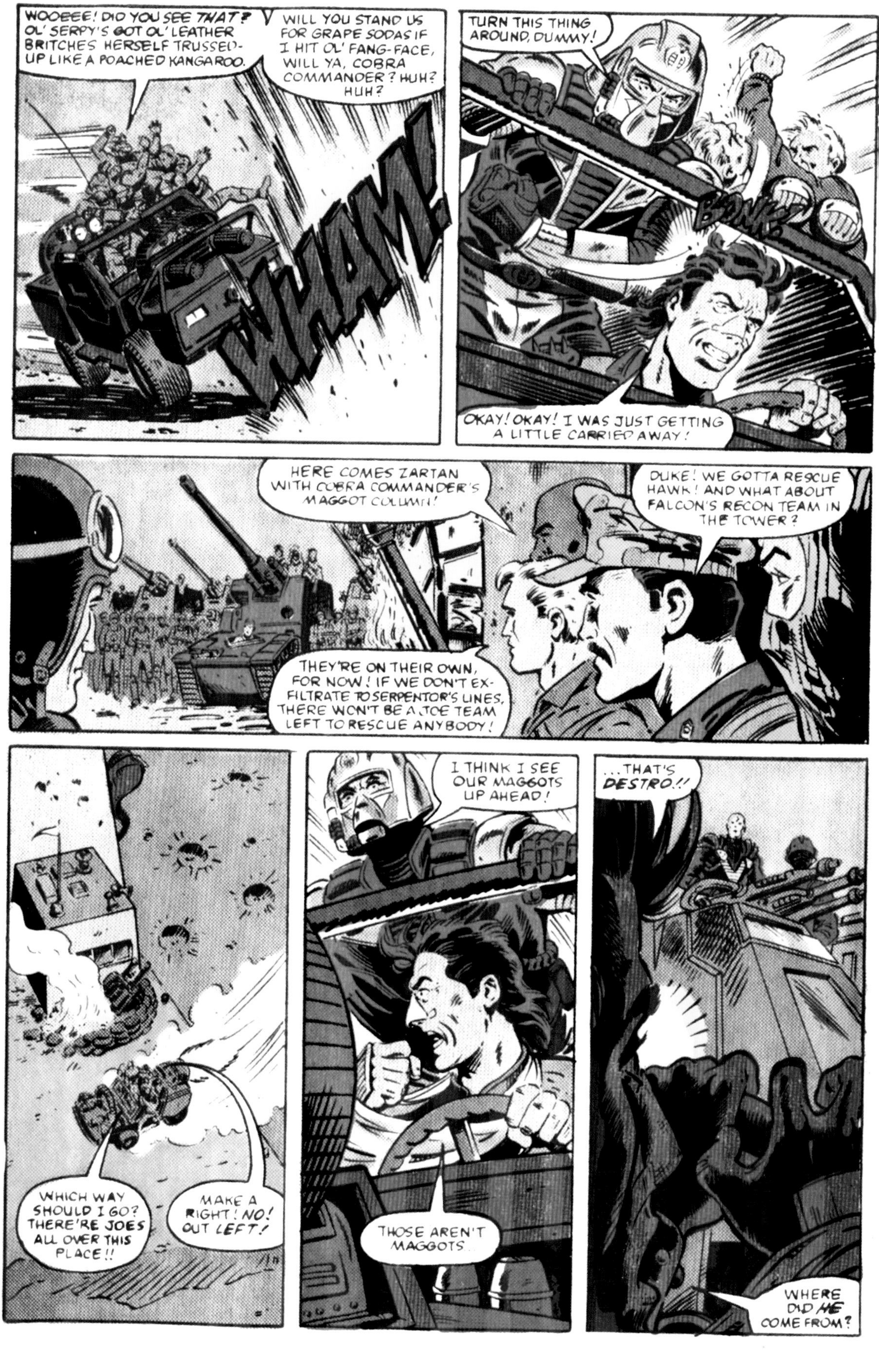
WOOEEE! DID YOU SEE THAT? OL' SERPY'S GOT OL' LEATHER BRITCHES HERSELF TRUSSED-UP LIKE A POACHED KANGAROO.
WILL YOU STAND US FOR GRAPE SODAS IF I HIT OL' FANG-FACE, WILL YA, COBRA COMMANDER? HUH? HUH?
WHAM!
TURN THIS THING AROUND, DUMMY!
BONK
OKAY! OKAY! I WAS JUST GETTING A LITTLE CARRIED AWAY!
HERE COMES ZARTAN WITH COBRA COMMANDER'S MAGGOT COLUMN!
DUKE! WE GOTTA RESCUE HAWK! AND WHAT ABOUT FALCON'S RECON TEAM IN THE TOWER?
THEY'RE ON THEIR OWN, FOR NOW! IF WE DON'T EX-FILTRATE TO SERPENTOR'S LINES, THERE WON'T BE A JOE TEAM LEFT TO RESCUE ANYBODY!
WHICH WAY SHOULD I GO? THERE'RE JOES ALL OVER THIS PLACE!!
MAKE A RIGHT! NO! OUT LEFT!
I THINK I SEE OUR MAGGOTS UP AHEAD!
THOSE AREN'T MAGGOTS...
...THAT'S DESTRO!!
WHERE DID HE COME FROM?

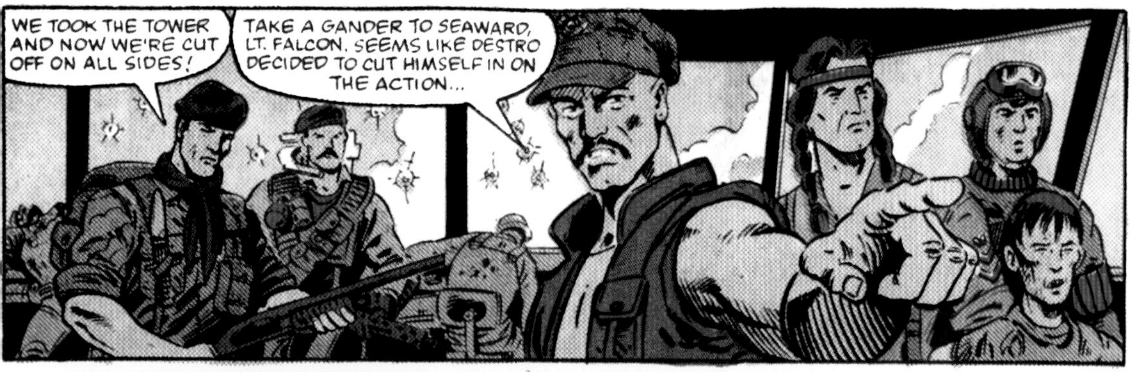
WE TOOK THE TOWER AND NOW WE'RE CUT OFF ON ALL SIDES!
TAKE A GANDER TO SEAWARD, LT. FALCON. SEEMS LIKE DESTRO DECIDED TO CUT HIMSELF IN ON THE ACTION...

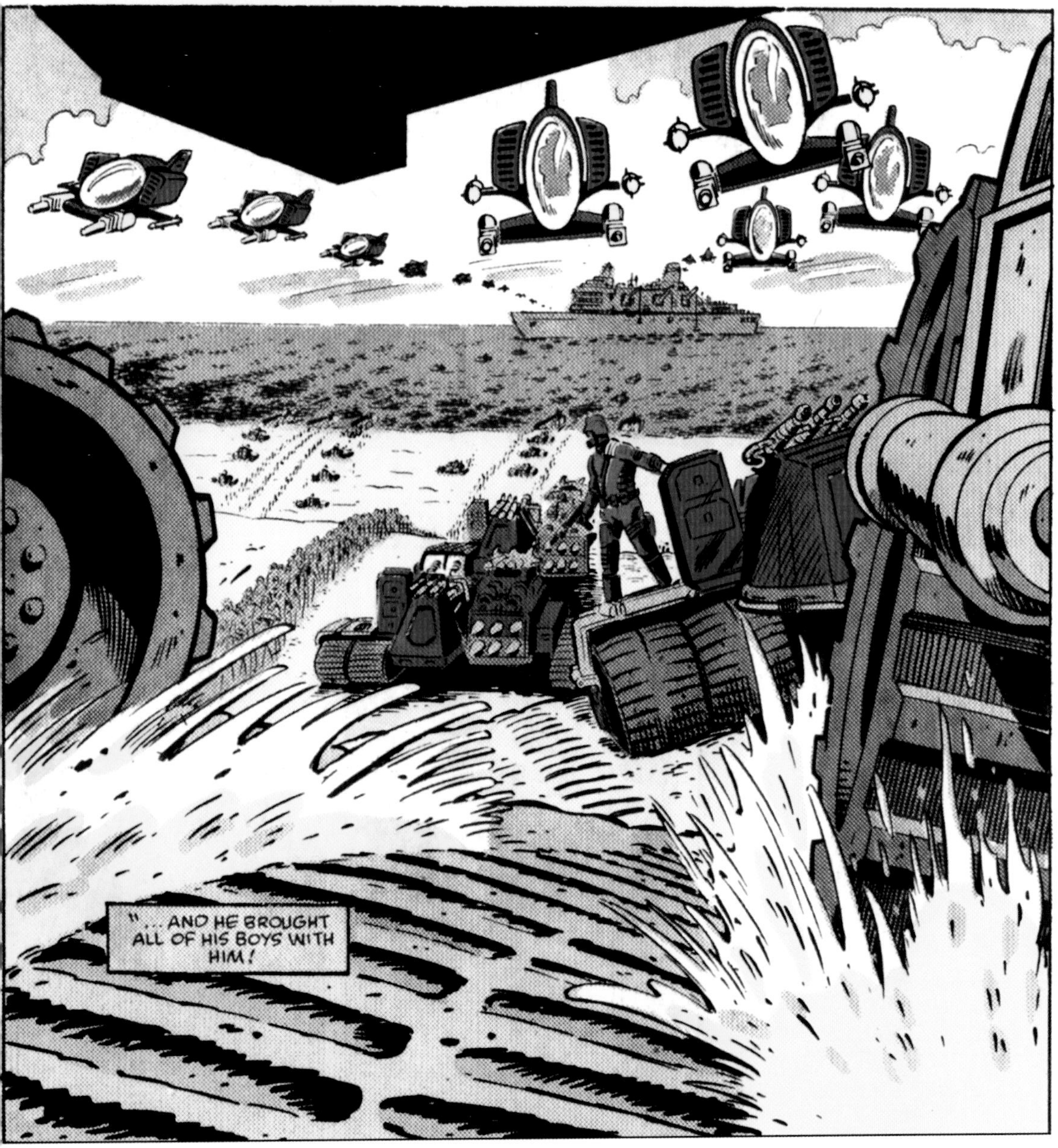
"... AND HE BROUGHT ALL OF HIS BOYS WITH HIM!

THIS CONCLUDES G.I. JOE BEST OF HAWK